Keel and Saddle
by Joseph Warren Revere

Copyright © 2019 by HardPress

Address:
HardPress
8345 NW 66TH ST #2561
MIAMI FL 33166-2626
USA
Email: info@hardpress.net

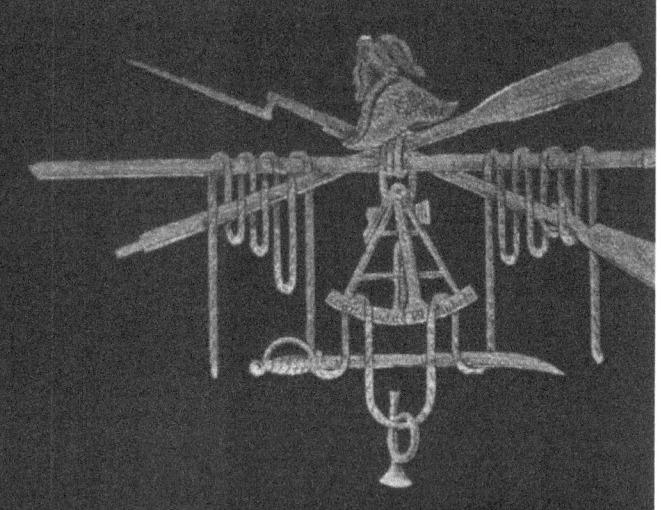

Geog.4208.72.2

Harvard College Library

FROM THE ESTATE OF

MRS. ELIZABETH C. GAY

OF

BOSTON

Received April 30, 1908.

Winslow Lewis

KEEL AND SADDLE:

A Retrospect

of

FORTY YEARS OF MILITARY AND NAVAL SERVICE.

BY

JOSEPH W. REVERE.

BOSTON:
JAMES R. OSGOOD AND COMPANY,
(Late Ticknor & Fields, and Fields, Osgood, & Co.)
1873.

Harvard College Library
From the Estate of
Mrs. Elizabeth C. Gay,
of Boston,
April 30, 1908.

Entered according to Act of Congress, in the year 1872,
By JAMES R. OSGOOD & CO.,
In the Office of the Librarian of Congress at Washington.

Boston:
Stereotyped and Printed by Rand, Avery, & Co.

To the Memories of

COLONEL PAUL JOSEPH REVERE,
(20th Mass. Infantry,)
KILLED AT GETTYSBURG;

AND OF

ASSISTANT SURGEON EDWARD H. R. REVERE,
(20th Mass. Infantry,)
KILLED AT ANTIETAM;

BOTH DYING ON THE FIELD OF HONOR IN THE
MOMENT OF VICTORY;

This Volume

IS AFFECTIONATELY INSCRIBED

BY

THE AUTHOR.

CONTENTS.

KEEL AND SADDLE.

I.

Introductory Remarks. — I enter the United-States Navy. — Cruises to the Pacific, the West Indies, and Gulf of Mexico. — Florida. — The Seminole War. — Osceola. — Major Moniac. — The Forty Thieves. — Coast of Cuba. — Piracy. — A Prize. — Treasure-Trove. — A Cyclone and its Effects. — Disappointment 1

II.

The West Coast of Africa. — A Waif on the High Seas. — The Old Quarter-master's Yarn. — "The Volador." — The Chase. — The Capture. — The Sargasso Sea. — We make Prize of a Slaver. — Her Cargo and Condition, — A Tropical Calm. — A Water Famine. — Are saved by Rum Toddies. — Phlogistic Regimen. — A Revolt. — Pandemonium. — Our Deliverance. — Arrival in Port. — Moral deduced by a Portuguese Trader. — Monrovia. — Swamped on the Bar. — Adieu to Africa 9

III

I pass my Examination. — The Frigate "Constitution." — Cruise to the Mediterranean. — The Baltic. — Cronstadt. — The Czar *incognito*. — Festivities. — St. Petersburg. — The Imperial Family. — Constantine. — At Sea. — A Russian Deserter appears among our Crew. — The Pole 17

IV.

Story of the Polish Officer.—Siberia.—The Exiles.—The Chains.—Rations.—Death and Burial of the Exiles.—The Prussian Allies of Russia.—Dreadful Privations.—Escapes and Recaptures.—Converts to the Greek Church.—The Poor Polak.—*Lèse-Majesté*.—The Mines.—Charity in Russia.—The Siberian Exile Dead to the World.—Inhumanity and Bestiality of the Government.—Maxim of the Imperial Government.—Russian Servility.—End of the Story of the Polish Officer 21

V.

Rome.—Gregory XVI.—An Interview with Letitia Ramolino.—Art Treasures.—The Coliseum.—Holy Stones.—A Practical Officer.—Sicily.—Anecdote of Calabrian Brigands.—The English Frigate "Barham."—Englishmen fixing the Price of their own Ransom.—Tariff for Rogues and for Honest Men.—The Adriatic and the Ionian Islands.—Athens.—King Otho.—A Patent Yankee Exterminator, the Grandfather of the Mitrailleuse.—Narrow Escape from Regicide.—*Sauve qui peut* 28

VI.

Levantine Society.—Smyrna.—The Casino—The Dardanelles.—Constantinople.—Sultan Mahmoud—His Skill in Archery.—The Ægean Sea.—A Heavy Storm.—Narrow Escape from Shipwreck.—Asia Minor.—Beyrout.—Sidon.—A Visit to and Interview with Lady Hester Stanhope.—A Midnight *Séance* with her Ladyship.—Her Theological System of Belief.—Sir John Moore.—Her Famous Mares.—Return on Board 35

VII.

St. Jean d'Acre.—Ibrahim Pacha.—His Appearance.—Jaffa.—Jerusalem.—The Dead Sea.—The Jordan.—Arab Sentiment.—Alexandria.—Reception by Mahomet Ali, Pacha of Egypt.—Emin Bey.—His Leap from the Walls of the Citadel of Cairo.—Kismet.—Portugal—Spain.—Journey with Gypsies.—Pedrecillo.—The Gitanos.—The Order of March.—Evora.—Estremoz.—Elvas.—Arrival at Badajos.—Travelling on Horseback.—The Spanish *Arrieros* 45

VIII.

Merida, the Spanish Rome.—Roman Bridge built by Trajan.—Its Magnificent and Stupendous Remains.—The Lake of Proserpine.—The Ruined Aqueducts.—The Circus Maximus.—The Forum.—The Reservoirs.—Estremadura. — Its Porcine Products. — The Hams of Montanches. — On the Road. — The Confessional of St. Peter. — Robbers. — The Diligence gone through by them. — An Irate British Subject. — We have it in our Power to relieve the Distressed. — Medellin and Trujillo, the Birthplaces of Pizarro and Cortes. — Caceres. — Romantic Ride. — Arrival at Alcantara. — The Famous Bridge. — Inscription 53

IX.

The Military Orders of Chivalry. — Peculiarity of the Catholic Church. — The Jesuits. — Our Journey. — Coria. — Montanches — Placencia. — A Lovely Maiden. — Beautiful Country. — Yuste, and the Convent of San Geronimo, the Last Retreat of Charles V. — Farewell to Estremadura 59

X.

The Kingdom of Toledo. — Talavera. — Toledo. — Arrival at Madrid. — The Royal Palace. — The Armory. — Pictures. — The Unwholesome Climate of the Capital of Spain. — The Museo. — Society. — Tertulias. — The Puerta del Sol. — I seek a Guide. — An Aficionado. — Journey Northwards. — The Escorial. — A Château en Espagne. — La Granja. — The Castle in the Air. — Peñalara. — Queen Christina. — Muñoz. — Blasco's Account of their Amours and Management of the King, Ferdinand VII. — Away with Melancholy. — Segovia. — The Alcazar 66

XI.

Col. Reyes of the Spanish Army. — The Road. — Valladolid. — Simancas. — Adventure of Manuel Blasco. — His Imprisonment and Release. — His Account of the Little Fiasco at the Hotel. — We set forth again. — Aranda del Duero. — Arrive at Peñaranda. — The Zuñiga Family. — Old Castle. — Blasco grows Sentimental 74

XII.

Story of the Fair Iñez. — A Roué of the Middle Ages. — His Prodigality and Profligacy. — The Abbot's Counsel. — Don Baltazar joins the Crusade. — He is highly successful in a Military Point of View. — His Piety. — Reform. — Return Home. — Thrift. — Feudal Justice. — Clear Conscience. — Prosperity. — Gypsies. — Their Impiety and Sacrilege. — The Gitana. — Imprisonment illy endured. — A Convert. — The Comadre. — The Old Count smitten. — The Golden Chain 80

XIII.

Continuation of the Story of the Fair Iñez. — Determination of the Count of Miranda. — July wedded to December. — Description of the Fair Iñez. —

Her Beauty. — Her Spirits. — Her Innocence. — An Old Man's Darling. — The Green-eyed Monster. — The Pages. — The Seignorial Throne. — Peril of the Page. — His Departure. — Its Consequences. — Sudden Return of the Page Damiano de Zuñiga. — End of the Story of the Fair Iñez. — Lerma . 86

XIV.

Burgos. — The Cathedral. — The Castle. — Las Huelgas. — Pilgrimage to the Tomb of the Cid. — Miraflores. — The Mausoleum of the Parents of Isabel the Catholic. — San Pedro de Cardeña. — Bavieca. — Inscription. — Tombs of the Cid, his Wife Ximena, and their Two Daughters. — The Start from Burgos. — Overtake a Carlist Expedition. — Doña Florencia. — A Brave Lady. — The Soldiers of Don Carlos. — Arrival before Logroño. — The Skirmish. — The Attack. — Entrance into the Town. — A Night Combat. — Daylight. — Martin Zurbano. — A Military Execution. — Shocking Episode of the Civil War. — Subsequent Fate of Zurbano. — Disappearance of Blasco. — He re-appears. — We again take the Road. — The Pyrenees. — Pamplona. — Journey to Paris. — Exploit of Blasco. — Béranger. — An Interview with the Great Chansonnier. — Return to Spain. — Granada. — Pepe Montes, the Famous Bull-Fighter. — His Adventure in the Plaza de Toros of Granada. — Indignant Retreat thence 96

XV.

Historical Retrospect. — Causes of the Decline of the Spanish Monarchy. — The Successors of Charles V. — Effect of the Expulsion of the Moors. — Of the Discovery of the Americas. — The Laws of the Mesta. — Incredible Folly of Similar Laws. — Natural Result. — Paralyzation of Industrial Pursuits. — Contempt for every Axiom of Political Economy. — Destruction of the National Prosperity — Unreasonable Reverence for the Kingly Power. — Degeneration. — Sketch of Ferdinand VII. — Christina. — Revocation of the Salic Law. — Death of Ferdinand. — Revolt of Don Carlos and Breaking-Out of the Civil War. — Españolismo the Curse of Spain 113

XVI.

Visit to Algiers. — Arab Sentiment. — Abd-el-Kader. — French Soldiers. — The Casbah. — Expedition to Blidah. — Skirmish with the Kabyles. — The Zephyrs. — Capt. Eylau. — Arrival on the Field of the Spahis. — Victory. — An Oriental Frenchman. — I meet Manuel Blasco. — Blidah. — End of Poor Blasco in Matrimony 122

XVII.

Return Home. — Voyage of Circumnavigation. — Madeira. — Zanzibar. — The Imâm of Muscat. — The Eunuch Ahmed. — A Valorous Vizier. — A *Coup-*

CONTENTS.

ix

PAGE.

de Main, and Capture of Mombas. — A Forlorn Hope. — Allocution of the Imâm. — Success. — The Red Sea. — Muscat. — Bombay. — March of Lord Keane's Army. — Splendid Military Spectacle. — Composition of an Indian Army. — Sumatra. — War with Malay Pirates. — Sickness among our Crew. Singapore. — China. — We pass through the Bashee Passage into the South Sea. — Arrival at Boston. — In the West Indies again. — I experience a Great Sea Bore. — Tragic Fate of "The Clio" 132

XVIII.

Cruise to the Pacific in 1845. — My Ship joins the Squadron of Com. Sloat at Mazatlan. — The Details of this Cruise previously published in "A Tour of Duty in the Pacific." — I here continue this Work as a Sequel to that One. — Taking Possession of the Californias, and hoisting the Flag of the United States. — Her Majesty's Ship "Cornwallis," Admiral Sir Michael Seymour, is forestalled by our Action. — Com. Stockton. — Gen. Kearney. — Kit Carson. — Expedition to recover the Pueblo de Los Angeles. — Passage of the River of San Gabriel. — Combat of La Mesa. — Cavalry Charges of the Mexicans. — They make no Impression on our Square. — Their Retreat. — Entrance into Los Angeles. — Capture of San José, Lower California, and Guaymas. — Occupation of Mazatlan. — Return to Boston. 143

XIX.

Appointment as Timber-Agent for the United States in California. — Discovery of Gold. — Rush for the Mines. — I sail for the Isthmus. — Arrival at Chagres. — Gold-Seekers. — Chocolate. — Its Uses for the Traveller. — Baron Steinbergen. — Our Embargo at Gorgona. — I take the Isthmus-Fever. — Start for Panama. — Meet with a Good Woman. — Meet a Friend in the Street. — I go to his House and am cared for. — I recover, and embark for San Francisco. — Change wrought in that City. — Singular State of Society. — I meet an Old Shipmate. — His Remarkable Hospitality. — Anecdote of the Maid of Mrs. Gen. Smith 151

XX.

San Geronimo. — Account of my Rancho. — Impossibility of engaging in any Agricultural Pursuit. — I resolve to visit the Placer. — Arrival at the Dry Diggings. — State of the Labor Market. — Prospecting. — Sales of Cattle. — Commercial Ventures. — Successful Operations. — Return to San Geronimo. — Visit to San Francisco. — Emigrants from Abroad. — Act as Pilot for the Sacramento. — The Peruvian Company of Miners. — Coca, its Use by them. — Pedro Beltran. — Account of a Coquero 158

CONTENTS.

XXI.

PAGE.

Crops at San Geronimo. — Dearness of Provisions. — San Francisco. — Readiness of the Emigrants in adapting Themselves to the Situation. — Their Pursuits. — Weakness and Imperfection of Human Nature. — Interview with a Digger. — His Account of Himself. — The Classics in the Diggings. — His Advice to me. — Improvements at my Place. — A "Herradura." — Indian Forays on our Horses. — Organization of an Expedition for their Suppression among my Neighbors 163

XXII.

Rendezvous of Rancheros at Baulinas. — Preparations. — The Start. — Beautiful Country. — Indians. — The Gentile Village. — Trading. — Don Pepe Armenteros. — Sudden Appearance of Don Juan Briones. — Lamentations of Don Rafael Garcia — The Gallant "Pinto." — We start on the Trail. — A Night March. — Arrival at the Village of the Horse-Thieves. — Lovely and Peaceful Scene. — Breaking of the Dawn. — Our Attack and Surprise of the Gentiles. — We are Victorious. — Our Magnanimity. — No Material Guarantee of Peace being Available, we seize the Personal One. — Return Home and Disposition of the Prisoners. — I resign my Commission as Lieutenant in the Navy 171

XXIII.

Alexander McGregor. — A Remarkable Character. — Description of his Appearance. — His Mental Accomplishments. — His Failings. — A Ship Ashore. — Flotsam and Jetsam. — A Rich Spoil cast up by the Sea. — Assembling of the Rancheros at the Estero de Los Tamales. — The Rancho of Don Rafael Garcia. — Rural Festivities. — The Captain of the Lost Bark. — End of the Great Fandango. — Submarine Exploit 180

XXIV.

The Golondrina. — Preparations for a Voyage. — My Crew. — A Cosmopolitan Company. — Sail for the Lower Coast. — The Gulf of California. — Indian Tribes inhabiting the Coast. — The Hiaquis. — The Guelphs and Ghibellines of Sonora. — Their Contentions. — A Brig Ashore. — We anchor near Her. — Action with the Indians. — Rescue of the Passengers and Crew. — The Custom-House Peculiarities in Mexico. — The Arancel. — Bribery and Corruption. — Mazatlan. — San Blas. — Smuggling Specie. — Twenty Years of Presidio. — The Captain of the Port. — A Strict Search. — The Captain leaves us. — McGregor reveals his Ingenious Concealment of the Gold. — We are discovered. — We dispose of the Inspector, and sail for the Offing. — Becalmed. — The Pursuit. — Clear Ship for Action. — British Interference. — Are threatened with Boarding. — Resistance. — We sink one of the Enemy's Launches. — The Rest sheer off 188

CONTENTS.

XXV.

PAGE

Arrival at Mansanilla. — Agree with the Resguardo on Favorable Terms to admit Cargo. — Visit to the Volcano of Colima. — Zapilon. — The Great Barranca. — The Volcanic Zone of this Section of North America. — Jorullo. — Tuxtla. — Volcanic Sympathy of Action. — Grand and Imposing Spectacle of an Eruption. — Return to San Blas. — Sale of "The Golondrina" — We land our Cargo. — Tepic. — Leaving Tepic for the Great Fair. — Guadalajara. — Highwaymen. — The Fair of San Juan de los Lagos. — The Meson. — Family of the Innkeeper. — Pancho. — A Foundling Castaway. — The Pintos. — La Chapita, the Maid of the Inn. — The Close of the Great Fair. — Trip Northward. — Arrival at Chihuahua. 198

XXVI.

The Bolson de Mapimi. — Silver Mines. — Santa Eulalia. — Working of the Mines. — Reasons why Capital is not employed. — Adventure at a Hacienda. — An Indian War-Party. — Army of Apaches. — Narrow Escape. — Traces of the War-Party. — I bid Adieu to my Friend McGregor. — His subsequent Unhappy Fate. — Durango. — The Indians of the Sierra. — Magic and the Black Art. — A Friend relates a Tale of Sorcery 206

XXVII.

Story of Bartola. — Witchcraft. — Don Alvaro Lopez. — A Model Mexican General. — Outrage upon an Indian Family. — Death of the Chief. — Condition of his Daughter. — My Friend is called to attend Lopez in Sickness. — His Malady. — Remorse. — Scene at the Hovel of Bartola. — Incantation. — The Odic Force. — Magnetic Influences. — Effects of a Determined Will. — A Duel à la Mort. — Double Death, and Bartola's Revenge 213

XXVIII.

Return to San Juan. — Continuation of the Story of the Maid of the Inn. — The Wedding. — The Nuptial Feast. — Its Sudden Termination. — The Somnambula. — Disappearance of Pancho. — Melancholy Catastrophe. — The Cemetery. — Departure from San Juan de los Lagos. — The City of Mexico. — President Arista. — The American Minister. — I accept Service in the Mexican Army. — My Rank and Duties. — Journey to Guanajuato. — Father Ipolito. — My Appointment with Him 220

XXIX.

The Vial of Lethe. — Insomnolence. — The Dutch Captain. — The Opiate. — Recollections. — Curiosity of Pancho. — Explanation. — Dario. — A Weird

CONTENTS.

PAGE.

Convert.— An Unseen Witness —Terrible Scene in the Cemetery of San Juan.— Indian Superstition.— Father Ipolito explains away the Mystery.— Dénoûment of the Story of the Maid of the Inn 226

XXX.

Expedition to Morelia.— The March.— The Diana.— Quajimalpa.— Toluca.— Hacienda de la Gabia.— A Magnificent Property.— Taximaroa.— Querendaro.— Our Cavalry engaged.— Ambush in the Defile of Los Trojes de Angangueo.— A Novel Light-Artillery Manœuvre.— The Column saved by Prompt Action of the Artillery — Mexican Horses and Riders — Patzcuaro.— Success of the Expedition.— Return to the Capital.— Place Hunters.— The Hotel de Iturbide.— A Street Acquaintance.— A Promenade.— Agreeable Impressions.— An Old Schoolmate.— A Rival.— Mutual Confidences — The Alameda.— Discontent of Valdes.— He moralizes.— The Old Cavalier.— Horsemanship à la Haute École.— Odious Comparisons 232

XXXI.

The Chase after the Hat.— Change in the Demeanor of Valdes.— A Free Young Lady.— A Siren.— A Recognition.— A Rebuff.— Counter Recognition.— Courtesans.— Dreams.— Morning Salutations.— Visit to the Minister of the Interior.— Unexpected Rencontre.— His Excellency is cool towards Antonio 240

XXXII.

A Critical Situation.— Polite Dismissal.— Valdes.— Rapid Exit.— Reflections in the Street.— Philosophic Determination.— A Pleasant Dinner.— Monologue upon Wine.— Generosity.— The Mistaken Door.— Post Bacchum Venus.— Finding an Ally.— Note from the Minister.— The Breakfast.— Moral, and End of the Story of Don Antonio Palacios 245

XXXIII.

I leave the Mexican Army.— Preparations to return to the United States.— Leave the City by Diligence.— My Travelling Companions.— Perote.— Robbers.— A Shot Right and Left with Both Barrels.— Pusillanimity.— Arrival at Vera Cruz, and, after, at New Orleans.— Proceed up the Mississippi.— Lieut. Thomas J. Jackson, United-States Army.— Astrology.— Jackson's Singular Opinions.— Strange Prediction.— His Enthusiastic Character 252

XXXIV.

Italy. — Strasburg. — The Russian Colonel. — The Old French Major's Story. — Military Discipline. — The Army of the Rhine of 1815. — Gen. Rapp. — A Military Revolt. — Causes of the Mutiny. — Dalhousie. — The Enemy still held in Check. — Discipline preserved in an Army in Revolt. — Success of the Mutineers. — Their Return to Obedience. — End of the Revolt — A Visit to the Cantinière of the Fourth of the Line, the Doyenne of the French Cantinières 258

XXXV.

Paris. — Major Philip Kearny. — His Opinions on the Approaching War of the Rebellion. — Adieux and Assurances. — Breaking-Out of Hostilities. — Sumter. — Great Movement among the People of the North. — Imbecility of the Administration. — Bull Run. — Worthlessness of the Militia. — The People outrun the Government. — I again enter the Service. — Am appointed Colonel of the Seventh New-Jersey Infantry. — Recruits in Plenty. — Arrival in Washington. — Condition of the Army. — Gen. McClellan. — Organization. — McClellan's Labors. — His Success 269

PUFFS FROM PICKET-PIPES.

The Lieutenant's Story 283

The Artillery-Officer's Story 293

The Major's Story 316

The General's Story 342

Monte; or, The Robbers 355

KEEL AND SADDLE.

I.

THE simple record of the career of almost any person, however humble, furnishes some useful lessons, from which may be derived either guidance or warning; and the story of an active life full of vicissitudes and strange experiences, lacking though it may the graces of rhetoric and the riches of scholarship, can hardly fail to point some profitable moral to the few, while it may possibly entertain the many.

These are the considerations which have led me to write the following pages at a time of life when my career may be regarded as closed, and leisure has been found to condense the diaries and memoranda I have always been in the habit of keeping.

Following the bent of an early predilection for foreign travel, I entered the United-States navy at the age of fourteen years, as a midshipman; and, after a short term spent at the Naval School at the New-York Navy Yard, I sailed on my first cruise to the Pacific Ocean on board the frigate "Guerrière," bearing the pennant of Com. Charles C. B. Thompson, in the summer of the year 1828.

For three years I served in the Pacific squadron, and was duly initiated into the tough discipline then in vogue in our navy, the rigorous practice of which had originated during the war of 1812.

Upon my return I enjoyed but a short respite, and in a few months found myself on board a corvette on the West-India station; and, having been transferred to the schooner "Flirt" and other vessels, was finally attached to what was called the "mosquito fleet," — a flotilla of small vessels and boats co-operating with the army in Florida.

Cruising in the Everglades in a barge, exposed to the weather for weeks, I found decidedly rough: but, though the Seminole War was in progress, no encounters with the enemy occurred to mitigate the tedium of my situation; for excepting a few prisoners I saw at Tampa, including the celebrated Osceola, I never beheld an Indian.

After vain efforts to "surprise" our wily foe, the cruise at last ended, having been signalized by the loss of one of our men from fever induced by mosquito-bites, and the disabling of several others from the same cause; and with the warlike trophies of one small squaw captured at a deserted camp, and a keg of powder, we returned to St. Augustine.

Here we found Gen. Jesup's army about to march to the Indian country; and the quaint little Spanish town was alive with excitement over the military preparations.

As I stood one morning admiring a fine regiment of Creek Indians, who were being mustered into the service of the United States, I was suddenly seized by the shoulders from behind, and saluted with the characteristic ejaculation, — "Ugh!" Turning instantly, I found myself in the embrace of a tall Indian, naked except for his breech-cloth and red-cloth leggings, his head shaved clean save the chivalrous scalp-lock; while the thick war-paint prevented me from recognizing his dusky visage. The warrior proved to be Moniac, a young Creek chief, who had been educated at the Military Academy at West Point, with whom I had been intimately acquainted in New York, and who was now a major of the Creek regiment. Although he had been accustomed for four years to the drill and discipline of West Point, had graduated with honor at that institution, had participated in the pleasures, and perhaps partaken of some of the pleasant vices, of civilization, Moniac, upon returning to his tribe, had declined accepting a commission tendered him as an officer of the army, and had chosen to resume all the apparent hardships and perils of savage life.

Perhaps he was right: but I never knew; for a few weeks afterwards, while gallantly leading his battalion, he was killed by his relatives (the Seminoles are descended from the Creeks) at the battle of Okeechobee.

Leaving St. Augustine for Tampa and Pensacola, I was ordered to Key West from the latter place, to take command of a large felucca-rigged boat, pulling forty oars, and armed with a long twelve-pounder; and received instructions to cruise in the Old Bahama Channel, and endeavor to capture a noted pirate named Benavides. Piracy was at that time a regularly-organized business in the West Indies; the capital being supplied by persons in Cuba and the United States, and the cut-throats by the "faithful isle." It was very difficult to secure the trial and conviction of the corsairs in Havana, however evident their guilt; for the Spanish authorities were notoriously interested in the profits of their nefarious calling. It is well known, that, not long before the time I am writing of, Com. David Porter was tried by a court-martial for landing at Foxardo to capture some of these gentlemanly marauders, — a rebuke which led to his leaving the profession of which he was so distinguished an ornament.

For a week or two we saw nothing on our new cruising-ground except a few small merchant-vessels, and heard of no pirates, until one evening a felucca appeared, crossing from Cayo Romano to Cuba. We immediately gave chase, but lost sight of her at nightfall. At early daylight she was again seen under the land of Cuba, but suddenly disappeared up one of those estuaries which inlace the low ground of the coast. Making our way into the one we supposed she had entered, we pursued our unseen but hoped-for prize up its sinuous course, the view being limited by the banks of the estuary, which were covered by a mangrove thicket, growing down into the water, as is the habit of this plant. I landed, however, at the entrance for a few moments, in order to put on shore a couple of men provided with means to signal to us if necessary.

After rowing in this way for about ten or fifteen miles, we came suddenly, at a turn of the estuary, upon a camp, and a bark-rigged vessel lying at a rude pier. Here we landed, with the usual precautions against surprise, and found the ship to be the French bark "Amedée" of Bordeaux, evidently not long since captured by pirates. Her cargo had been nearly all removed from the vessel, and probably taken in lighters to Havana or Matanzas; but the evidences of a hurried "breaking bulk" were everywhere to be seen. The sails of the bark had been burned (for we found the incombustible parts), the rudder unshipped, and both anchors let go; so that it would have been impossible to remove her from the place. Many knick-knacks, which apparently did not suit the taste of the pirates, lay about, the *embarcadero* being strewn with various "articles de Paris." The cabin furnished evidence that it had been tenanted by passengers of both sexes; and it was fearful to think of what had probably been their fate, although we met with no positive proofs that murder had been done.

In the afternoon I wished to return to the sea, but found that some of my men had straggled away into the country:

so, leaving the galley in charge of a petty officer, I started with a small party to hunt them up, ascending the hills which rose above the landing-place to a considerable height. Our search was vain, however: we saw no traces of the stragglers; and, after a walk of about two miles along the crest, we returned towards the pirates' camp down a ravine, in the hollow of which ran a brawling rivulet.

The sides of the ravine were precipitous, and covered with huge bowlders, while the dense and almost impenetrable verdure of the tropics clothed its surface. I tried to cover as much ground as possible with my men, in order to explore the country as thoroughly as we could; for I feared my lost ones had stupefied themselves with liquor obtained from the French bark. Suddenly one of my scouts high up the bank of the ravine shouted to us to ascend; and, thinking he had tidings of the runaways, we scrambled up to his elevated position. I found him at the entrance of a hole, or cave, which was partially concealed by a bowlder of great size, the ground around it bearing the marks of footprints, with staves and iron spikes scattered about. Bringing my little band together, I delegated a young and agile foretopman to enter the hole first; which he did, shoving his carbine before him as he went in, and disappeared from our sight into the bowels of the earth. We prepared to follow: but the first who entered met the second one returning; and, as neither could pass the other in the narrow entrance, we hauled the last man out by the legs. The foretopman reported that he had passed into a large chamber inside; but that, owing to the darkness, he could say nothing as to its size or contents.

Determined to prosecute the search, I improvised tapers made of the torn leaves of a book I had in my pocket; and, thus equipped, we crawled in. At about twenty paces from the entrance we found ourselves in a circular chamber, evidently an excavation, some fifteen feet in diameter. Our means of illumination being scanty, we had not time to examine the contents of some kegs and barrels, which, together with some old rusty muskets and cutlasses, and other objects pertaining to seafaring men, composed the contents of the room.

As we were about to withdraw, one old tar, determined not to go without carrying away some memento of the place, rolled out a keg before him, thinking, doubtless, it contained a supply of liquor; but which, being upset, gave forth an ominous rattling sound, that indicated something more substantial. We rolled the keg down to the camp, which I desired to reach before the approaching sunset; after which, in the tropics, there is no twilight. I found, upon my arrival, that our stragglers had returned, my fears having been unfounded as to their drinking; for the pirates had evidently consumed, or effectually concealed, all liquors.

Sentinels having been placed around the camp, we went to sleep after supper, pleased with visions of untold wealth to be secured in the morning at the cave, which we imagined must contain the fabulous treasures of Aladdin; for the keg we had brought with us was filled with newly-minted Spanish dollars. Shortly after midnight my dreams were interrupted by a sentinel, who reported that a fire was burning brightly at the entrance to the estuary. As this was the signal agreed upon in case our presence was required, I had no alternative but to start at once; and we manned our row-galley, and sped down the creek as fast as forty pairs of vigorous arms could propel us. The day was breaking as we arrived at our destination ready and eager for action; for we thought it probable that the pirates were returning to their haunt, which was as secure a *puerto escondido* for those buccaneers— "friends to the sea, and enemies to all who sail on it"— as could be found in Cuba.

My lookout men reported having seen a light at sea, which

we soon saw, and, boarding the vessel, found her to be His Majesty's schooner "Monkey" on a cruise; and her commander handed me a despatch from the commander of the United-States schooner "Grampus," directing me to join him at Havana as soon after I received it as possible. Reluctant to abandon our promising investigations, we squared away the long yards of the felucca before the trade-wind, and next morning rounded the Morro Castle, ensign and pennant flying, and anchored near "The Grampus." The secret of our discovery was religiously kept, and the keg of dollars divided amongst the crew, each receiving about fifty dollars; and we cheered each other by the prospect of soon returning to the *cache*, and enriching ourselves with the pirates' hoarded treasure.

A few days after our arrival, one of those terrible cyclones which periodically devastate the West Indies came on; and it seemed as if the city would be torn down by the mere power of the wind. Several vessels were destroyed by being dashed violently against the wharves at Regla; houses were unroofed; the belfry of a church of great solidity was blown down, the heavy bell being hurled to the distance of several squares from the building. Ponderous cannon, *en barbette* on the walls of the Cabaña, were blown into the sea, and many lives were lost. The damage to vessels at sea was immense; and the hurricane was long afterwards remembered and chronicled as the heaviest known for years. In the interior, plantations were ruined in a single night; millions of dollars worth of crops destroyed; houses blown down; machinery wrecked; and even ancient landmarks either removed altogether, or transported to incredible distances, by the wind.

"The Grampus" and "The Forty Thieves" safely rode out this tremendous gale; and, after its fury had abated, our crews were instrumental in saving much property and some lives in the harbor.

About a week after this catastrophe, the weather becoming settled, and the trade-winds having resumed their usual direction, we started again for our former cruising-ground, and soon reached the *embarcadero*, near the underground treasury. On landing, we found everywhere marks of the passage of the hurricane. The French bark had been completely torn to pieces, as if the centre of the cyclone had passed over her. A heavy anchor which was upon her deck at the time of our first visit, and her capstan, lay far up the hillside, and were embedded in the earth as if they had been shot from guns. The rude sheds which had sheltered the pirates were tossed about like paper; the whole landing-place had been deluged with water; and enormous rocks from above cumbered the ground.

With doubting steps, and hearts saddened by the sight of such terrible havoc, we took our way to the cave; but the fair face of Nature seemed to have undergone an all-pervading change. In places where, on our first visit, there were levels, now were hollows, or mounds of earth and rock; and where mounds had once been was now level ground.

The entrance to the cave, the object of so many hopes and fears, had disappeared; and although we searched for two whole days with all our force, and brought all our ingenuity to bear, we could not discover it. At my previous visit I had hurriedly taken the cross-bearings of the entrance by a couple of lofty ceiba-trees on the opposite side of the ravine; but these also had been levelled with the earth; and the huge rock which had sentinelled the entrance to the cave had been hurled from its lofty place, and doubtless lay undistinguished from others in the bed of the rivulet. Every evidence of the existence of the cave had been obliterated; and we returned to our boat as poor as we came.

II.

MY next cruise was to the coast of Africa; and most monotonous it was. We spent our time almost entirely on board ship without society, at sea almost constantly, and not daring to pass even one night on shore in that pestiferous atmosphere. Occasionally a chase of some slavers would vary the usual routine of duty, and afford some little excitement: but, for the most part, we were thrown entirely on our own resources; and those inclined to such employments had ample time for study and improvement. The several ports we visited gave our officers little pleasure or profit; and we all agreed that "the coast" was another Pandemonium on a very limited scale. At sea we alternately were drenched with the heavy equatorial rains, and scorched by the fierce tropical sun; and the boat service in the rivers was simply detestable.

One day, while cruising, I got leave to lower a boat in order to pick up specimens of the nautilus, which are very large and handsome in some parts of what is called by mariners the Sargasso Sea. Quite absorbed in my search, I went some miles from the ship, which lay becalmed "like a painted ship upon a painted ocean;" and suddenly espied a large object rising and falling on the long swell. It proved to be a cask covered with barnacles, and, as was evidenced by the long seaweed that trailed from it as we lifted it into the cutter, had been a long time in the water. It turned out to be a forty-gallon cask of old Santa-Cruz rum, of fine taste and flavor, evidently acquired in its long voyages. On its head were branded some almost illegible characters, among which could be made out the word "Volador." That night I had the middle watch; and, as the ship went easily along under the influence of a light breeze, the old quartermaster at the "con" spun me the following yarn: —

"It seems to me, sir, that I have sailed before to-day with that cask which you picked up with such remarkable luck. [I suppose that if I had found a diamond as large as the Koh-i-noor, it would not have possessed such value as the cask had in the old tar's estimation.] Just two years ago I was returning to the West Indies from this coast in a clipper schooner, a slaver. We were bound to a port on the south side of Cuba, and had approached the Sail-rock Passage, calculating the handsome profits we should reap from our cargo of blackbirds, when we fell in with a British man-of-war, which immediately gave chase.

"Our vessel was very fast; and we flew along before a fresh trade-wind, with every rag set that would draw; and for several hours we seemed to beat His Majesty's cruiser: but towards evening our captain took it into his head to shorten sail, haul up on the starboard tack, and try to gain the shelter of the land under San Domingo, when we might evade our pursuer. This ruse is not unusual with slavers, and might have succeeded: but, after an anxious night, the dawn showed us that our manœuvre had been anticipated by the commander of the war-brig; for he was in shore of us, and not far off. That he was alert was very apparent; for, although under easy sail when we first saw him, his royals and steering-sails were instantly set, his courses dropped, and his course altered to a point converging towards our own, so as to close; and soon a puff of white smoke from his bow-gun accompanied the rise of the red-cross flag to his main peak. The chase lasted until two, P.M., with little advantage to either side; but we managed to keep out of range of his guns, although we could see that he was steadily gaining on us.

"His best point of sailing was 'going free,' while ours was 'close hauled:' so we took in the steering-sails, and attempted to bring the schooner by the wind. The evolution failed; and we had neared him by attempting it, and lost ground also, as every attempt to 'luff' was met by a lee helm on board the brig, while his occasional shots came nearer and nearer. We started our water, slacked up the lanyards of the standing rigging, knocked the wedges out of the partners to give the masts play, and finally sawed several deck-beams in twain; but nothing availed us. We then began to lighten the schooner, first throwing over the deck-load and all the spare spars and boats; and finally all the provisions, even the cabin-stores, including, I believe, that precious cask you fell in with to-day, for I had, on rare occasions, tasted its contents by especial favor. But our efforts were all useless; and the head of our foremast having been shot away, and carried with it the jib-boom and head-sails, and the schooner almost reduced to a wreck, we were taken by the cruiser, and carried into Port Royal, Jamaica, where the vessel was condemned, and the crew set adrift. I shipped in a vessel bound to New York, being without money or even clothes; and thus ended my cruise in the saucy 'Volador' ('Flying-Fish')."

Eight bells struck as the old quartermaster finished his yarn; and, having been relieved, I invited the old man down to my room to taste again the contents of that cask "he had sailed with before." I have no doubt it was the same, and that the cask had followed the current westward until it fell in with the Gulf stream, which carried it eastward again, and, passing by the shores of Europe, deposited it in that great receptacle of seaweed and other waifs, the Sargasso Sea, where we found it.

I believe that some day this enormous deposit of weed will be made available for agriculture, as it is especially rich in soda and the phosphates, and easily collected; while, being on the high seas, no nation can claim the exclusive privilege of gathering and shipping it.

Off the mouth of the Bonny we gave chase to a slaver which incautiously hoisted American colors, thinking our ship an English cruiser; and this made him a good prize under existing treaties. I was directed to take her into port after the capture, and boarded her with a boat's crew of sixteen men; while the corvette left us, and stood away for the northward.

The slaver was a schooner of about a hundred and fifty tons burden; and in this little vessel were confined over three hundred slaves, in a condition to which no description could do justice.

The officers and crew had been sent on board the corvette; and here we were left to muse on the comforting assurance of the Portuguese captain, that his "cargo" were ferocious and untamed savages from the interior of Africa, who, so far from appreciating our philanthropic efforts to save them from slavery, would inevitably massacre us all in case they got possession of the vessel, not knowing the difference between one set of white masters and another. They were all under hatches covered with strong gratings; and looking down upon them from deck seemed like looking into a certain place, which may be hotter, but not more uncomfortable. The slaves were thus divided in this *malebolge:* the main hold contained all the adults of the male sex, shackled by the leg to long bars running fore and aft in rows; and the women were in the steerage abaft them, unshackled, but separated from the males by a strong bulk-head.

The tierces of rice and water-casks were in the fore hold; and there were others under the steerage, with a few water-casks on deck; on which, abaft the foremast, were the slave-coppers for cooking, set in brick. On taking possession, I stationed sentinels at the hatchways, with orders to permit but two persons to come on deck at once, through an aperture in the grating; took every possible precaution to guard against a rush from below; and organized such other measures against surprise as seemed necessary.

A pretty fresh sea-breeze was blowing, and I had little doubt of getting into port on the next morning; for the low land was already in sight, and the wind seemed steady.

At nightfall, however, the breeze gradually died away, and at midnight had ceased entirely; while the absence of the usual land-breeze indicated that one of those calms common to the African coast, and which sometimes last for ten days or a fortnight, had come upon us.

I had brought in the boat only rations for my men for two days, and no water save that in the boat's breaker, — about sixteen gallons; and now my men reported that there was but a forty-eight hours' supply of water left in the casks below.

The rascally slaver's crew had started some of the casks before leaving the vessel. What was to be done in case the calm lasted? True, we could get ashore in our boat; but then we should have to abandon the prize and our " liberated" captives. This was not to be thought of: so I went to the main hatchway, and took a look below. None of us could understand a word the slaves uttered: indeed, they appeared hardly to possess the organ of speech, so deeply guttural and barbarous was their uncouth dialect, — more like the chattering of baboons than any human jargon. Many of them were fine athletic figures, curiously tattooed; and some had their teeth filed to a point, this serrated jaw giving them a most demoniac aspect when they grinned. As to intelligence, they evidently knew not the difference between an American gentleman and a Portuguese blackguard; and the change of masters they regarded with supreme indifference.

The first day passed without a breath of air. We lay upon deck under the awning, trying to keep cool, and sheltered from the burning sun; the vessel swaying idly on the long ocean-swell, with her sails flapping, and no sound to be heard save a groan from some block aloft, or the jaws of the gaffs as they swung around the masts. The second day passed in the same way; two slaves being still permitted on deck at a time, and our seamen walking about, and whistling for a breeze. On the third day our water which was on deck gave out; and, going below, we found that the slaves had got at the only remaining cask there, and had emptied it also.

Some rain fell, however, on this day; and we caught about ten gallons, which I carefully placed under guard for my own men. Several waterspouts formed in our neighborhood, threatening to deluge us with more water than we needed; thus adding a new and sombre feature to the situation.

At the end of the twenty-four hours we had no water left, and the slaves grew clamorous, and reasonably too; for thirst is the most terrible punishment one can suffer in that heated atmosphere, amid the reflections from the glassy sea. There was no alternative, however, but to continue to keep them below; for our lives depended on retaining them in subjection. Our provisions had been consumed; and we were compelled to eat the slave-rice, cooked with salt water, which fearfully increased our thirst. Under the cabin-floor, in the run, I had discovered a half-puncheon of rum and a box of muscovado sugar; which prizes had been carefully watched to prevent my men from intoxicating themselves. I now determined to try the spirit, as the poor fellows must keep up their animal vigor in order to perform their duty: so I detailed a trusty hand to mix toddies, and gave each man a drink every two hours.

This diet — phlogistic, I suppose, it must be termed — appeared to afford nourishment to the men; and indeed they soon looked eagerly for grog-time. We speared a dolphin on the fifth day, which afforded us all a hearty meal; our satisfaction being increased by the unexpected discovery of a cask of water.

The sailors by unanimous consent served it out to the slaves, retaining none for themselves; toddies, they said, being quite sufficient for them. The fifth day passed uneventfully, and the sixth brought no promise of a breeze: we found, too, that the vessel had drifted nearer the land; and with a glass I could see the cocoa-palm trees, and the surf breaking on the beach.

About two in the afternoon, while taking a nap on deck, I was aroused by a tumult in the hold; and, running forward, found that the bulk-head between the men and women had been broken down. Some of the slaves had slipped their irons; and all were mixed up in dire confusion, yelling, screaming, and fighting like demons. They had conspired to break down the bulk-head; and, having got access to the rum, had just commenced an orgy, which transformed them into incarnate fiends.

We hastily recovered possession of the steerage and cabin, and removed the rum to the deck; sent a strong guard below with cutlasses and pistols, which soon restored order; and, having separated the sexes again, replaced the bulk-head.

The fight had lasted about half an hour, and several slaves had been killed, whose bodies were brought on deck, and launched overboard. We then drenched all the blacks with bucketfuls of salt water, which seemed to assuage their thirst in some degree. On the seventh day the sun rose clear and calm as usual, but in half an hour retired into a dense cloud; and then I knew that our deliverance was at hand. So it proved, for a fine land-breeze sprang up, succeeded by a glorious sea-breeze; and we sailed up to our anchorage in fine style. On landing, I proceeded to the residence of the consul, who took charge of the schooner and her lading.

Although our troubles were over, those of the blacks were not; for said a Portuguese trader to me, "What for you Yankees take so much trouble about these niggers? They no better off than they were before. Suppose they no go to the West Indies to work, then they get eaten up here in Africa;" meaning that all the efforts of our philanthropic government do not alleviate the condition of the native African. While on the coast, I had occasion to see that these efforts are generally made in the wrong direction; and all of them avail nothing toward preventing evil. In my opinion, extensive colonization is the only practical mode of benefiting "benighted Africa."

At last we hove to off Cape Mesurado for the last time before leaving the coast. I went on shore to make arrangements for the homeward voyage; but was not destined to escape entirely from this accursed place, as we were swamped on the bar in returning to the ship in a large heavily-laden cutter.

There were twenty persons in the cutter altogether; and, finding myself in the water in a heavy surf, my first impulse was to seize an oar which floated near me. My situation was still full of peril; for all around I could see the dorsal fins of huge sharks, always cruising in these localities, gliding ominously through the water, and often quite close to me: but I struck out boldly, and made all the noise I could without exhausting myself, until boats from the landing-place at Monrovia came to our assistance. Our danger seemed an age in duration; but, in fact, we had been only three-quarters of an hour in the water. Only fourteen persons, including myself, were saved from drowning and the sharks.

III.

IN 1832, having passed my examination for lieutenant, I sailed in the frigate "Constitution" for France; whence we brought home Mr. Livingston, our minister to the court of Louis Philippe, who had successfully negotiated a treaty with the French Government, allowing our spoliation claims under the Berlin and Milan decrees. We went to sea again immediately, bound for the Mediterranean, where our vessel was to be the flag-ship of Com. Elliott.

I served for several years on this station in different ships, and, during the time, visited almost every port in that classic sea, besides making a trip to the Baltic. I always look back to this period of my life with pleasure; for I had many fine opportunities of seeing places and persons of historic interest. I will endeavor briefly to describe an episode which came within my experience during this part of my naval life.

One fine evening, in the short summer season which succeeds the rigorous winter of the Baltic Sea, our ship entered the harbor of Cronstadt, anchoring in that part of it allotted to ships-of-war. The sails were furled, and every thing made snug, as is customary in our ships after entering a harbor, when a government barge was reported approaching the ship. Soon it came alongside, and a Russian officer mounted to the deck. Ostensibly his visit was one of courtesy; and, in the usual manner, he tendered the facilities of the port and dockyard to our commander.

While the officer was engaged in the cabin, several of the boat's crew ascended to the deck, and among them the coxswain, a tall man in the dark green uniform of that humble office, and bearing no other insignia of rank than the silver chevrons of a petty officer. This person walked round the ship, descending to the main deck, where he minutely inspected the battery and other warlike appurtenances. He evidently wished to remain unobserved; but his imposing stature and noble air did not fail to command attention.

Our old North-Sea pilot at last observed this *incognito* seaman, and reported to the officer of the deck that a personage of the highest rank in Russia was on board; and the captain was immediately apprised of his presence and station. Our commanding officer at once comprehended and respected the wishes of the unknown, but directed such preparations to be made quietly as are customary when a personage of his condition is received.

In due time the Russian officer came on the quarter-deck: his boat was manned at his request; and, the tall stranger having taken his place at the helm, the boat shoved off from the ship.

As soon as this was done, the shrill call and hoarse summons of the boatswain was heard: a few active topmen sprang aloft, the life-lines were rove and the yards manned, and the thunder of our thirty-twos burst forth in an imperial salute, the Russian standard at the main. All the ships-of-war around us, aroused by the report, instantly began their preparations; and, before the reverberations of our guns had ceased, their yards were manned, and their cannon and those of the castle prolonged the deafening acclaim. The barge lay for a few moments abreast of our ship. The tall coxswain rose from his seat at the tiller, and gracefully lifted his cap in acknowledgment. He was Nicolas, Czar of all the Russias.

The czar treated our captain and all the officers with distinguished hospitality during our stay; and for a fortnight we had our fill of visits to St. Petersburg and its vicinity, with balls, parties, dinners, and *fêtes* of all kinds, intermingled with the opera and reviews, and concluding with a reception at the Palace of Zarsko Zelo. After the lapse of so many years, I still remember the Emperor Nicolas as the handsomest man I ever saw in any country, and the most perfect embodiment of the regal power and dignity that the imagination can picture. Hamlet describes his appearance exactly. In his imperial palace he acted his part with courteous dignity, and moved through those courtly halls with the lofty bearing of a king and the quiet ease of a well-bred gentleman. Like Saul, he was greater than other men, and at a ball could be seen towering over the throng a full head and shoulders above men of even lofty stature. At the review he was "locked up in steel," wearing the uniform of the cuirassiers of the guard; and, mounted upon a powerful black charger, he rode, as heroic a figure as was ever imagined by Homer. The imperial family were also remarkable for their personal beauty, inheriting it from both parents; for the empress was a most lovely and amiable person: and this distinction still clings to the house of Romanoff.

"There is a black sheep in every flock;" and this one was not exempt from the application of the proverb. Constantine, the son of Paul, the brother of the czar, was in appearance, as in other things, an unmistakable Calmuck. The grand duke, however, entertained us most hospitably at his magnificent château near St. Petersburg. At this interview a Polish officer speaking French and English acted as interpreter; for, unlike most Russians of station and education, Constantine spoke nothing but his own language. This officer seemed high in the esteem and confidence of the grand duke; but what was our astonishment, and the indignation of our commander, when, after we had got well out of the Baltic, we saw this audacious Pole appear in the midst of our crew as if dropped from the sky! The poor man, in the disguise of a seaman, had been secreted in the depths of the cable tier, and nourished there by some of his countrymen, musicians and marines, in pure commiseration, ever since we left Cronstadt.

It was at first decided to return, and deliver up this fugitive, as the spiriting-away of a subject of the emperor might have led to serious diplomatic complications; but finally we kept on, and the Pole remained on board. One day I called to this person, and asked him why he so earnestly desired to escape from Russia.

"Sir," said he, "that question is easily answered in one word, — Siberia!" — "But," said I, "we saw you enjoying a respectable military rank, and apparently possessing the confidence and esteem of the brother of the emperor, as well as an important post in his household; all of which you have suddenly given up, and are here as a fugitive, without money, friends, or any prospect for the future."

"Ah!" returned the Pole, "you know not Constantine or his tiger-like nature. With him there is no such sentiment as friendship, especially towards one of my race and nation. His crimes against my unhappy country call loudly for retribution from Heaven, as you must have heard: and, although I never experienced aught but kindness and favors from him, I felt that any moment, and for the most trifling cause, I might feel the heavy weight of his displeasure; while the consequences would be to me, as to others I have known, of the most terrible character. It is not my unfortunate countrymen alone who tremble at the name of Siberia: the Russians themselves of every class never hear the word spoken without a thrill of anxiety, and a glance about them to make sure that they are still in their own homes."

IV.

"SIBERIA," continued the Pole, "comprises all that vast and desolate tract of country that stretches from those northern shores of the Polar Sea, lined with eternal glaciers, beneath which dive rivers as large as the Volga, to the illimitable steppes which terminate in the rugged range of the Altai. On the east it is bounded by Behring's Straits; and, towards Europe, by the nearly impenetrable forests of the Ural, guarded by the fierce Bashkirs and Calmucks. Its soil consists of gravelly plains, interspersed with marshes, from whose sparse mosses and lichens the few reindeer draw their scanty subsistence.

"In the southern parts of this dreary tract may be seen at long intervals the wretched 'yourts' of the miserable inhabitants and the rude huts of the poor exiles, who labor hard to raise a few vegetables to keep them from starving during the long winters. From the first of August to April the nights are twenty-two hours long, and the temperature twenty degrees below zero. For the succeeding four months the sun never sets: it is necessary that his rays should be incessantly poured upon the indurated soil in order to ripen its scanty productions.

"Into this dreadful gulf the Russian Government throws *pêle-mêle* with the infected masses of their own criminals the best blood of Poland. The chains leave St. Petersburg and Moscow daily, regardless of the severity of the weather. Men and women alike are hurried along by their savage Cossack guards to the inhuman solitude they are destined to people, and, if necessary, urged on with the stick and the knout. Once daily, and on Sundays and feast-days, there is a halt at wretched sheds provided for the purpose, twenty-five versts (fifteen miles) distant from each other.

"In these they are huddled together, without even straw to sleep upon : and, should these shelters be occupied by the soldiers of the czar, the chain sleeps beneath the canopy of heaven ; for they cannot be expected to share the quarters of the defenders of holy Russia. Their rations are just enough to keep them from starvation ; consisting daily of a handful of buck-wheat flour and oats, a few vegetables, and a loaf of sticky black rye-bread, powdered with salt, cooked by the exiles themselves. If they dare to complain of insufficient fare, they are treated to a *hors d'œuvre* of seasoned ash or oak, administered on their backs and shoulders. The commander of the escort is the sole judge of the quality and quantity of the victuals issued to the chain. If it pleases him to economize them, selling the portion saved, for his own profit, or if half the chain die on the road from hunger, it is nobody's business to examine into the cause of the mortality. The dead are silent ; and the living take care to forget the circumstance in Russia, where an imprudent word may be fatal.

"The journey from St. Petersburg to Tobolsk is about twenty-two hundred miles ; and is accomplished by the chain in four and a half months, at the rate of about sixteen miles daily.

"So long a march is not executed without accidents and sickness : so there are hospitals, so called, on the route. They are mere open barns, built of logs, infested by the filthiest vermin, presided over by a person called 'doctor,' who is either an empiric or a barber, at a salary of twenty roubles (twelve dollars) per annum. When a patient dies, his body is enveloped in a coarse winding-sheet, or laid naked in a rude pine-coffin, which is drawn over the snow to a place where the bodies of men and beasts are together interred : a shallow grave is dug in the hardened soil; or, if the soil be frozen too hard, the corpse is left there in the snow to await a thaw. There is no religious ceremony; for what need of prayers has an exile? He was banished for offending the czar; and therefore, by the Greek Church, is held to be in a state of mortal sin, of which he can be purged only in hell. If the deceased be a Pole, he is perhaps thrust through a hole in the ice of the neighboring river. The Russians reserve all their hatred, fury, and caprice to vent upon the 'Polak.'

"Their sovereign loves not Poland; the Pole exasperates the czar: so let us torture and even kill him, should he fall into our hands; and these ferocious savages act accordingly.

"During the long march of a hundred and fifty days, it sometimes happens that some of the boldest escape, often carrying with them the arms of a soldier of the escort. Flight is not difficult: but it is not easy to get out of the country, or to subsist in the trackless forest; and, if any succeed in doing so, it is only to fall into the hands of the Prussian *gens d'armes*, who instantly return the unhappy fugitive to their Russian allies. If recaptured by the latter, the exile has his flesh cut into ribbons by the sharp, angular lash of the terrible knout. Should he survive the fearful punishment, his heel is pierced, and an iron ring inserted between the bone and the Achilles tendon. He is then sent to end his days in a mine, and to ponder there over the paternal justice of his monarch and father. But the runaway exile usually sells his life dearly, knowing the price that will be exacted for it.

"To recount all the horrors of this fearful transit would be to disgust you with your species; and I shall not further weary you with the loathsome details.

"Should any one, actuated by a sentiment of generous pity,

denounce all these atrocities to the emperor, he himself would be denounced, and his ruin effected, for conspiring against the state, the czar, and religion. He would immediately be knouted, to give him a lesson of prudence, silence, and discretion. The czar is not ignorant of the facts: but in Russia one may see every thing, hear every thing, yet beware of expressing a single sentiment of surprise or pity; for it is the crime of *lèse-majesté*.

"Upon their arrival at Tobolsk, the Pole and those destined for the mines are immediately sent to their place of exile, in order to get them at once as far as possible from the frontier. The rest — the bandits, assassins, poisoners, and other felons — are set free, with leave for a fortnight to rest from the fatigue of the journey: after which they receive a route-ticket, and a leathern purse containing about eighty cents in copper coin; and are obliged to go to their destination without any further directions, and to find the master to whom they are allotted.

"But the mines, — those deep and darksome gulfs in which men are forever plunged, never again to behold the light of day, and doomed to spend their lives in digging coal, — who shall tell of the anguish, the misery, of these abominable sepulchres, in which the unfortunates, consigned to a living death, toil continually, until completely worn out, their joints paralyzed, and their members rendered powerless by neuralgia?

"Those who are allotted to service are placed with some colonial master who exercises a profession or business, or cultivates the soil. He may be a humane person: if so, so much the better; for the unfortunate may expect a sort of relative happiness. Should he be a cruel one, however, so much the worse for the poor soul; for all hell's torments heaped upon a single head would not be the measure of the sufferings and anguish which he must endure. The government does not occupy itself with such details, nor does it protect its subjects from cruelty.

"True, there are plenty of 'ukases;' but, though emanating from the brain of the czar, they are never executed, seldom even read. If the exile be a Pole or a Georgian, and consequently a Catholic, he is trebly unfortunate; for he has a halter permanently around his neck. The master is bound to provide food, lodging, and clothing for his servant, and to deposit with the *golowa* the sum of sixty cents monthly, which represents his pay; certainly not much. For the time of his apprenticeship of hard servitude, he must give up the most modest, the most inoffensive enjoyments, — even tobacco, unless it is bestowed upon him in charity. Charity indeed! that is a coin uncurrent in Russia. By a strange contradiction, the government, which treats the human race worse than the brute creation, and to which the life of a man is worth no more than that of a crow, exerts every effort to people this vast solitude, called Siberia. It tolerates neither celibacy nor widowhood, permitting the departed of neither sex to live isolated. 'It is not good for man to live alone,' says Holy Writ. 'Man must work, and people the earth,' adds the czar. Upon Siberian soil the exile dons a new skin: he loses his name, and is rebaptized; he is a new being, and is expected to found a new family. To that which may be left behind him he is dead and buried. Should he have property, it is taken by the State, to spare his heirs the trouble of a division; or, if his parents have any, his portion is seized by the same paternal authority. Reconcile these monstrosities if you can.

"But one saving grace remains: which is, that, in case his wife and children solicit the favor of sharing his banishment, they are permitted to do so on condition of submitting to the penal regulations which govern the Siberian population; of which I will spare you the recital, for fear of their giving you a nightmare.

"To proceed. The condemned person works for three years, and at the end of that time enters into possession of about twenty-five dollars of your money, with which he buys a cow and a few articles of prime necessity, clears a few acres of land allotted to him, builds a log-hut, and becomes, in his turn, a master colonist.

"As to the manner in which the women convicts are treated, I shrink from the task of describing it, and beg to leave it to your imagination. Suffice it to say, they are compelled to submit to the same rules with regard to marriage that are imposed on men; and these enforced unions are made with scarcely more respect than is usually paid to the coupling of animals.

"As elsewhere in Russia, the government endeavors to realize with sanguinary fury the fundamental maxim of the first Nicolas, — 'Political unity by means of religious unity.' There is need for no other belief than that foul and ignoble orthodoxy on which is pinned the faith of the Russian clergy: so the Pole is urged to become a convert to the Greek religion. Should he refuse, all hell's torments are discharged upon his devoted head; and when, breathless and lost, the unfortunate succumbs under the superhuman griefs and pains of the knout, the stick, and the whip, his executioners cry to him, 'Embrace the religion of our father the czar, and all thy punishment shall cease!' Should the poor creature assent, he is instantly immersed in the next brook or pool; and, lo! a convert to the Greek Church.

"If I ever dared to allude to all the ingeniously fiendish tortures inflicted upon my countrymen during my forced residence in Russia, I was met with the remark, 'They complain not of their fate, but pass, without much regret, from their easy but *harassed* condition in their native country to this life of labor, fatigue, and servitude, which may not be so painful as you imagine.' All Russians have the strange and servile habit of praising all the acts of their autocrat; which indicates an utter absence of moral sense, and an impenetrable thickness of skin to which that of a rhinoceros is but the thinnest paper. Every other consideration must be ignored when it is a question of the worship of the great national fetish.

"And now," said the Pole, "that I have given you but a partial account of the dreadful fate which constantly menaced me in Russia, can you wonder I should wish to escape from a country in which such crimes can be committed with impunity, and from a doom which has been meted out to so many of my countrymen? No! I know you do not; although your own free and enlightened nation has always had a sort of sympathy with Russia, the ground for which is, I shrewdly believe, that you expect to divide the world between you by and by. While you are subduing a mighty continent by the enterprise and energy of your people, Russia is imitating your example in Europe and Asia; and, by means diametrically opposite, silently accomplishing a similar purpose.

"Truly the ways of the Almighty are inscrutable, and we, his creatures, but the passive, involuntary means of their fulfilment."

V.

GREGORY XVI. was pontiff at the period of my first visit to Rome, during the Mediterranean cruise I have referred to; and, of the famous personages then residing in the Eternal City, the one I most desired to see was the mother of the modern Cæsar, Napoleon I. Madame Mère, or Madame Letitia, as she was usually called, being requested to grant an interview to a small party of American officers, of which I was one, graciously assented, and fixed a day for the reception at the palace she occupied.

Repairing thither at the hour appointed, after a short detention in a spacious ante-chamber we were ushered into one of those lofty saloons common to Italian palaces, handsomely, not gorgeously furnished, and opening by spacious windows into a beautiful garden. There, with her back towards the subdued light from the windows, we saw an elderly lady reclining on a sofa in a graceful attitude of repose. She was attended by three ladies, who all remained standing during our visit. In the recess of one of the windows, on a tall pedestal of antique marble, stood a magnificent bust of the emperor; while upon the walls of the saloon, in elegant frames, were hung the portraits of her children, all of whom had been kings and queens, — of royal rank, though not of royal lineage. Madame Letitia received us with perfect courtesy, without rising from her reclining position; motioning us gracefully to seats with a polite gesture of a hand and arm still of noble contour and dazzling whiteness. It was easy to see where the emperor got his small white hands, of which he was so vain, as we are told; while the classic regularity of his well-known features was clearly traceable in the lineaments of the lady before us. Her head was covered with a cap of lace; and her somewhat haughty but expressive face, beaming with intelligence, was framed in clustering curls *à l'antique*. Her eyes were brilliant, large, and piercing (I think they could hardly have been more so in her youth); and the lines of her mouth and chin gave an expression of firmness, courage, and determination to a fine physiognomy perfectly in character with the historical antecedents and attributes of Letitia Ramolini. Of the rest of her dress we saw but little, her bust being covered by a lace handkerchief crossed over the bosom, and her dark silk robe partially concealed by a superb cashmere shawl thrown over the lower part of her person. She opened the conversation by making some complimentary remark about our country; asking after her son Joseph, who resided then at Bordentown, N. J.; and seemed pleased at receiving news of him from one of our party, who had seen him not long before. She asked this officer whether the "king" (*le roi d'Espagne*) still resembled the portrait in her possession, which was a very fine one; and upon our asking permission to examine the bust of the emperor, the greatest of her sons, told us that it was considered a fine work of art, it being, indeed, from the chisel of Canova; adding, I fancied with a little sigh of melancholy, "Il resemble beaucoup à l'empereur." After some further commonplaces, she signified in the most delicate and dignified manner, more by looks than by words, addressed to the ladies of our party, referring to her rather weak state of health, that the interview should terminate; and, having made our obeisance, we left her.

I may be excused for making an exception to my general

rule of silence with reference to the marvel of antiquity and art in Rome in the case of the Coliseum, of which every writer is expected to say something.

Rome having become mistress of the then known world, and having imposed her yoke on every foreign nation, rendering all tributary to her, erected this vast edifice, capable of seating a hundred thousand persons, as the principal place of amusement of her citizens. The Romans had ceased to labor for their subsistence: they inhabited a city built entirely of marble, through which they idly sauntered, bent on pleasure, or the enjoyment of the baths they had constructed with such luxurious taste and lavish expense. Their chief excitement was found in the bloody scenes of the arena; and their passion for this could be gratified only by the wholesale slaughter of the brute creation and the murder of the human species. The terrible appetite grew by what it fed on, until tamer diversions seemed insipid; and its indulgence produced those storied monsters of antiquity who disgraced humanity. It was in the decadence of the empire that this great amphitheatre arose, and soon found imitations in every province.

Christianity came in to divert it from its original use; and we have still before us, as a lesson, the mighty ruins, which seem destined to endure to the end of time.

While reflecting after this fashion in the great amphitheatre, I turned to our first lieutenant, and asked him for his views on the Coliseum.

The worthy officer, who was entirely devoted to his profession, — a martinet on the subject of clean decks, combings, ladders, brass railings, and belaying-pins, — replied curtly to my inquiry, waking up from his revery, "Well, I was just thinking what a fine lot of 'holy-stones and bibles' I could get out here, if I could only transport them aboard the ship."

A strange event happened during this cruise, while we lay at Messina.

An English tourist, in search of the picturesque, was taken prisoner by the brigands of the Abruzzi in Calabria. The British consul at Reggio, having entered into communication with the chief of the robbers, — it would have been useless to ask help from the Neapolitan Government, — inquired what sum was required for his ransom. Ten thousand ducats, was the answer. The consul, who had come in person under a safeguard from the brigand chief to the conference, could not help an exclamation of surprise at the enormity of the demand. He abruptly broke off the negotiation, and sent to Malta for a ship of war to intimidate the brigands. In a short time his Majesty's ship "Barham," of sixty guns, arrived at Reggio; and at last the troops of King Ferdinand took the field against the robbers.

The brigand chief was equal to the emergency. He disappeared from the neighborhood with his prize, taking refuge in the inaccessible defiles of the mountains. The hostile demonstrations of the consul having failed, he again sought an interview with the chief, and re-opened his negotiations. "Now, *amico mio*," said the consul, "tell me what ransom you really mean to take for your prisoner?" — "Twenty thousand ducats," replied the chief; "and it is my last word. Let me have my answer soon; for provisions are scarce with us, and it costs something to keep an Englishman. Above all, take care to make no more hostile attempts against us; for, in that case, the ransom will be trebled."

The consul saw the point; and after some time it was agreed that the Neapolitan Government should pay one half the amount, the British Government paying the other. Word was sent to the chief that his proposition was acceded to, and a time and place agreed upon for the redemption of the captive and the payment of the ransom. The high contracting parties met at the rendezvous, the consul, as before, accompanied by a strong guard; but the robber chief came alone.

The prisoner was delivered up, and the money counted out to the brigand; but the consul could not help remarking, in some excitement, upon the magnitude of the amount of the sum demanded. "Abbiate pacienza, Signor Consule" ("Be calm, sir"), said the brigand: "it is yourself that fixed the sum." — "How I?" — "Certainly, sir. You remember, last year, a ship came to Naples from England, with foreigners on board, intending to revolutionize our country and upset the government of our good king." (The brigands pretended to be desperately loyal to King Bomba.) "The ship was seized, adjudged a lawful prize, and condemned as such. The crew, including one Englishman, were cast into prison. England was indignant at the outrage upon one of her subjects, threatened the king's government, and, abusing her superior strength, compelled Ferdinand to restore the ship, and to liberate the Englishman, and, in addition, to pay him the sum of ten thousand ducats. The tariff for a rogue being thus fixed by yourselves, we could not think of asking less for the ransom of an honest man. As to the other ten thousand ducats, that is the price you must pay for the presence of your ship-of-war at Reggio, and the attempt to coerce us by employing soldiers to hunt us down; for know, Signor Consule," added the brigand with a haughty gesture, "we are not children, who can be frightened into compliance with your wishes."

"The Barham" came over to Messina afterwards, and we met her officers frequently amid the festivities of that gay city. We heard that the fair Sicilians frequently asked their guests how they liked cruising after brigands in the mountains of Calabria.

From the Adriatic we visited the Ionian Islands, the west coast of Greece, and the Morea, touching at Napoli di Romania and Hydra; and off Cape Colonna we met the British frigate "Portland" bearing away from the classic land old King

Louis of Bavaria, who had been on a visit to his son, King Otho of Greece. Then, sailing up the Gulf of Salamis, we entered the harbor of the Piræus, and anchored in view of Athens, with Mount Hymettus towering above the city.

The young king had just ascended the throne, and offered us every facility for visiting the objects of interest in his kingdom: for which, I fear, we made but a poor return; for his visit to "The Constitution" at Piræus nearly cost him his life. It happened in this wise: —

On a lovely morning His Majesty came on board, accompanied by a numerous suite of ladies and gentlemen of the court, and civil and military officers, whom we received with all the honors. The ship was in her best trim; and, at the close of the reception-ceremonies, the drum beat to quarters, and the crew were exercised at the great guns and in all the details of a naval engagement, at the king's request. Now, we had on board certain repeating rifles, invented by some cute Yankee, intended to clear an enemy's deck at close quarters, and, generally, to "beat all creation." This arm, formidable alike to enemies and friends, consisted of seven rifled gun-barrels welded together *en faisceau*, the repeating principle lying in the peculiar form of the bullets, which were cylindrical, with a hole for a fuse through their axes; thus communicating with a charge of powder between each pair of bullets, and, *seriatim*, from that nearest the muzzle to the breech. The lock was near the muzzle of the arm, and each barrel contained twenty-five charges. A shower of leaden hail could thus be thrown, which was to continue until all the hundred and seventy-five projectiles were discharged; for, the piece once fired, its contents must all be thrown out before the volley could be stopped. It was poised upon a swivel, intended to be inserted in a top rim or ship's rail, and directed by a long handle called a "monkey-tail."

At the close of the exercises, the king and the rest of our

guests, with the officers of the ship and those of a French frigate in the harbor, assembled on the quarter-deck to witness the performances of this wonderful engine, which was swivelled upon the taffrail. Our old gunner seized the monkey-tail to control the fire, pointed his piece at the target, — which consisted of some barrels lashed together and dropped astern of the ship, and pulled the lockstring.

The "infernal machine" began its work in an exemplary manner, with the rolling fire of an infantry platoon, and smashed the target at once. One, two, three barrels were emptied; but the piece then became hot, and gave evidence of a strong desire to emancipate itself from control, and to wheel upon its pivot, and turn its muzzle inboard. The gunner held on manfully to the monkey-tail until all but the last two barrels were discharged; when the piece became completely unmanageable, and suddenly bore upon the deck, distributing its leaden sugar-plums indiscriminately in every direction.

Sauve qui peut was the word; and the spar-deck was quickly cleared. Our commodore, with great presence of mind, seized the king in his arms, and made a plunge down the after-hatchway leading to the main-deck; and all the company dived below through other hatchways, the ship's officers gallantly following the example of the commodore with the ladies of the court. The king was dressed in a splendid Albanian costume; and the ample white kilt spread out like a fan while His Majesty made frantic efforts to escape from the parental embrace of the old commodore in what he considered a most undignified retreat from danger. The ladies took it more quietly; but the exodus was general as well as speedy, and the quarter-deck was left to the undisputed possession of Brother Jonathan's patent exterminator, which continued to rake the spar-deck fore and aft until the bullets were all expended.

VI.

FROM Greece and the island ports of the Ægean Sea our summer cruise was continued to Smyrna, which we found the most agreeable and hospitable of all the Levantine ports. The society was of a nature which is always the most entertaining, and was composed of refined and highly educated people, — Americans, English, Italians, Spaniards, French, Greeks, and Armenians.

Of the native Turks I cannot speak, as unbelievers are not admitted to the privacy of their dwellings, with the rare exception of a few official persons; judging from whose reports, we had no desire to know more of the Osmanli.

The Christian element, of which I have spoken, is most harmoniously fused in an institution, common to the cities of the Levant and Sicily, known as the *casino*. This is what we should term a club: but, social enjoyment being its object, its privileges are shared by both sexes; which community gives the institution a more civilized and refining character. The casino is established and maintained by subscription; all the members being on terms of perfect equality, and retaining there the same independence they enjoy in their own homes. The casino at Smyrna was, and probably still remains, a model of its kind. The house was large and spacious, its saloons magnificent, with suites of elegant apartments for cards, billiards, conversation, and music, including a fine ball-room; all handsomely furnished. A restaurant and buffet was attached to the establishment, which had a large staff of attendants under the superintendence of a major-domo, who performed his multifarious duties subject to the direction of a committee of members of the casino. The subscribers maintaining this splendid institution were all merchants, either of Smyrna or the neighborhood, including all the foreign consuls, who, in the East, enjoy a *quasi* diplomatic character. There was a weekly ball, except in the season of *villegiatura;* and the rooms could be used by the members for private re-unions if they pleased. This last advantage of membership I should think worthy of imitation elsewhere, as it precludes the necessity of turning one's own domicile upside-down for a single evening, to say nothing of the saving of expense. All strangers were introduced by a member; after which they enjoyed all the advantages of the casino.

At these casino balls, I have heard the officers of all nations agree, were to be seen the most attractive and beautiful women of every clime, bewildering in variety of charms, bewitching in character, and all in toilets more or less splendid and fanciful. In fact, nothing was wanted to complete the accessories of elevated and refining social enjoyment.

Having received our firman from the Sublime Porte, after considerable diplomatic negotiation and delay, we left Smyrna and its fair women, its gay balls and parties at the casino, its delicious fruits, its pleasant hunting-parties in the woods of the neighborhood, where wild boar and venison were abundant, and sailed for the Dardanelles, touching at the plains of Troy, and anchored in due time off Seraglio Point, at Constantinople. Although desirous of seeing this far-famed city, we did not find the change agreeable in many respects.

I never could feel any admiration for the Easterns, especially the Turks, who, after all, are but a strange, nomadic, and still barbarous people, albeit prominent in European politics, and who may be said, at the present day, to be merely encamped in Europe. Hardly more sympathy can be felt for them by the people of Western Europe than is felt by the people of the United States for the Mormons or the aborigines.

As to the sights of Stamboul, they are chiefly natural; and those esteemed very wonderful by the Turks may be dismissed as altogether unworthy of serious notice. The antiquities are few, and the museums and palaces contemptible, except those of the sultan, which have a sort of mixed French and barbaric splendor. The population is bigoted, intolerant, and insufferably dirty in appearance and manners; and altogether you cannot resist a strong desire to expel these Oriental humbugs to the Asian deserts from which they came.

Sultan Mahmoud, the slayer of the janizaries, and one of the wisest monarchs who has ever held the sceptre of the prophet, and the first who had ventured upon the work of reform in the empire, was at that time at the height of his power. Strolling through the Almeidan one day with a few companions, we became aware that a distinguished party was entering the place. First came a squadron of cavalry, which occupied the different avenues leading to it; while a smaller party of richly-dressed slaves following them drove away every one but ourselves, telling us we might remain; and, forming in line, drew their sabres. They were the eunuchs of the imperial harem. The ancient lists having been cleared, a target was set up at one end of them; and we learned that the commander of the faithful himself was momentarily expected to enjoy his favorite practice of archery, in which he excelled. To this one of the ancient customs of the padishahs, his predecessors, he still adhered. A group of Turks, evidently of station and consequence, followed; and then, riding alone on a noble chestnut horse, came Mahmoud himself. He dismounted immediately, and, taking a bow and arrows from an attendant, placed himself at a stone which marked the base, and began to fire at the target, at about the distance, I should think, of a hundred yards.

The sultan was at that time in full health and strength, and had a considerable share of good looks. He was of medium size, with aquiline features, piercing black eyes, and a full beard of the same color, which probably owed its glossy look to dyes and cosmetics. His dress was a blue cloth tunic, made like a single-breasted military frock, with embroidered cuffs and collar; light-blue trousers in the Frankish style; and a star of brilliants on the breast of his coat. On his head was a scarlet fez, with an aigret of brilliants in front, holding a straight heron's plume, the imperial ghika; and by his side hung a gorgeous sabre. On dismounting, he threw off a capacious scarlet cloak. The commander of the faithful proved to be a skilful as well as graceful archer, striking the target with every arrow. After about a dozen successful shots, the target was removed; and the sultan began his exercise with the bow for distance, which was marked off by several marble pillars. He stepped forward, and quickly despatched about a dozen more arrows, firing with great rapidity. I should think he sent his shafts at least two hundred and fifty yards.

The sultan then became aware that we were observing him, and graciously sent us the information by an officer, that he had, in the last trial, sent an arrow beyond any of those recorded by his predecessors. He then mounted his horse and rode off, followed by his eunuchs; but the cavalry remained for about an hour, engaged in the national exercise of the jereed, which I need not describe.

Although Mahmoud was fond of and highly skilled in the old warlike sports of the Mussulmans, he still took care to provide his army with muskets and bayonets of European manufacture, and clothed them in the uniform of the Frank; which certainly did not improve their appearance to the eye accustomed to behold the models they imitated. These reforms, and other departures from the time-honored customs of the Moslems, led to a serious revolt, which he extinguished with resolute vigor; but discontent still existed, and his regular troops were called, in derision, "tacticos."

Leaving Constantinople, we sailed down the Ægean, touching at Scio and Tenedos, and sustaining a heavy gale, in which we narrowly escaped shipweck. The storm was heaviest just before nightfall, when we were to the northward of Myconi, and that island was close under our lee. The sun went down red and angry; and the wind, increasing with the darkness of night, became almost a hurricane, accompanied by sharp lightning and driving rain and hail. We lost sight of the high and rocky shores; but, at midnight, could distinctly hear the roar of the surf as the waves broke on the rocks, so near to them were we. Our ship held on well, with the lee hammock-nettings almost in the water, as she careened under the pressure of close-reefed topsails and whole courses. In an open sea she would have been hove to under storm-sails; but here we were compelled to carry on, even if the masts went out of her. Our old Greek pilot stood between the night-heads, accompanied by several officers; and our first lieutenant — a splendid seaman and accomplished officer — had the deck, and stood immovable at his post, trumpet in hand. The ship dashed gallantly through the waves at a high rate of speed, but trembled like a living thing under the unwonted pressure of canvas. Every officer and seaman was at his post, and perfect silence prevailed: no sound was heard save the roar of the blast, and the dashing of the waves as the ship threw them from her bows.

Just at a critical instant, when the breakers were reported

ahead, and the command for tacking, "Ready about!" had been given through the trumpet, a heavy squall passed over the ship, and the clouds broke away for a moment in the southern horizon, showing clearly the passage between the Islands of Tino and Myconi, for which our pilot had been anxiously looking. Instead of tacking, the ship was put before the wind; the mainsail hauled up. Up went the helm, and she flew into the passage like a bird, that, having been struggling against an adverse wind, suddenly abandons its purpose, and flies with the gale.

The old pilot then gave his directions to the helmsman to "port" or "starboard" as we rushed through the narrow passage, "conning" the ship by the luminous appearance of the breakers on either hand as we approached them; and in half an hour we rounded to under the lee of the land, and were saved.. Not so a Turkish line-of-battle ship, which had been in company with us all day. We heard afterwards that she went ashore upon Tino that fearful night, and was lost, with every one on board, — five hundred and sixty souls.

A few days later, having run down the coast of Asia Minor, our good ship anchored in the road of Beyrout.

Having visited the ruins of Balbec and the famed city of Damascus, we sailed southward close in with the land of Syria, and, passing Mount Carmel, anchored again at Sidon.

From this ancient seaport I was sent by our commodore with a message to Lady Hester Stanhope, who had her residence not far off on a hill; and arrived there just at nightfall.

This eccentric English lady, the niece of the great Earl of Chatham, had led a solitary life in the East for several years, during which she occupied herself in travelling over the country, in becoming acquainted with the places celebrated in biblical history, and acquiring the various languages and customs of the Oriental countries.

Her relatives were much concerned about her eccentricities and voluntary exile, as she had once moved in and adorned the highest society, and possessed an ample fortune. Several reasons were assigned for her voluntary exile, the most plausible of which, probably, was that her mind was somewhat unsettled in consequence of the death of her affianced husband, Sir John Moore, killed at Coruña, — the hero of the fine ballad, —

"Not a drum was heard, nor a funeral note,
As his corse to the ramparts we hurried," &c.

Lady Hester had expended a large portion of her property during her sojourn in the East, roaming the wilds and deserts at the head of her hired soldiers, and making treaties with the wild Bedouin sheiks in the spirit of a Semiramis. She was certainly generous and fearless; but I fancy she sometimes owed her safety, while travelling in the desert, to the high respect and deference yielded by all Orientals to persons whom Allah has deprived of the full measure of reason. No doubt, also, her ladyship's *bucksheesh* was acceptable to these untutored children of Nature, who are quite as mercenary as other barbarians or the Thugs of civilization.

The American consul at Sidon, our surgeon, and myself, arriving rather late at the rambling buildings which composed the residence of the English lady, found the gates shut and guarded by her ladyship's Albanian soldiers; but after a parley, in which our ambassadorial character was reported to the chieftainess, they were opened to us, and we dismounted in the court-yard. We were then invited into the house, and provided with toilet-conveniences, and a comfortable supper, *à la Turque*, on temperance principles, but with plenty of kibobs and coffee. After this refreshment we were told that Lady Hester would receive us, and, following an attendant, were conducted into a large, dimly-lighted room very scantily furnished, with windows high up in the walls, so that any view from without was impossible. At the farther end of this room, on a divan, sat a bundle of Turkish female habiliments, which, upon a nearer approach, proved to contain a lady, who was smoking a long chibouk, which she scarcely removed from her lips to bid us welcome.

Without rising, she removed the "yashmak" from her face, and gracefully motioned us to seats, her attendants bringing us pipes like her own; and for some minutes we all sat silent, as if smoking the calumet with some Indian potentate. My message and invitation to the ship having been delivered and duly acknowledged by the lady, silence reigned again for a brief space, during which we had time to observe and admire the truly noble and expressive features of the singular woman before us.

Suddenly the silence was broken by Lady Hester, who commenced a long tirade against the British ministry, which had incurred her lady's displeasure by divers acts, as we now learned for the first time from her own lips, but in the merits of which we surely could not be expected to feel the slightest interest. Having scolded and abused the unconscious objects of her displeasure at considerable length with an energy of speech not much milder than vituperation, Lady Hester asked for news of Ibrahim Pacha.

When we had given the required information as to his Highness, who had been especially polite and hospitable to us at Beyrout, her ladyship proceeded, with undiminished volubility, to pour out the vials of her wrath upon the head of the pacha, whose crimes seemed to be rebelling against the sultan his master, and neglect of her ladyship's advice. She finished her diatribe by announcing her intention to seek out the pacha, and to lead him by the beard to the footstool of his rightful lord, the padishah, and to crush the revolt by imprisoning the father of Ibrahim, Mehemet Ali, Pacha of Egypt.

As she declared her determination, Lady Hester rose from her seat, dropping her chibouk, which was picked up by a little black girl at her feet, and stood revealed to our sight, — a tall, elegant figure, clad in loosely-flowing robes, and looking like an inspired sibyl.

After having vented her anger as to her two pet grievances, she conversed very agreeably on general topics, antiquities, &c., for some time, during which she appeared in her real character, — that of a high-born English lady. The lucid interval was not of long duration, however; for soon she again broke forth, and this time her theme was religion.

Apart from her interesting account of places hallowed by the traditions of Bible story, her discourse was a rhapsody rather than a discussion, and altogether failed to settle the knotty points she so flippantly assumed to decide. Her theology seemed to be a strange mosaic of Judaism, Christianity, and Islamism, ingeniously dovetailed together into a creed or faith, of the absolute truth of which, if unrevealed to others, she had convinced herself, at least, satisfactorily. She evidently was a firm believer in the doctrine of private judgment in faith, even to personal infallibility.

We could easily see that her ladyship had not such good listeners every day; and she availed herself to the fullest extent of the opportunity, continuing always the speaker, and running from one subject to another with rapidity and ease; and at last, meeting with neither denial nor criticism from us, she arose majestically from her divan, and bade us good-night. She took leave courteously, offering us her hospitality, and amiably saying that she had a right to feel a peculiar interest in our native country, holding, as she did, so near a relationship to Lord Chatham, our oldest friend and advocate : then, kindly giving us leave to see her celebrated mares on the next morning, she retired with graceful dignity.

We were astonished to find that the interview, which began about eight, P.M., had lasted until long after midnight.

We did not again see our hostess; but before leaving, after breakfast next morning, paid a visit to the famous mares. One of these animals had a remarkably hollow back, a sort of natural saddle, and was destined for the use of the Redeemer of the world at his second coming; while the other was reserved for Lady Hester herself, who, with her divine companion, was to ride triumphantly into Jerusalem. The animals were in fine condition, never being used; and stared at us as if they marvelled greatly at our appearance.

We had a pleasant ride back to Sidon, stopping at a Maronite convent half way, the prior of which shrugged his shoulders when he heard where we had been, tapping his forehead significantly: he then drew forth a bottle of excellent native wine for our refreshment.

On comparing notes, we found the impression received by all of us was the same, — that Lady Hester was partly deranged, and partly a religious enthusiast; and that Gen. Sir John Moore, by his glorious death on the battle-field, had escaped a more painful fate.

VII.

ARRIVING at St. Jean d'Acre, we found that Ibrahim Pacha had preceded us, and was actively engaged in repairing the defences of that celebrated place in preparation for the conflict between his sovereign and himself that soon after broke out. Ibrahim was a man of mark in the East, and used all his power to sustain his father, the rebellious pacha, then struggling to make his pachalic hereditary in his family; and doubtless dreamed of independent sovereignty, which they would doubtless have achieved but for Russian interposition.

I often saw him. He was of low stature, with a meagre face and figure; but had a soldierly carriage, and a mien of authority and dignity.

Unlike most Turks, he was of a restless and uneasy temper and active habits. His efforts to improve the Egyptian army and marine were untiring; and he employed many foreign officers in the work of reform. His dress was always the same, — that of a private soldier, — a simple white linen tunic, baggy trousers of the same material, with blue cloth trimmings, and gaiters; his head coifed with the inevitable fez, and a plainly-mounted sabre at his side. Yet, simply attired though he was, the pacha was always the central figure of his large and brilliant staff.

Of course, all the officers had opportunity to make a pilgrimage to the Holy City under the most favorable auspices, and protected by the authorities. I visited all the scenes of our

Lord's earthly sojournings,— his sufferings and passion,— with gratitude for the precious privilege; and treasured up memories ever after recurred to with sincere pleasure.

These places have been reverenced by the followers of the Messiah for nearly two thousand years as the actual theatre of those memorable events. I can have no sympathy with those who go to the Holy Land with determined scepticism as to the identification of the spot held sacred in Catholic history. The Catholic pilgrim certainly has the advantage of the Protestant in this respect; for he can, reposing in the religious reverence in which he has been reared, ask confidently, "Is not this the place where the 'mortal put on immortality'? Was it not here that the sacrifice of the Man-God was consummated?"

Under the guidance of an intelligent Greek kavass we visited Bethlehem, the Dead Sea, and the River Jordan; and, while encamped at the latter place, were visited by a party of Bedouin Arabs. Though they may have come with plundering intent, they found that nothing was to be gained by force, and contented themselves with begging for every thing they saw. With Spiridion as interpreter, I entered into conversation with a venerable sheik, who sat gravely before the low tent of striped cloth, stroking his long white beard. We spoke of the ruins at Balbec, Palmyra, and other localities, with all of which he was familiar, and of the unknown and unremembered people who had once possessed them. These sons of Ishmael are accustomed to converse in poetry; and, at the termination of our discourse, the old sheik said, taking hold of his tent-cord, "This string of camel's hair which supports my tent is but a slender one; yet it has seen the rise and fall of Babylon, Tyre, and Palmyra, as well as all the gorgeous remains of the cities we have been talking about."

We were hospitably received at Alexandria by the pacha, Mehemet Ali, who then reigned as independently as any sovereign monarch. He was a fine, venerable man of about sixty, with a delicate, fresh-colored complexion, and a long white beard of silky texture. At his reception in the palace overlooking the harbor, he did the honors in a graceful and dignified manner, more like a Western European than any Turk I had yet seen. He wore the Nizam dress of fine brown cloth, slenderly embroidered in black; for the "tactico" dress had not as yet been adopted in Egypt. Looking at his benevolent face, no one would imagine that he was the ruthless and determined destroyer of the Mameluke Beys, the only survivor of whom was pointed out to us at the reception. This was Emin Bey, who leaped his horse from the wall of the citadel at Cairo down fifty feet into the fosse, and thus escaped the massacre that overtook all his comrades in the court-yard. The horse was killed; but a few days afterwards an old woman in rags presented herself at the divan of the pacha, begging for mercy from the truculent chief. Mehemet, recognizing the "kismet," — the doctrine of fatalism of Islam, — not only pardoned Emin, but afterwards took him into his confidence, — a sure road to wealth and honor

Some months after leaving the Levant I was temporarily detached from duty in the squadron, and ordered to report myself to the American minister at Madrid, as bearer of despatches from him to the legation in Paris; and, in pursuance of my instructions, landed at Lisbon about the first of September, 1836, and proceeded with the American consul the next day to the village of Aldea Gallega. I supped that evening at the posada in company with the gypsy chief with whom the consul had arranged to conduct myself and servant safely to Badajos across the frontier. This worthy, Pedrecillo by name, — gypsies scorn surnames, — was a dark-skinned, sun-dried specimen of his race, forlorn and miserable enough in appearance, though possessed of the keen black eyes of the Gitanos, that seemed perpetually on the lookout for snares and pitfalls, as became his vocation of contrabandista. His usual employment, when occupied with any business, was smuggling tobacco and other forbidden merchandise by the aid of his band, although their ostensible employment was trading horses and mules.

I was assured that I could trust implicitly to the protection of the gypsies, and that I might feel as safe on my journey as if I had an escort of cavalry. Having agreed to conduct and protect us for a fixed compensation, Pedrecillo, I was told, would fulfil his engagement to the letter; although, under some circumstances, he would cut our throats as readily as a chicken's. I had hoped to enjoy a quiet night's rest at the posada; but Pedrecillo informed me at the close of our repast that I and my *mozo*, a boy I brought with me from Cadiz, must set forth at midnight, and join him at a place on the highway just outside the town, near which the gypsy crew were bivouacked. The announcement was made after the chief had demolished a puchero, the greater part of a pair of fowls, and a pudding, washed down with a bottle and a half of Collares wine; and I assented, concluding that these gentry transact their respectable commerce only by night, in order to escape the onerous taxes laid by the *resguardo* (custom-house). I yielded only to necessity; for my guide stipulated that I was in all things to obey his instructions while travelling under his protection. I already owned a fine mule: but my first transaction with Pedrecillo was a horse-trade; and I found myself in possession of a good Andalusian roadster, at a price not more than twice his real value. My mule was transferred to my *mozo*, who carried the *provant* for the journey, my valise, and *alforjas*.

We found Pedrecillo waiting for us at the rendezvous, and started forward in the moonlight at a brisk canter, which soon brought us up to the gypsy troop, which had preceded us. They seemed a shabby cavalcade of men, women, and children, of all ages, on all sorts of mounts, from fine Cordovese horses to humble *boricos* (asses); and all were laden with packs composed of camp equipage and contraband luggage. At daylight their appearance, although picturesque, — rags are always so, — did not improve. I should except from this remark the chief, who, being now on his "native heath," dropped his whining tones and sneaking demeanor, and assumed a jaunty and swaggering air. He was mounted on a fine stallion; and before him, across the saddle, was an enormous *trabuco* (blunderbuss), capable of holding a pint of musket-balls, with a flaring muzzle like a bass horn. The column of vagabonds was marshalled like cavalry on a march, — an advance of gitanos, who examined the road with searching glances; then the main body, with the *carjadores* (muleteers), with their pack-mules of contraband goods; then the gypsy women, with their household goods, and bantlings strapped to their backs; and lastly a rear-guard of stout fellows, who pushed every one ahead of them, suffering none to lag on the route. The chief, his wife and son, with Juanito and myself, rode at the head of the main body in the place of honor.

In this manner we advanced in an easterly direction, at a steady trot, through a rough and uncultivated country, interspersed with dry water-courses and groves of cork-trees, until about eight, A.M., when we saw a large town north of us, and halted in an oak forest at a spring to breakfast. I desired to visit the town, which was Evora; but the chief objected, as he did not wish it to be known that his band was in the neighborhood, for excellent reasons which I could readily appreciate. I therefore took a nap instead; after which we all mounted and rode on, and, leaving the main body at Estremoz, arrived by noon at a miserable village beyond that town, called Alcarvizas; thence through Elvas, from which the chief alone conducted us to Badajos, at which town we arrived late in the evening.

The gypsy crew had been left behind near the frontier for some reason which did not appear, and Pedrecillo signified to me that he had fulfilled his contract. I expressed my satisfaction at his fidelity, paid him in full, adding a handsome *douceur*, and bade him farewell. The gypsy thanked me with the lofty manner of a true Spaniard, which leaves you in doubt as to whether you are not really the obliged party, and took leave, returning to his band.

In my experience with these people, I have always found it best to treat them with politeness and consideration, as a matter of policy, if from no better motives. Offer them a cigar, call them *caballeros*, and occasionally confer upon them a *gratificacioncita* of a few reals: in this way you will conciliate them, and they will repay your condescension by ministering to all your little wants not formally set down in the agreement.

Badajos is usually described as a *grande place de guerre, premiere classe ;* but I found it only a dull frontier-town, with its famous fortifications decaying for want of repairs. It is, however, most interesting to a military man as the scene of the siege conducted by the Duke of Wellington, and so graphically described by Napier in his "Peninsular War." It is situated on the Guadiana; above which river the fortified heights of the strong city rise several hundred feet, with a bastioned front towards the land side. A strong *tête de pont* commands the bridge across the river, which is also commanded by the citadel of San Cristobal, into which the indomitable Philippon retired with his scanty garrison after the taking of the town by storm.

I visited the famous bastions of Santa Trinidad and Santa Maria, where the main attack of the English failed with such terrible losses; and the San Vicente bastion, where Picton, converting a feint into a real attack, by a felicitous inspiration, carried the town.

With these frowning walls and deep ditches, the flanking batteries which defend them, and the solid masonry of their construction, the strong city seems impregnable if resolutely defended; and we must agree with Napier, that " no age ever sent forth braver troops than those who stormed and carried Badajos." Beside the cathedral, erected 1248, containing a few doubtful pictures of Morales, and which is sadly in want of repair, — for it is in Spain, — there are no other objects of interest to the passing traveller.

Not being pressed for time, I determined to continue as I had begun, and perform my journey on horseback with no other companion than my *mozo*, or such chance wayfarers as I might meet. So I sent my *impedimenta* to Madrid by the carrier; and towards the last of August we cantered gayly out of Badajos over an extensive dreary plain. If you have no ladies or other companions, this is always the best mode of travelling in countries, which, like Spain, have a sort of demi-civilization. Besides your horse, equipments, and a servant, who must always know enough of the country to act as guide, you must provide a pair of *alforjas* (saddlebags of woollen) for yourself, and *capachos de esparto* (hempen panniers) for your servant, with a leather wine-bottle and provant, — all of which is carried by your *mozo* on his mule; and with your arms, and a good cloak of the excellent Spanish cloth called *paño pardo*, you are equipped for the road.

You are then independent, bound to nobody, travelling at your own will and pleasure, can start when you please, stop when you please, and are not restricted to the regular highway, or subjected to the dislocating jolts of the lumbering diligence over execrable roads, with the prospect of a runaway or an upset, or the probability of robbers. It is the only plan, even now, by which you can visit the sights best worth seeing in the country. The Spanish *arrieros* (carriers) are perfectly reliable, and may always be trusted. They form a class of themselves. Like many of their countrymen, they are vain, boasting, and great liars (*embusteros*); fond of telling tremendous yarns about the country they pass through; but are honest and industrious.

We had a monotonous and sultry ride across the plain I mentioned until a short time after high noon, when we entered the superannuated city of Merida.

VIII.

EVEN in Spain, where every thing speaks of the past, and nothing of the living present, Merida, the ancient capital of Lusitania, retains more memorials of by-gone ages than any other city; and, although very seldom visited by tourists, can boast of remains as interesting as those of Rome itself. Indeed, it might with reason be called the Spanish Rome. It is proudly seated upon the Guadiana, and has an imposing and lordly aspect.

My first visit was to that marvellous structure, the bridge built by Trajan across the Guadiana, which still serves the citizens of the place, and which seems as durable as a work of Nature. It is said that the Moslems, unable to realize that it had been erected by man, attributed it to the djinns, or genii. It is built of stones of enormous size, far greater than those used in any modern work, whose transportation must have demanded immense mechanical power, and which are still perfectly joined together by cohesion only. It is more than twenty-five hundred feet long, and thirty wide; and the roadway rests on eighty-one arches, thirty-five feet above the river.

Over this bridge passed the Roman legions with their banners inscribed S. P. Q. R.; and, after the lapse of eighteen centuries, here also have crossed the eagles of the modern Cæsar. Both hosts must have felt their hearts swell within them at the matchless prospect. A dike of the same enduring masonry serves the bridge as a bulwark against inundations, and has undoubtedly saved it from being seriously damaged in past times. This island-buttress is now a retreat for the washerwomen of Merida, who resort to it in crowds to ply their vocation. A mixed Roman and Moorish alcazar serves as a *tête de pont;* and, on the other side, the episcopal palace, once a Moorish castle, and afterwards occupied by the knights of St. John, is raised upon the Roman foundation, still distinctly visible, although the upper part was blown up by either Wellington or Marmont.

In the town stands a magnificent triumphal arch, also built by Trajan, but now sadly dilapidated. Mosaic pavements, the remains of richly-carved Corinthian columns, and huge stone-blocks that seem as if quarried by the Titans, also abound in the city. The forum is traceable near the convent of the Descalzos (barefooted friars); and another very perfect Roman bridge still spans the rivulet of Albaregas, a tributary of the Guadiana, which would be celebrated in any other locality. In this neighborhood is a splendid Roman aqueduct, with three tiers of arches built partly of granite, and partly of brick. This was but one of the many aqueducts of Merida in its palmy days; yet, ruined as it is, by its grand proportions, the solidity of its materials, and its unmistakable utility, it puts to shame all modern works of the kind. The circus maximus, or hippodrome, still exists, just outside the town, and might easily be used for equestrian performances without alteration. Its outer walls are of tremendous thickness, and thousands of spectators could be accommodated in its eight rows of seats. A small theatre is still occasionally used for the national game of bull-fighting.

[Let me remark here, that, in writing of this tour in Spain, I shall speak at length only of such out-of-the-way places as Merida, which are seldom visited by tourists; passing by without particular mention those which have already been generally seen and much written about.]

I spent a whole day in inspecting and wondering at the great water-reservoirs in the neighborhood, which are truly stupendous and unique in Europe, far surpassing even the celebrated works of the same kind at Constantinople. At the Charca de la Albufera, there is an enormous wall of solid granite, serving as a dam to what is called *El lago de Proserpina*, — a subterranean artificial lake, so grand and marvellous in its construction, that the observer might be pardoned for doubting that it could have been made by human hands. Several massive towers connected with this wonderful structure contain stairs still perfect, descending into the huge subterranean lake, which even now might be repaired and used if required by a numerous population. Alas! such a probability is infinitely remote; for the ancient Emerita, which once numbered her hundreds of thousands, now counts but three or four thousand poor people.

Having replenished our provisions for the road, and exhausted the sights of Merida, we rose at daylight one morning, and again set forth on the king's highway, — "*camino real.*" Estremadura is famed through Spain for the excellence of its pork, the dried *sopresada* (a sort of smoked sausage, flavored highly with red pepper, garlic, and anise-seed) being especially notable, while the hams of Montanches have a European reputation. Of these savory viands we had furnished ourselves with a bountiful supply, Juanito having purchased enough to subsist a dozen persons for a month. Continuing our route for about three hours, we came suddenly upon the diligence, which had left Merida the day before, its mules gone, and the passengers surrounding the vehicle with rueful visages. They had fallen among thieves: their luggage had been ransacked, and the team carried off by the robbers. The *zagal* and *mayoral* had left them in quest of other animals; and the wretched travellers were compelled to await their return, occupying the interim with boisterous lamentations. A Briton, of the species "commercial traveller," was especially wrathful, cursing Spain, its roads, and particularly its government, calling down upon them all inverted blessings, as soon as he found out that I understood his language. I learned from a son of the country, a passenger, that this part of the high-road is called *el confesionario de San Pedro*, — ominous name, on account of the numbers of poor travellers sent to Hades unshrived by the *salteadores* (highwaymen) who infest it.

Having fasted since the day before, the passengers, nine in number, were ravenously hungry, and made a fierce onslaught upon our stock of provisions, while Juanito gallantly engaged in preparing chocolate for the three ladies of the party. Travelling by diligence in Spain is simply odious. The cumbrous vehicle is invariably behind time; the stoppages, relays, and delays innumerable; and the *ventas* (wayside inns) have wretched accommodations, and are overrun with vermin.

The conductors having arrived, Juanito and myself cantered gayly off, and escorted the diligence as far as Medellin. This small place is noted as the birthplace of Hernan Cortes; but I could find in it nothing to commemorate him. Yet it is pleasant to behold places associated with the lives of men who have stamped their names and characters upon the history of their race. Among these, surely, may be counted the chivalrous and daring leader who devoted to his country's aggrandizement forty years of his life; to use his own words, "with small allowance of food, less sleep, and constantly under arms and in harness;" and who filled with his deeds one of the most dazzling pages of history. To a military man, Cortes presents the model of a partisan officer; and the moral of his career as such is, that its success was mainly due to his boldness, and apparent contempt of all caution : only apparent; for, in reality, the marquis was shrewd and cunning as well as daring.

On the next day we arrived at Trujillo, the native town of

another of the heroes of Estremadura, — Francisco Pizarro. A tomb is here shown in the church as that of the conqueror of Peru, upon which reclines his statue in armor; but, having seen another in the cathedral of Lima said to be his, I took the liberty of doubting its genuineness. Pizarro was of humble origin, the son of a swineherd, and is said to have been suckled by an Estremenian sow, — an appropriate nurse for a native of this province, though somewhat humbler than that of the founders of ancient Rome. His house is near the plaza, easily to be recognized by the statues of Indians in chains on its front and at the corners.

Leaving Trujillo, we diverged from the main road, as I desired to see more of the country; and passed the night at Caceres, which rivals Cincinnati in the rearing of swine. The country around it is fruitful and picturesque, pleasantly contrasting with that we had been travelling. The houses of the Estremenian aristocracy have a feudal aspect, their portals being decorated by shields of the armorial bearings of their owners. The district is fertile, and produces the finest wheat, fruit, and wine. The streets of Caceres are neat and clean, well watered by running brooks: and there are some Roman remains, objects of antiquity being found in the vicinity, which are doubtless genuine; for the Spaniards, unlike the Italians, have not sufficient ingenuity to reproduce these articles of *virtu.*

From Cæsar's camp — the name is derived from *Castro Cæsaris* — we had a most delightful ride past old Gothic castles, Moorish alcazar, and Roman ruins, to Alcantara; which ancient town, with its crumbling walls, and thin, flanking towers, its grim old castle, weather-stained houses, and narrow streets, on its bold eminence hanging over the Tagus, would delight an artist like Prout or Ruskin. As all the world knows, this ancient town was founded by the celebrated military order of Alcantara, under the rule of St. Benedict.

Amongst those mixed orders of monks and knights which shed so much lustre on the middle ages, the Benedictines were foremost in arms, as in erudition. Like the Templars, these knights, originally poor, became rich and powerful; and, exciting the jealousy of the crown, the king was appointed their grand master two centuries after their foundation. His Majesty found no difficulty in disposing of the superfluous wealth of the order; which, having fulfilled the object of its existence, soon fell into decay. They have left here a splendid convent, containing their church, with the tombs of many of the soldier-monks.

The great sight of Alcantara is the bridge, which, I think, is the most remarkable in the world. It bestrides a gorge with walls of solid rock, through which rolls the lordly Tagus; and the river expands into a lake above it. It is very deep, and is said to rise in a freshet to the height of a hundred and seventy feet. There are six arches, the two central ones having a span of a hundred and ten feet; and it is two hundred and ten feet from the parapet to the water in the ordinary stage of the latter. The architect has given his name to posterity in the inscription near the entrance: —

"PONTEM PERPETUI MANSURUM IN SECULA MUNDI
FECIT DIVINA NOBILIS ARTE LACER."

IX.

THE organization of the military orders, it is well known, dates from the time when not only Spain, but Europe also, was threatened with an irruption of Moslems, whose efforts were directed towards the supplanting of the cross by the crescent. The domination of Christianity being threatened, there sprang into existence the Templars, the Hospitallers, the orders of Santiago, of Calatrava, of Alcantara, and others, which, with true military foresight, carried the war into Asia, there to fight the battle to the end, their vows compelling them never to make peace or truce with the infidel. The crusaders, who are generally but erroneously thought to have been barbarians, fanatics, or enthusiasts, gave to the European peoples the much-required ascendency over the hordes of Islam. They stimulated the military spirit and strengthened it, united Christians fraternally, and made of them a homogeneous and compact brotherhood. They developed the dormant sentiments of the human mind, improved the condition of the serfs, and slowly but surely undermined the feudal system. They created navies (witness the knights of St. John), encouraged commerce and manufactures, and gave society a powerful impulse in the direction of enlightenment.

For themselves, the military orders renounced all those things which command the exertions of mankind, being vowed to celibacy, poverty, and obedience, many of them condemning themselves to perpetual mendicity. They also spread themselves everywhere, laboring to convert souls to Christ, and devoting their most strenuous efforts to release the host of captives held by the Mussulmans.

Centuries afterwards, the existence of the Church was again threatened by the schism of Luther: and, the ancient orders having fallen into decay, a brilliant Spanish knight, laying aside his carnal arms, betook himself to a preparatory course of prayer, seclusion, and fasting; after which he founded the order of Jesus.

At this juncture fleshly arms were unavailing to help the Church: the age required her defenders to put on the armor of learning and astuteness. The mere mention of the name of the Jesuits suffices to invoke vague fears in the minds of many, — a sentiment of indefinable dread, as of an irruption of savage Indians, like those who threatened society in the early days of our republic. We are as alarmed at the establishment of a school or college of this order as if it were to be made the means of our enslavement. Shutting our eyes to the vast and increasing corruption of the whole machinery of our government, the open bribery, the lack of education, and the predominance of ruffianism, in our governing classes, we cry out against the dangers of priestcraft with furious animosity.

Men do not despise the Jesuits: they fear them. It may be seen immediately, that he who attacks them believes himself opposed to no insignificant adversaries. In his heart he believes that every thing relating to the Jesuits is a grave matter, and that the least indulgence of them is dangerous, the least negligence fatal.

The spirit of the age is essentially one of scientific and literary progress; and, knowing this, the Jesuits act accordingly.

For this reason so many learned and eminent men are found among them. Their knowledge and influence are always exercised in extending the beneficent teachings of the Church, in pursuance of which they have already encompassed the globe; and having preached the gospel everywhere in person, and not by the distribution of books, they return to add their valuable treasures of experience to the common fund of science and education. These are the crimes for which they cheerfully endure obloquy, persecution, and death.

At the establishment of the military orders, the world cried out, "What an unnatural alliance!—the ecclesiastical character combined with that of the soldier! How incompatible!" But it was soon seen that those institutions were in conformity with the natural order of things at that period. It was a strong remedy for immense evils, which threatened anarchy, and retarded civilization. And so with the foundation of the order of Jesus. Men could not successfully combat their arguments, or vanquish them in the field of controversy: so they cried out against their influence over the mind.

And still the most prejudiced cannot deny that these orders of which I have spoken all acted with utter self-abnegation, and that through their efforts much good was effected, while in their institution and action we plainly see the finger of God directing them.

Returning from this little digression, we will resume our itinerary.

After leaving Alcantara, we were ferried over the Tagus, and took the road to Placencia, passing through Coria, famous for its Pelasgian walls thirty feet in thickness, and a remarkable tower of the middle ages, a fine example of Gothic construction, with corner bartizans and machicolated summit.

We entered Placencia to the sound of the cathedral-bells sweetly ringing the Angelus, and rode at once to the posada, which we found very comfortable. We were served with an excellent supper, including a dish of the delicate trout of the vicinity, famous for their size and flavor, and with the fine wine of the country. The attendance of the most beautiful young woman I had yet seen in Spain gave a zest to our repast.

She was the *moza* of the posada: she had large, liquid black eyes, regular and pearly teeth, a brilliant complexion, perfect figure, and an abundant glossy black *chevelure*.

Even the usually demure Juanito was carried away by the exquisite loveliness of this Estremenian maid, and acknowledged, that, even in his own province of Andalusia, he had never seen such a vision of beauty; "Although," he added deprecatingly, "Que lastima falta el meneo Andaluz!" ("What a pity she should want the graceful carriage of an Andalusian!")

In the morning, leaving Juanito to enjoy the society of the fair maid of the inn, I sallied forth with a person I picked up, who had nothing better to do, — there are always plenty such in Spain, and really intelligent ones too, — to view the sights of Placencia.

The old town is indeed "pleasant;" for even at this time, after travelling in all parts of the wide world, both before and since my visit to it, never have I beheld such varied changes of view, and all charming. It is girdled by the silver Xerte; and the twin-valleys of the Valle and La Vera are perfect gems of landscape. The artist will find here all scenic accessories that he could wish. The river, the rocks, and the distant mountains of the Sierra de Bejar and de la Vera; the ancient houses, domes, and steeples of the town; the "flanking walls that round it sweep;" city, castle, aqueduct in ruins, and picturesque figures to embellish the foreground in appropriate costume, — are all to be found in perfection. Let me add that the climate is mild and salubrious, and the sky of the true ultramarine tint; and he would be hard to please indeed who could fail to find here subjects for his pencil. The scenery far exceeds that of the famed Valley of the Arno in its variety and richness.

This part of Estremadura is fertile, the land producing abundant cereal crops,— vegetables, the vine, and the olive. Its grazing-grounds furnish rich pastures for cattle. There is good shooting in the neighborhood, and the mountain-streams abound in trout. No wonder Charles V. selected it as the place of his retirement, familiar though he was with every part of Europe. I ascended to the roof of the cathedral, and stood entranced by the magnificent and smiling panorama of which it is the centre; and again climbed to it on the morning of my departure to carry away with me the freshest possible memory of a spot so lovely. Thirty years have elapsed since that last look, and in the interval I have seen many noble prospects; but I reflect upon fair Placencia as surpassing them all.

It is eight leagues from Placencia to Yuste,— the retreat of Charles V.,— which I intended to traverse rapidly; but was delayed by involuntary halts to contemplate the ever-recurring and varying prospects on the way.

We passed and exchanged frequent salutations with parties of women and girls, who walked, balancing baskets on their heads. They were carrying provisions to their male relatives, the vine-dressers, who were busily engaged in harvesting the grape-crop in the vineyards of the Valley of the Vera. Merrily they tripped along, clad in their picturesque costume, with stockingless, sandalled feet, beguiling their way with songs and laughter. It seemed like a scene in a comic opera.

Arriving shortly after noon at the farm of Magdalena, in sight of the old Convent of San Geronimo (the emperor's celebrated retreat), we lunched there on our own fare; after which we ascended to the monastery. I was so lucky as to secure as *cicerone* here Father Alonso Caballero, a venerable priest, who took holy orders, as he told me, in October, 1778, and who showed me all the interesting historical places of the conventual remains, which are much dilapidated.

The convent is entered by a gateway; near which stands a patriarchal walnut-tree called the *nogal grande*, under which the august recluse has doubtless often mused. The church and the chambers occupied by the self-dethroned emperor are still intact. From the former a door communicates with his bedroom; and the chamber has a window which commands a view of the altar, so that the bed-ridden monarch could witness the elevation of the sacred elements in the mass. Here also hung the celebrated Gloria of Titian, as we are told, which accompanied the emperor in his journeys, and upon which his last gaze was devoutly fixed.

Charles desired that this picture should be hung wherever his body rested after death; and his son, Philip II., transferred it to the Escorial. Here is the cabinet of the emperor, and several other rooms with fireplaces in them, — a domestic luxury rarely seen in Spanish houses, — the *brasero* being mostly used. The windows of these rooms command fine views; and they communicate by a cloister with the private garden, in which still may be seen the antique sun-dial of which we read in history. The emperor did not long enjoy the pleasant retirement he had promised himself here; for he died in about a year after taking possession.

In reviewing the splendid career of this monarch, — if I may be permitted to express an opinion, — I should say that his history has yet to be written, so unjust, querulous, and fault-finding have been those who have hitherto undertaken the work. This is especially true of those writers who are accepted authorities in this country; for in considering his motives and actions during the wars he waged, — chiefly religious wars, — they do not seem to take into the account the customs, manners, and sentiments of the period. In laying down his imperial power, Charles has given us the evidence of his greatness, even had he not been born to a throne; for the step was caused by no morbid misanthropy or disgust with the world in which he had played so important a part. His retirement was due to sheer weariness of worldly matters, and a desire for absolute repose and reconcilement with Heaven, before whose tribunal he knew he must soon appear to render an account of his stewardship. He wished to finish his reign of sovereign power, during which he had overrun civilized Europe with his hardy Spanish veterans, by making expiation for his sins and misdeeds before it was too late. He set about this immediately upon arriving at Yuste, and, as the event proved, not a moment too soon for his salvation.

By the kind permission of the good prior, I slept in the bed-chamber of the mighty dead, the darkness of which was somewhat relieved by the solitary altar-lamp shining through the window, undisturbed by any visions of its former occupant. In the early morning I attended the first mass, being one in a small congregation consisting of two or three friars, a couple of poor women, and a beggar. At the termination of the service, I bowed a long farewell to the altar upon which had been fixed the last dying gaze of the great Charles V. Then, mounting our beasts, we slowly recommenced our wayfaring eastward, and soon bade adieu to Estremadura, and entered the kingdom of Toledo.

X.

OUR next halt was at Talavera, situated on the Tagus, in the midst of a beautiful and fertile vega, or plain, and famous as the scene of the battle which raised Sir Arthur Wellesley to the peerage. As this battle is so well described in Napier's excellent "History of the Peninsular War," I merely refer the reader to it, as giving a trustworthy account of the success of a campaign which seemed to be already lost by Wellington, but in which Fortune, proverbially fickle in war, deserted the French eagles, to perch on his victorious standards.

At Talavera I reluctantly discharged my *mozo*, Juanito, who was long enough away from his relatives, and who, as he told me, *quiero a descanzarme* ("wished to rest himself"). I then sold my animals, and proceeded by diligence to Madrid, stopping a couple of days at Toledo by the way.

I shall not describe the capital city of Spain, as it has been already "done" so often by travellers and tourists; and will merely say that there are many other cities of the Peninsula decidedly preferable to it on every account. It is notoriously an unhealthy place, the climate being subject to extreme variations of heat and cold; and even its native inhabitants have to go about *embozado* (covering the mouth with the cloak).

The country around Madrid is desolate and inhospitable, and its situation as the geographical centre of Spain is a disadvantage; for all supplies coming seaward must be transported at immense expense, which makes it the dearest capital in Europe. The wealth of the Spanish capital in art-treasures is inestimable: the *museo* contains pictures, even to name which makes the eyes of the connoisseur glisten with delight. Here is that celebrated canvas of Velasquez, called familiarly "Las Lanzas," a representation of the surrender of Breda, in which is produced the curious effect of an actual glitter of the lances of the guard, so magical are the lights and shadows. Here also is that picture of Raphael, known as the "Pearl," sold by Cromwell to Philip IV. for two thousand pounds, and which the present British Government would be too happy to repurchase at fifty times that amount; the Pasmo de Sicilia, the virgin of the fish; and Titian's Charles V., said to be the finest equestrian portrait in the world. The emperor is arrayed in the suit of armor still to be seen in the royal armory.

The collection of arms and armor in the royal palace is unparalleled; and, in viewing it, one is carried back at once to the heroic age of Spain. These swords and lances were wielded by her noblest champions; these helmets covered the heads of her wisest warriors; and beneath these corselets beat the hearts of those forever famous in history, and embalmed in poetry. The silent but eloquent records are for the most part genuine; and the flaunting, moth-eaten banners on the walls were actually taken from the enemies of Spain, either Moslem or Christian.

As to society, there are few dinner-parties except in the foreign diplomatic circle; for Spaniards seldom entertain in that manner anywhere, but *en revanche* there is an institution of a national character well worthy of imitation. I refer to the *tertulia*, which, as in other Spanish cities, is held every evening somewhere. It is simply a meeting, by tacit understanding, among persons of the same social circle at each other's houses in rotation. The lady of the house is the supreme autocrat of the evening; even its master considering himself merely a guest for the time being. Having assembled at a rather early hour, the ladies amuse themselves with cards, conversation, games, or music, as they please; and, the gentlemen arriving later in the evening, these amusements are succeeded by quadrilles, waltzes, and *contradanzas*. One of these latter is known in America as the German; but, years before its introduction here, I have often seen it danced in Spain at *tertulias* under its true name, — the *contradanza Español*. No entertainment is given at the *tertulia*, the rule being rigidly enforced, *un vaso de agua y buen venida* ("a glass of water and welcome"). Thus many who move in the best society, who may indeed possess fine houses, but who cannot afford to provide expensive entertainments, are not therefore "tabooed" from social enjoyment. This plan also saves many heart-burnings, Mrs. B. not being able to triumph over Mrs. C. in the elegance and richness of her viands.

While awaiting the orders of the American minister I had ample time for seeing all the sights of Madrid, and to take part in the amusements of the capital. I also visited Cordova and other places of interest in the South. Granada I had already seen; but, as they are so well described by others, do not deem it necessary to go into details of my observations.

As the time of my departure drew near, and as it was more desirable than ever to travel on horseback on account of the civil war then raging in the Peninsula (the diligence, in addition to its other inconveniences, being alternately robbed by Christino guerrillas and Carlist bands), I frequented the Puerta del Sol daily in order to secure attendants for my journey. While watching one day the *empleomaniacos* (office-seekers) and others who are perpetually engaged in polishing the pavement of this well-known rendezvous of the

Madrileños, chance threw in my way the very man I wanted. Absorbed in my contemplations, I was saved from contact with a donkey laden with firewood by a robust person who swung the little animal clear of me by his "narrative" in a nonchalant style, chaffing his driver at the same time in terms any thing but complimentary. I accosted this person for the purpose of thanking him for the service he had rendered me, excusing myself for my abstraction.

All Spaniards, high and low, have a grave, high-bred air; and my unknown friend was no exception to the rule. I saw at the first glance that he was of a class very popular in Spain, although not of the highest respectability. He was evidently one of the *aficion,* or what we should call the "fancy;" in short, a *toreador* (bull-fighter). He seemed about forty. His round bullet-head, bald on the forehead and temples, surmounted by the Andalusian montera; his mutton-chop whiskers on a face otherwise cleanly shaved; his club-cue, tied with a black ribbon; broad shoulders; tapering waist; and long and sinewy arms, shown to advantage by the *majo* costume; together with an indescribable jaunty air, — all proclaimed the *aficionado.* There was a roguish twinkle in his one eye; and I observed that he had a halting gait, the left leg being bent under him, and shorter than its companion.

Having frequently seen their exhibitions in the arena, I had acquired a strong sympathy with this class of people, inspired by the very manly and dashing qualities they display in pitting their skill and agility against the mere brute force of the *toro* (bull). In none of our modern games can be witnessed a greater display of virile courage, nerve, and dexterity, than in the Spanish bull-fight. Deprecate it as we may, it is a nobler test than the disgraceful "P. R." tolerated among us. To see a young, graceful, elegantly-attired man, armed only with a slim, shining sword, facing a huge, ferocious brute of twenty times his strength, awaiting his onset with a keen, determined glance, relying only on his eye and agile muscle, yet confident in his ability to slay his powerful adversary, is a truly thrilling spectacle. And when the bull, confiding in his strength, lowers his stately head, levels his long sharp horns, and rushes upon the man as if to sweep him out of existence in a moment, the *toreador*, stepping lightly aside, masks the furious animal with his *capa* ; while in the same instant the keen weapon, quick as the levin bolt, pierces the spinal process at the nervous centre, and the bull falls headlong, to die in a few minutes.

I soon found that my new acquaintance was accustomed to travel; having already, in the practice of his calling, visited every part of the kingdom, even so far as remote Galicia.

By his references I also learned that he was a man of courage and tact, and as honest and truthful as could be expected. He was, too, versed in cookery and in foraging, — no mean accomplishments in Spain. He had recently been severely hurt in an encounter with an enraged bull while essaying some foolhardy exploit; and his lameness thus occasioned disabled him from appearing in the *cuadrilla*. He was therefore open to an engagement, which I soon concluded with him. The name of my squire was Manuel Blasco y Gusman, a native of Triana, a suburb of Seville.

I was amused by hearing the name of Gusman, one of the noblest lineages of Spain; but found that this was no uncommon instance of a lofty patronymic borne by a person of humble station. The great lords of ancient days often gave their names to their slaves upon manumitting them; and some of these latter, becoming famous, were ennobled in their turn: which complication has led to such confusion in names, that some travellers have asserted that *all* Spaniards are of noble blood.

Our preparations having been completed, *El Tuerto* ("the one-eyed") and myself, followed by a *mozo* with a pack-mule, rode out of Madrid by the fine road connecting the city with the Escorial, which runs for some distance along the Manzanares. The noble bridge across that stream, with its tall bridge house and stone statues, would command admiration if it only bestrode a river; for the muddy gutter which creeps beneath its high arches seems ashamed of its own insignificance. The country is barren, and the population sparse and poor, in the neighborhood of the capital; and we were glad to see at the fifth league the palace of the Escorial rising in dreary, solitary state by the side of the lofty sierra.

By invitation of an officer I had known in Madrid, I spent the rest of the day and night in this magnificent monument of the Spanish kings, which contains a royal palace, a monastery with a superb church, the remains of a fine library, and the royal mausoleum. But I will not attempt a description of the Escorial; for I experienced no other sentiment than that of oppression amid its gloomy splendors. It is seldom used by the court, and remains a monument of misspent millions, which, used in almost any other way, might have unspeakably benefited the nation.

We resumed our journey at early dawn, taking the road which ascends circuitously the steep and rugged sides of the Guadarrama range, and arriving before noon at San Ildefonso and La Granja. This *château en Espagne* is called the "castle in the air," standing nearly four thousand feet above the sea-level, and is a truly noble royal residence, amid magnificent alpine scenery, rocks, forests, and waterfalls, surrounding it in picturesque profusion; while above all towers the lofty peak of Peñalara to the height of eight thousand feet.

It was here that the imbecile Ferdinand VII. in 1832 signed the obnoxious decree revoking the repeal of the Salic law; which, however, remained but a short time in force, when he again repealed it, and declared Isabel II. his successor; which measure caused, ultimately, the civil war now raging.

The artificial accessories of this royal retreat, including the irrigation of the gardens, cascades, canals, and fish-ponds, are wonderfully complete. There is a model farm in a sunny nook called *La Quinta de Quitapesares* ("The Farm of away with Melancholy"); and here the modern Dido — Queen Christina — first met her Eneas, — Muñoz. From La Granja we descended the mountain by easy grades; and Manuel Blasco enlivened our wayfaring by his version of the story of Doña Christina, her palace intrigues and bold strokes of policy with silly old Ferdinand VII., his brother Don Carlos, and the soldier Muñoz. His being also the popular version, I shall give it hereafter.

Before he had finished we arrived in the plain, and saw before us the crumbling walls of Segovia, and the pointed roofs of the towers of its curious alcazar, called by Le Sage, in "Gil Blas," a tower; though there are several included in the edifice.

Having refreshed and restored ourselves, we took our way to the old castle, which I was curious to inspect. It exhibits both Gothic and Moorish characteristics, and rests upon a Roman foundation. Its keep is tall, square, and massive, with turrets at the angles, dating back to the twelfth century, and is replete with historical souvenirs.

From its lofty walls the worthy and magnificent Isabel the Catholic was proclaimed Queen of Castile; and from its gateway she issued alone, on horseback, for the purpose of quelling a mob, which she awed into subjection by her majestic appearance and strong will.

Here Ripperda, the daring minister of Charles V., was confined; and here came Charles I. of England, a suitor for the fair hand which he failed to obtain; and here, too, Gil Blas was confined, as we are told in his veracious autobiography.

Beside this picturesque and venerable relic of the past glories of Castile there is a chapel of the Templars, a Geronimite convent, a curious little church built on the model of the Holy Sepulchre, and the ancient mint, which in former times used the water-power of the Eresma, — a brawling little brook running through the town: it is probably the oldest mint in Europe. The Roman aqueduct, which was in use up to 1433, when it was repaired by Isabel the Catholic, is also interesting, especially to an engineer.

XI.

AT Segovia I met with Col. Reyes, an artillery-officer, with whom I had acquaintance; and as he was conducting several batteries and some recruits to the army of Espartero, and politely invited me to accompany him northwards, I accepted the offer, rather to the discontent of my squire El Tuerto, who was a Carlist in politics, although he warily concealed his opinions. We accordingly set forth together; and passing by Medina del Campo and Simancas, in the castle of which latter place Col. Reyes kindly aided me in inspecting the interesting archives there deposited, arrived on the fourth day at Valladolid.

In the fifteenth century this was without a peer among Spanish cities. Says the proverb, "Villa por villa, Valladolid in Castilla;" but now it is sadly on the wane. Its inhabitants boast themselves as genuine old Castilians still, and are grave and formal, all hidalgos, and, let us add, terrible bores. Its very stones are historical, as is well known.

I here took leave of my kind friend Col. Reyes, who passed through without stopping, but not until he had introduced me to the governor and some other valuable acquaintances. Having seen the various sights of the old capital of Castile, I prepared to prosecute my journey, and held a council with Blasco on the subject of our route to the north.

The man of the single eye preferred the road *viâ* Lerma, with which he was familiar; "And besides," said he, "we shall not in that case have to travel with *chapelgorris* (Christino militia) and other *gente sin verguenza* (low fellows), but shall have the road to ourselves." He also urged that the main road to Burgos was infested with highwaymen and *rateros* (foot-pads); adding with a lofty air, "I, sir, who address you, am accustomed to the society of *caballeros* (gentlemen) and *toreadores valientes* (valiant bull-fighters), and, rather than travel with such persons as we have been with for the past week, would much prefer to be alone with your worship and Pedro the *mozo*."

These and other cogent reasons were urged with such force by *El Tuerto*, that I accepted his view of the case, although with some suspicion that he had a private purpose to serve by diverging from the usually-travelled road.

On the dawn of the day appointed, I arose, performed my toilet, broke my fast, and awaited the appearance of Blasco with the beasts; but he did not arrive. At last Pedro came, and said that my squire had been arrested on the evening before, and was now in prison awaiting trial for his life by a military commission. His alleged crime was an aggravated assault on a sergeant of artillery. In Spain, summary execution so often follows an arrest in times like the present, that I was seriously alarmed, and immediately went to visit poor Blasco at the *carcel militar*, expecting to find him in the depths of despair. On the contrary, he was neither penitent, nor in the least alarmed; carelessly puffing his cigarette, and laughing at the suggestion that he was in peril. He regretted extremely that he should have caused me the least inconvenience, but expressed no apprehension for himself, declaring that the commanding general would set him at liberty immediately on my application to that effect. "For," said he, "you know, *teniente mio* (my lieutenant), that we are attached to the honorable American legation near *su magestad catolica*, and so are exempted from all ordinary interference while travelling on service."

Blasco was right in his conclusions; for my application to the military governor was successful, and the order for his liberation given immediately.

This little episode, as frequently happens in like cases, was brought about by the universal *casus belli*, — a woman. My squire was a devoted ladies' man, as I had already observed; and, on the evening in question, was engaged in the kitchen of the Fonda up to a late hour, entertaining the cook. The sergeant of artillery entered, and joined in the conversation, doubtless, as M. de Trop. The *séance* continued peaceably enough until an argument arose between the two gentlemen concerning the merits of their respective provinces, the sergeant being a Galician.

After disparaging Andalusia and her sons at some length, the sergeant became personal, and drew forth a bitter retort upon the Spanish Bœotia (Galicia) from *El Tuerto*, who, answering the reflections on his province and the contemptuous allusion of the sergeant to his single eye at one blow, with characteristic wit repeated the proverb, "En la tierra de los ciegos, el tuerto es rey" ("In the land of the blind, the one-eyed is king").

The soldier rejoined by applying to Blasco a name which signifies a bull which shrinks from encountering his enemies in the arena, — *un blando*. To call a man by such a name in the presence of a lady was to inflict an unbearable insult. The *aficionado* rose from his seat, moved towards his rival, and addressed him: "Know, friend sergeant, that I am not a *blando*, but that I am *duro chocante, carnicero y pegajoso*" (a bull which kills horses, upsets the bull-fighters, and clears the arena), in the slang of the *plaza de toros*, at the same time giving the soldier a sound box on the ear.

The latter sprang up, and drew his sword; but the one-eyed man, quick as lightning, disarmed and overthrew him, placing his foot upon his neck. The cook screamed murder. Servants, soldiers, and outsiders generally, hurried to the scene, but stood shrinking before El Tuerto, who faced them, his foot on his foe, his one eye glittering with rage, and his sabre describing the *moulinet* round his head.

At last the patrol appeared, commanded by an officer: but even to him Blasco refused to surrender save on terms of honorable capitulation; these being, that his opponent should be placed in arrest, while he himself should be put in the military prison, instead of the *calabozo*, the latter being the place of incarceration of vulgar criminals. His conditions being allowed, he gracefully yielded his sword to the officer.

This weighty matter having been brought to a satisfactory conclusion, our little cavalcade set forth, contrary to our usual custom, in the afternoon; and that night we slept at the village of Olivares, at the house of some one whom I took to be an intimate friend of Blasco, judging from the hearty *accolade* between them upon meeting, — a welcome also warmly confirmed by the friend's wife, with whom my companion's relations must have been exceedingly friendly; for he retired with her to the kitchen, and, by their joint efforts, an excellent supper was soon provided. Next morning we took the road, and arrived before noon at Aranda on the Duero. Here my guide turned aside from the *camino real* running from Madrid to Burgos, and led us through a most romantic country, in which each step revealed an ever-changing prospect, to Peñaranda del Duero, which we reached about two, P.M.

Having rested at the humble posada of the little village, I strolled forth to inspect a ruined castle I had observed perched upon a bold hill, the base of which was surrounded by dilapidated, Prout-like houses, about which lounged beggars in Murillo-like rags.

"This," said Blasco, "is *Peñaranda de la perra*, from a tradition which says that the Moors once held the castle obstinately, being besieged by the Christians with unavailing patience, until one day some of the besiegers saw a bitch (*perra*) move out of a hole, which was a secret passage into the castle, and which they marked well. That night a forlorn hope entered the stronghold by this passage; and, the assault being given at the same time, the fortress was taken, and its garrison put to the sword. The castle is the *casa solar*, or family seat, of the Zuñigas, counts of Miranda."

Ourselves and our beasts having been refreshed, we mounted, and rode leisurely northward through a fine country. Having a long ride before us, and being inclined to conversation, I dropped alongside of my squire, and offered him an excellent *puro* of Havana, which always put him in a cheerful mood. The Spaniards, generally, retain many of the Oriental customs and manners, and, among these, have a great weakness for stories, both as narrators and listeners. This is especially true of the Andalusians, who, born in the land of the Moors, and nearer the sun than others of their countrymen, partake in a greater degree of the temperament of their former Moslem masters. These *cosas de España* are often mentioned by foreign writers; and all the world knows that these propensities have brought upon the Andalusians the satire of their neighbors, the French: indeed, but for them, we should never have had the wonderful exploits of Don Quixote, as detailed for the world's amusement by the immortal Cervantes.

Blasco was somewhat given to story-telling: and, having gently urged him to exercise his power in this direction, I was not surprised that the dreamy air of the autumnal weather seemed to stimulate his faculties, as he withdrew his cigar from his lips, and answered me, "It always saddens me, *señor mio*, to contemplate such ruins as those we saw to-day, even for the fortieth time; and I cannot help figuring to myself the persons who once occupied them, who wept, or were merry, and who, perchance, thought the same thoughts that we are thinking, or suffered the same griefs and enjoyed the same pleasures that are ours.

"The place we have just left behind has its traditions of a past generation; and I shall be happy to relate to your worship, if you have the patience to listen to a story of the country, a tale of events which happened in the very neighborhood."

I gladly assented to the proposition of my worthy squire; and Manuel Blasco, signing to Pedro to approach nearer in order to give him what he knew would be a gratification, began his story. It is impossible for me to give the reader an idea of the air and gesticulation of the narrator, or to convey to the ear his sonorous tones as he rolled out the magniloquent Castilian sentences of his romance; but I will endeavor, in the following chapter, to give his story an English translation.

XII.

"Many years ago, when Moor and Christian were still contending for the possession of the Peninsula, the town and castle of Peñaranda were held in fief by Baltazar de Zuñiga, Count of Miranda. You may yet see his tomb at the *colegiata* in the village, and that of his wife, with others of that ancient family.

"Count Baltazar was a dissipated young man, and passed his time mostly in hunting and chivalric employments, varied by frequent carousals with his riotous and debauched companions, making love to all the pretty women of the neighborhood, and availing himself to the letter of his feudal *derechos de señor* (seignorial rights). After succeeding to the titles and estates, he began the burning of the candle at both ends; and his course of profligacy at last alienated from him all his respectable friends. The only ones who remained to him were the drunkards and gamblers, whose society he seemed to prefer.

"As might be expected, he finally squandered all the ready money left him by his father, and all he could borrow on his personal property; but the fief of Peñaranda, being a *mayorazgo* (entailed estate), he could not alienate.

"His creditors, the Jews, held the count in great dread; for when they came up to the castle to dun him for the payment of their dues, loaned on usurious terms, he worried them grievously with his boon companions, and sometimes kicked them down the superb staircase you were to-day admiring into the court-yard, whereby their bones were often seriously damaged.

"I pointed out to your worship, as we passed it, the ancient Convent of San Domingo de Silos, the tutelar of which worked many miracles in his lifetime, and delivered so many captives from slavery in Africa, that, in gratitude, they performed pilgrimages thither to hang up their chains at the gates. The abbot was not free from the popular contempt for the Jews, and upheld his neighbor the count in this treatment, who, he declared, was an example of feudal and seignorial excellence in his just scorn of the Hebrews; and he counselled Don Baltazar to go on with the good work. He further told the count, that, in order to carry out this work, he ought to take the cross without delay, and proceed to Granada, where our sovereign lord and lady, Ferdinand and Isabel, were prosecuting a holy war. There, while slaying infidels, he would undoubtedly, at the same time, acquire great store of treasure, wherewith, returning to his native heritage, he might enjoy *una vida descansada* (a lifelong rest).

"Don Baltazar, convinced of the excellence of the worthy prelate's advice, both spiritual and worldly, immediately assembled his vassals, put on his armor, and departed for the land of the infidel, to the great joy of all his neighbors and most of his friends. Arriving at his destination, he set to work vigorously, slaying Paynims, sacking towns and villages, and conducting himself in all ways like a valiant Christian knight.

"In his new vocation, which was very agreeable to God, the king, and himself, Baltazar gained great renown as a good servant of the Church and the State, after the fashions of the times. He also amused himself much in that distant country; oftener giving a golden ducat to a pretty girl than a silver penny to a beggar.

"Several years passed by, and people had almost ceased talking about the count and his mad pranks, when he suddenly re-appeared in Peñaranda with a numerous following of vassals and foreign slaves, bearing great treasures of gold and precious stones, the spoils of war. Those who had come back without any thing save wounds and holy relics were consumed with envy at the count's good luck. But, you know, this is an envious world. The very first meritorious act of the count was to add liberally to the wealth and possessions of the Convent of San Domingo; to atone, as he avowed, for the sins of his early life. It has also come down to us, that, from a profligate and graceless youth, the count grew to be a good and wise man, and was completely reconciled to God and the Church.

"The king made him a commander of Santiago, and captain-general of the district; and he conducted himself with such discretion in his high office, that he was soon greatly beloved. Instead of being choleric, as in his youth, he became gentle in his deportment; and the change confirmed the saying, that 'gray hairs bring wisdom.' The only thing that seemed to ruffle his temper was disrespectful mention of God or holy things: any one guilty of such an offence he would drive ignominiously from his presence, the old Adam re-appearing as in the days of his hot youth.

"He repaired and added to the castle, and furnished it anew in a royal manner, astonishing the neighbors with its Saracenic splendor. He greatly ameliorated the condition of his serfs, established mills on his domains, and increased his flocks and herds. By stimulating agriculture, and otherwise improving his seignorial fiefs, he soon augumented their value and population; and at any time could have summoned to his banner a thousand fighting-men from his own domains. In such good works did the Count of Miranda grow old upon his estates, governing his vassals paternally and benevolently, and administering impartial justice as their lord and suzerain.

"Sometimes, however, he put in execution his right to hang incorrigible criminals, when justly convicted before his judgment seat; thus vindicating the majesty of the law and his feudal privileges. He was especially rigid with all robbers and marauders, saying that they were to be regarded as wicked beasts of prey; and summarily consigning them to the gallows, which stood before the castle-gates. Justice having been dealt upon them, he permitted their bodies to be buried in consecrated ground, declaring that they were sufficiently punished by the loss of life. He continued to persecute the Jews, it is true, but only when they were bloated with ill-gotten wealth: and until they had acquired it by usury, and waxed fat, he let them severely alone; then he pounced upon and despoiled them for the profit of the church and the king, reserving a small share for himself. This, with grim wit, he styled tax-gathering.

"Thus this bluff and hearty lord acquired the esteem of every one in his district, rich and poor, great and small, by his protection of life and property. The consciousness of duty performed gave cheeriness to his visage; and the Abbot of San Domingo coming to visit him one day, and remarking this, accosted the count with, 'Ha, ha, my good lord! you are merry: you must have had some one hanged to-day.'

"When, attended by his train, mounted on the strong white hackney he brought from the land of the infidel, he passed through the village, the children would run fearlessly by the side of the cavalcade, and shout, 'Ah, ha! this is court day; here is the Señor Conde: buenos dias, Señor Conde!' And the old count would smile graciously, and say to them gayly, 'Amuse yourselves well, my children.' And they, 'Ah! si, si, Señor Conde.' Thus every thing seemed to prosper with the count, who was now an old man with a venerable white beard.

"In those days, besides the marauding bands, the curse of the period, who avoided the count's jurisdiction, there roamed about vagabond *gitanos*, or Egyptians, as they do now in Spain, who are not of our blessed faith, mocking at it when they can do so with impunity; and one of these bands came to Peñaranda on the Eve of St. John. They encamped on the plaza, and were seen by some of the villagers scoffing at the statue of our Blessed Lady; one of them, a very pretty young woman, dancing and posturing in very abbreviated garments. For this sacrilege it was agreed by the authorities that she should be burned as a wicked spawn of the Devil, — a fate not uncommonly meted out to these heathens in those days.

"But the old count came to the rescue, and by his logic proved to the people that it would be a much more agreeable thing to our Blessed Lady to rescue this poor lost soul from the claws of Satan, and to convert her to the true faith, as the fagot would only consume her body, without burning the devil who inhabited it, and her soul would be lost forever.

"The matter having been referred to the archbishop, the count's reasoning was found to be sound, his conclusions wise, and even canonical, and in conformity with Christian charity and the holy evangel. But the ladies of the town and other respectable persons loudly proclaimed, that, by the change of programme, they would be deprived of a *gran funcion;* also urging that the proposed conversion of the gitana would be merely nominal and insincere. Perhaps they had reason; for the girl, deprived of her liberty and the free air and light to which she had been accustomed, was as impatient of duress as a young kid, and passed her time in weeping, refusing food, and bemoaning her hard fate continually. 'So,' said the gossips, 'she will pretend to be converted, if only to recover her liberty.'

"To this the count replied, that, should the unfortunate stranger wish to embrace our religion, he would give them a much more splendid ceremony than the *auto da fé* they anticipated, making it the occasion for even royal festivities; and that he himself would stand godfather to the new convert.

"The Morisca did not hesitate between the fagot and baptism: so she was placed in a convent near by, the sisterhood of which undertook to prepare her for her new destiny. Here, in due season, she took the vows of holiness, and was baptized and confirmed; while at the first ceremony there was a great feast, with dancing and revelry, in honor of the Church and the new convert, at the count's expense. The promise of the latter was thus nobly redeemed; the festivities being indeed of royal magnificence, and even commended by the party originally in favor of burning.

"Now, at the baptismal feast, the count, acting as godfather, had for *comadre* (godmother) a very beautiful young lady, the daughter of one of his oldest and most valued friends, an ancient comrade in the Crusade, the Lord of Aranda.

"Your worship well knows how sacred and intimate with us in Spain is the relation between *compadre* and *comadre*, and how that connection confers peculiar privileges. The Lord of Aranda, having assumed the cross at the same time with the count, was taken prisoner, and was still held captive for lack of means to pay the heavy ransom demanded, which was the greater in that he was a most doughty and valorous knight. His wife, the Lady of Aranda, had pledged all the revenues of her fief with the Jews, hoping to accumulate the necessary sum, and lived with her daughter in humble lodgings in the village, with scarce a blanket to her bed, but proud as the Queen of Sheba, and brave as a lioness in the good cause she had undertaken.

"Seeing her ill-concealed distress, the old count bethought himself of acquiring the right to serve this admirable lady by inducing her daughter to become his *comadre* at the baptism of the Egyptian; for those old nobles were very punctilious. The worthy Count Baltazar had another object in view; and at the wedding clasped a heavy gold chain round the neck of his fair *comadre*, to which he would have been but too happy to add his broad domains, his good sword, his white beard, and his white hackney, so well known in the country round.

XIII.

"THE Count of Miranda had of late years perceived that he actually required a wife to assist him in ruling over his manorial possessions; and it saddened him to think of his approaching senility, while his desires governed him tyrannically as do those of all old men. So, during the festivities, he thought of his wounds, and of the eighty years that had passed over his head, and of the feebleness that prevented him from joining in the dance, in which the young Lady of Aranda floated with the grace of Psyche. The count also reflected, that, if he was ever to enter into the state of matrimony, he had no time to lose; and, to shorten a long story, he proposed to the mother of the young lady, was accepted, and the marriage followed in as short a time as it could be accomplished by the rules of the Church.

"The lovely Iñez de Aranda was only eighteen at the time of her union with the count, beautiful as a vision, graceful as an Andalusian, as full of life and gayety as a young mountain-kid, and blessed with a physical organization that defied all bodily fatigue. She would run all day long in chase of butterflies, or romping with her young companions; and then dance all night, if permitted, without the least sign of weariness. With all her gayety and high spirits, she had been most carefully brought up by her mother; and never had an unmaidenly or impure thought been permitted to enter that snowy bosom. She had not the remotest idea of the passion of love, both her mind and body being virgin to every coarse sentiment; and she needed only wings to make her fit for a denizen of paradise.

"Such was the fair young creature who suddenly quitted her humble abode to become the Countess of Miranda. Lowly and innocent as she was, she did not escape the ill-will of all the young ladies of the district. They envied her for the long blonde tresses, of which she had made a net to catch her superannuated lover; for the robe of rich stuff trimmed with gold, à l' antique; the magnificent jewels presented by him; and even the great golden chain of the Saracen emir, which now bound her irrevocably to the old count.

"The nuptials were celebrated in a manner becoming the lordly house of Zuñiga, the old nobleman being attired in a gorgeous wedding-suit. But the contrast between her bloom and his wrinkles, his tottering gait and her agile and graceful movements, was too palpable not to be noticed and commented upon. At the sound of the marriage-bells ringing a joyous peal, the gay procession, and all the pomps and vanities of the ill-assorted wedding, the ladies before mentioned were seized with sudden desires for crops of slain Moors, a deluge of rich old noblemen, and even a repetition of Egyptian baptisms.

"Immediately after the marriage, the Lady of Aranda received from her son-in-law a notable sum of money; with which she set out for Granada to ransom her husband from captivity, escorted to the frontier by the armed vassals of Miranda. She took leave of her daughter, giving her into the charge of the count with a recommendation of implicit obedience to his will, entreating him at the same time to guard her well.

"I may as well say here, that she succeeded in her mission, and returned in due time with her lord, who had contracted the leprosy in his imprisonment: and, as lepers in those days were secluded in order to avoid contagion, his wife, faithful unto death, accompanied him into his retirement in a distant district; where I shall leave them.

"The nuptial rejoicings lasted for three days, to the great delectation of every one; and, on the fourth, the count carried his bride in great pomp to the castle, in which the marriage-couch had been solemnly blessed by his friend the abbot.

"Coolly reflecting on the step he had taken, the intoxication which prompted him to it having passed away, the poor old count began to perceive that he had not exactly done the proper thing in allying his senility to so much youth and vigor. He accordingly attempted to supply his shortcomings by all the means in his power, and to supplement them by extraordinary indulgences. He gave up to the countess the keys of all his treasures and stores, turning over to her also the full control of his domains and hereditaments; and she, poor thing! wholly inexperienced in the affairs of life, and innocent of heart, was in an ecstasy of delight at the gallantry of her goodman. The fair Iñez, thus suddenly placed in possession of every thing heart could desire, and gifted, as we have said, with high animal spirits, betook herself to field-sports, and was soon engrossed in all the mysteries of hunting and falconry.

"She chased the deer and the roe on plain, valley, and mountain-side, mounted on the famous white hackney presented her by the count; and was never so happy as when flying her falcons and attending to their training. The poor old man at first attended her to the field, but was soon compelled to give up that pleasure in consequence of his increasing infirmities, after having been several times unhorsed in the vain attempt to renew the sports of his youth. Then, in the evenings at home, she would be seized with a desire for dancing, and would force the ancient castellan to accompany her; but he, loaded with his warm and heavy clothing, soon wearied of the violent exercise. At last the count was compelled to abstain from these saltatory entertainments altogether, and content himself with holding the candle for her to dance.

"Now, when the count had ceased to accompany his wife on her hunting and falcon-flying expeditions, he had delegated a page to perform those duties for which he was too enfeebled; and Doña Iñez was not slow to perceive the immense difference between the eighty years of her husband and the twenty-three of this young gentleman. Although not of noble birth, the gallant was a skilful hunter and falconer, as well as an accomplished cavalier, sitting his horse upright as a dart beside her rein, as they flew together over hill and dale, chasing the deer, or following the lofty flight of her falcon. The contrast and the preference of Iñez could not but be apparent to the count, who for the first time felt the pang of jealousy: so he dismissed Enrique from the post of lady's page, and sent him to display his accomplishments as a horseman among the *ganado mayor* (horned cattle) of a distant estate. He then replaced Enrique by a mere boy of his own lineage, of comely appearance.

"The countess resented the exile of her favorite with all the malevolence of the female sex. It now was, 'My dear count, I want this;' 'My dear count, I want that;' 'Come, husband, let us do this;' 'Come, my lord, let us go to this place.' *Vamos*, count, here, there, and everywhere, until the poor man was more worn by her fantastic longings than he ever had been by any experiences in his life, although he persisted in discouraging her outdoor amusements.

"Iñez, meanwhile, feeling the want of something to do, employed herself with giving reading-lessons to her page; and this exercise usually took place while the old count took his siesta in the middle of the day. At that hour, the huge antique chair in which the old lord usually sat was unoccupied;

and, naturally, the countess filled it, while the page sat upon a footstool near by to receive his lessons. The page proved an apt scholar, I ween; for, after a time, he watched anxiously for the hour when his beautiful mistress seated herself in the great seignorial throne for her task, while the old count loudly snored on a neighboring sofa.

"Damiano de Zuñiga, the page, as beseemed a youth of gentle blood and knightly qualities, was exceedingly devout and loyal in the observance of his religious duties; and, some weeks after he had begun to receive lessons from his fair mistress, he resorted, as was his wont, to the abbey, to confess himself to his spiritual adviser. What passed between them was under the seal of confession; but Damiano retired from the interview pale and distressed, and immediately sought the presence of the count.

"The old warrior was seated at the entrance of the castle on a stone bench, watching his armorer, who furbished the harness, whose weight the ancient knight could no longer bear, but which he insisted upon keeping polished as brightly as a mirror. He contemplated these arms with much pleasure, as they reminded him of many a stoutly-contested field and gallant tourney; their hacks and dints being silent records of his doughty feats of arms.

"Damiano approached, and bent the knee to the count, as his suzerain; at which the old lord was somewhat surprised. 'My lord the count,' said the page, 'send these people away; for I have something for your private ear much concerning you and myself.' The servitors, having retired out of ear-shot, stood respectfully watching the grim old warrior and the youthful page, who stood in a humble attitude before him, his fine eyes cast down, his head bared; and seemed to communicate something to the count which moved the very depths of the old man's soul, for he suddenly turned pale as a ghost.

"Instantly, however, he recovered his self-possession, and with it, apparently, all his youthful strength; for he seized from among the arms that lay there a heavy steel mace with which he had struck down many a Paynim.

" He brandished the mighty weapon aloft as if it had been a mere straw; then stayed it for an instant over the head of the boy, who retained his attitude of humility, but raised his eyes fearlessly to those of his master. His firm bearing doubtless saved his life : for, casting his weapon far from him, the old man uttered a passionate exclamation ; and, by his gesture, the wondering servitors saw that he commanded the page to leave him. This the boy did, withdrawing sorrowfully and slowly, retiring down the steep descent leading to Peñaranda.

" The count proceeded in the contrary direction, taking the path to the gardens, in which the countess was then walking. The servitors cautiously followed, and overheard the angry old man accost her with dreadful imprecations; telling her the truth was known, and she must prepare to die, and that he had already killed Damiano.

" The shock of the announcement threw the fair dame into a dead faint. Her women rushed to the rescue, and carried her into the castle.

" The count then raved, and tore his beard, accusing himself of killing his wife by his cruelty, and despatched messengers in every direction to seek the page, in order to show her he was alive; but the boy was nowhere to be found. He was last seen by a peasant, from whom he borrowed a horse, which he mounted and rode off, telling the countryman he was going to the land of the infidel to take the cross in pursuance of a vow, to accomplish a penance laid upon him.

" The countess learning all this, and that her loved Damiano had left the country, probably for ever, subsided into a state of melancholy, from which it was impossible to rouse her.

Her lamentations filled the castle; and the old count, now sensible of his many faults and crimes, tried every means of assuaging the grief of his wife in a parental manner. Nothing he could do, however, would console the countess for the loss of the *petit page d'amour;* and her radiant charms soon paled under the shadow of her grief.

"In those times, the secrets of the inner life of the nobility were seldom known beyond the walls of their castles so that all these circumstances I have related did not come out until long after they happened, when the actors in them had all passed away.

"Thus it was that the true history I am recounting to your worship was preserved by the gossips, and handed down by them to our times, long after the deaths of the fair Iñez and her child."

"Child!" said I: "what child? Was there a child?"

Just at this moment the slanting rays of the setting sun fell upon walls and towers, and the single-eyed story-teller informed me we were about entering Lerma.

This is a fine old town, situated upon the little River Arlanza, in a lovely country, abounding, I was told, in game both finny and feathered, but little frequented by travellers. It conferred the ducal title upon the celebrated cardinal minister of Philip II., and contains a splendid palace built by him. We spent one day here, in order to make some repairs in our travelling equipments; and I improved the opportunity to inspect the palace and other mementoes under the guidance of an excellent cicerone provided for me by Blasco. That worthy was absorbed in his visits to his old friends during our stay, but was punctual in starting on the following morning; and at noon we stopped for lunch at the small hamlet of Madrigalejo. When we were fairly on the road again, Blasco signified that he felt like talking, and resumed his story:—

"Yes, your worship, there was a child. It arrived in the due course of time, much to the delight of the mother; and the circumstances of its birth were unknown to all outside the castle. The count had provided for that; for in those times inconsiderate scandal might compromise the life of an offender: so the old man received all the credit of its paternity.

"To any one, however, familiar with the fine ingenuous features of the page Damiano, the similarity to those of the beautiful and lusty infant was too apparent to be denied; and the old cuckold must have felt very strangely at the likeness.

"So the news went through all the country-side that the Count of Miranda had still vigor enough to leave a son and heir to the name, titles, and estates of the Zuñigas.

"Iñez conducted herself with the strictest propriety. Not a word was breathed abroad to her discredit; and all her time was occupied with the care of her child. The poor, decrepit old count seeing the boy daily and hourly, and witnessing the love of the mother and the gambols of the innocent little being, from sheer force of habit ended by loving him also, and would have resented any wrong done to him as earnestly as if he had been his own child.

"Iñez, considering herself now more than ever bound to Damiano, continued to humor the old man; and, after the custom of those ladies who hoodwink their lords, rendered him so contented, that he lived altogether in the bosom of his family. One day, however, he was sitting in his great chair, his wife and the child playing together near him, when he suddenly fell back, exclaiming, 'Ah! Iñez, my love, my Iñesilla! it grows dark! I can't see thee!' and, saying it was night very early, he slept the sleep of the just.

"The great and powerful lord was gathered to his fathers; and Iñez mourned for him as for a parent, fell into melancholy, and would not listen to a proposition of a second marriage, although her friends strongly urged it. She was in the prime of her youth, and an excellent *parti;* but she devoted herself to her child in her widowhood. This seclusion and celibacy greatly astonished people; for it was not known that she had a heart-spouse, and that she was a widow in sentiment as in fact: for she had heard nothing from Damiano since he had taken the cross, except a vague rumor that he had been killed, which caused her many sleepless nights. The countess thus lived for fourteen years in the memories of a few weeks of love and happiness, and her son had attained the age of some months less, when she received one day a small party of visitors come to the castle to pass the day. Seated in the old count's great chair, her favorite seat, she was conversing with her guests, when the young count, her son, came running into the hall, blooming as a rose. He was more like the page than ever, resembling his putative father in nothing except the name he bore. He threw himself on his mother's neck, exclaiming, 'O dear mother, here are strangers! I have just seen a pilgrim in the court-yard who kindly embraced me.' — 'Ha!' said the countess, turning to the boy's attendant, 'have I not forbidden you to allow my son to speak to strangers? Go! I discharge you from my service!' — 'Alas, sweet lady!' said the servant, 'the holy pilgrim wished the dear young count no harm; for he kissed him, weeping bitterly all the while.' — 'He wept,' said she: 'ah, it is his father!' And, with these words, she leaned back her head in the great chair fraught with so many memories, and the color deserted her cheeks.

"The guests all pressed about her, thinking she had fainted, and applied all the usual restoratives; but the heart of the poor lady had ceased to beat forever. No one could ever learn whether her death was caused by sudden joy at the unexpected return of her lover, or by fear that he had a second time left her.

"At the funeral ceremonies of the Countess Iñez, which were marked with all the pomp observed when a member of the house of Zuñiga is taken away, a pilgrim was present, who, though still young in years, bore the traces of much hardship and sorrow, and who, when the fair body of Iñez was entombed, suddenly left the place. This was Don Damiano de Zuñiga, who, driven to despair by the death of his sweet mistress, completely lost heart, and, seeking for his woes the consolations of religion, became a monk in the Monastery of Santo Domingo de Silos."

As my friend Manuel Blasco ended his story, the twilight deepened; for the close of the autumnal day and the end of our long ride approached together: but I had no time for musing on the loves of the fair Iñez and the gallant young page, as we saw before us the lights of a large town, and soon, clattering over an ancient bridge, entered the famous old city of Burgos.

XIV.

BURGOS, like Venice or Prague, still seems in the condition of centuries ago; and we feel in her streets that we should not be surprised at meeting her citizens walking abroad in jerkin and trunk-hose, or a procession of mail-clad knights on horseback. It was the cradle of the Castilian monarchy. It rose: but its decay followed soon after its efflorescence; for, the Castilian kings having removed their court from it in the fourteenth century, its prosperity was destroyed; it gradually declined, and the French invasion by Napoleon completed its dilapidation.

The venerable old town has a noble seat, rising grandly on the banks of the Arlanza, with its dominating castle, and the graceful spires of its unrivalled cathedral proudly announcing the city to the approaching traveller. This wonderful temple is well known to all admirers of mediæval architecture as among the finest specimens of florid Gothic in the world. It is, indeed, a "poem in stone;" and its western façade is probably the finest of its kind in Europe. It would require a volume to record all the wonders of this noble fane. The three aisles, the octagonal dome rising two hundred feet from the pavement, enriched with carvings called the work of the angels, the sculpture and paintings, the carvings of the choir and stalls, and the magnificent high altar, fill one with delight and religious fervor. Although its adornments are profuse, there is nothing meretricious or overloaded in their general effect.

Besides the cathedral, there is the castle, beautiful in its decay, and rich in historic reminiscences, several palaces of the ancient aristocracy, and a fine promenade on the banks of the river. In the neighborhood is the Convent of Santa Maria la Real, called "Las Huelgas" ("The Delights"), with its chapel, in which were once crowned the Spanish kings; and the tomb of the Cid.

Being so near, I felt that I must pay the homage of a visit to the last resting-place of this famous warrior; and accordingly set forth, accompanied by a friend whose acquaintance I had made in Burgos, and who, besides being an intelligent and learned cicerone, was an enthusiastic admirer of the great Spanish hero. We first directed our course to the Carthusian Convent of Miraflores, where there is a royal mausoleum erected by the magnificent Isabel with filial piety to the memory of her parents. The eye can hardly take in all its wondrous glories. It is sculptured all over with costumed figures, animals, birds, and foliage, cherubs, apostles, saints, and angels, delicately carved in Oriental alabaster, and illuminated by painted glass of gorgeous tints. As said my good friend, "Faltan ojos para mirarlos" ("One wants eyes to see them all").

Continuing our route to San Pedro de Cardeña, we alighted in front of the noble gateway, above which the Cid, mounted on Bavieca, rides down the hostile Moors. No one was ever allowed to mount the noble steed after the death of her master; and here she lies buried. The tomb of the Cid bears the following epitaph, composed, it is said, by Alonso the Wise, who also caused the tomb to be built:—

"BELLIGER INVICTIS FAMOSUS MARTE TRIUMPHIS CLAUDITUR HOC TUMULO MAGNUS DIDACHI RODERICUS."

Here are also the tombs of his wife Ximena, and their two

daughters, Maria Sol and Elvira, queens of Aragon and Navarre. His only son was killed at the battle of Consuegra, with others of his faithful followers, including Alvar Fañez Minaya, his cousin, whom the Cid was wont to call his right arm.

Having passed several most agreeable days in Burgos and its vicinity, our little party set forth, intending to make our next halt at Logroño; sleeping one night on the road at a hospitable estate of another friend of Blasco, — a retired *aficionado*, who, having given us an excellent breakfast, after many affectionate *accolades* to my squire, sent us on our way with *vayan ustedes con Dios*. We saw a cloud of dust ahead; and found that it proceeded from a column of troops, of which we soon overtook the rear-guard. They were Carlist infantry. We were not permitted to precede this guard, the officer in command saying he was compelled by his orders to prevent any one from doing so; and were forced to linger along in their rear among the usual camp-followers, almost stifled by the dust. Blasco was instantly engaged in animated conversation with our new acquaintances, with whose party, as I have already said, he was in active sympathy. For my part, seeing a lady in the crowd riding a fine horse, and attended by a couple of servants, I entered into conversation with her. She proved to be the wife of the lieutenant-colonel commanding a Basque regiment, the second in command of the force before us; and she informed me that she always accompanied her husband on the march, and even under fire. As she was extremely affable, like all her countrywomen, I was soon on excellent terms with Doña Florencia Soler; and we exchanged information about acquaintances in Madrid.

About noon the column halted, and the lady improved the opportunity to introduce me to her husband. From him and others we then ascertained that the Carlist force of about nine hundred was commanded by colonel, the Count of Leso; and

I learned also that its destination was Logroño, which town they expected to surprise and capture with some persons of importance. They had made a forced march from Bilbáo for that purpose. The Carlist troops, whom I now saw for the first time, appeared to be young, sturdy, active fellows, apparently possessing more of the true military spirit than the queen's soldiers. They were in the usual dress of the Basque peasants, and wore the national red beret. The Count de Leso was very polite to me, regretting that my journey should have been delayed, but telling me, that, so soon as Logroño was in sight, we would be at liberty to go wherever we pleased. In less than twenty minutes the little Biscayans were again on the road, tripping gayly along with the elastic step of the mountaineer, so different from the lounging gait of the Christinos. The lengthening shadows soon fell upon the walls of Logroño, and the column halted: the line of battle was promptly formed, the skirmishers trotted briskly to the front, and the whole force advanced at the double-quick to the attack, under cover of their rifles, shouting gayly; while their bugles sounded the charge. A grand guard stationed in the suburbs was driven in, and we could see the Carlists hotly engaged with the enemy; then lost sight of them as they entered the town, as it appeared to us, pell-mell with the Christinos. Blasco, Pedro, and myself witnessed the combat from a slight elevation; and my squire soon told me that the sharp rattle of musketry, now incessantly heard, came from the direction of the plaza, the possession of which seemed to be hotly contested. Doña Florencia had left us; and the one-eyed man said she had joined her husband in the fight. The fire at length became scattering, and receded beyond the town; and Blasco said we might enter it. We did so, passing in the streets some corpses and wounded men, but none of the inhabitants: all were, I was told, shut up in their houses. We proceeded immediately to the plaza, where we found the Carlist colonel and his staff surrounded by a number of citizens, some of whom were municipal officers; and with these he was alternately threatening, expostulating, and promising, with some volubility, after his victory.

The fight had evidently been a stubborn one at this point; and women (among whom I saw the religious habit) were bewailing the loss of some friend, or assisting wounded persons to a place of security and rest. After mildly congratulating the Carlist colonel, I retired to the inn on the plaza; while Pedro took our animals to the stable in the rear, and Blasco was going and coming with news in the evening in a great state of excitement.

He informed me that several persons, whose names I had never before heard, but whom he appeared to think of consequence, had been taken prisoners; that the Carlist chief had ordered the alcalde to provide wine and provisions for his soldiers, and had laid a contribution upon the town, to be forthcoming at an early hour the next morning; and that Doña Florencia was with her husband, who had command of the guard posted at the bridge which crosses the Ebro on the farther side of the town, and by which the discomfited Christinos had retreated.

Wearied by the excitement of the day, I lay down on the bed without quitting any but my upper garments, and was soon fast asleep; for silence prevailed in the town, and only the occasional barking of a dog, or the *alerto* of some vigilant sentinel, was distinctly heard through my open window, which looked directly into the plaza. I must have slept soundly; for I was awakened by a terrible noise of shouting and swearing in the plaza, mingled with military commands and the sound of firearms. I rose, and for a moment stood gazing at the indistinct masses of men below, and the usual tumult of a heady fight. A taper was burning in my apartment; and I was admonished by several bullets singing through the window to extinguish it; which I did, retiring to a safer position; but not before I saw that the red berets were getting the worst of it, — probably overpowered by superior numbers.

The dawn soon appeared, and with it my *mozo*, Pedro, who came to seek protection from both parties; and, my valise being at hand, I put on my uniform, and awaited the issue of events.

The noise of the battle now receded westward in the direction by which we had come to Logroño; and the plaza was deserted, save by the fresh crop of dead and wounded that had been harvested since the evening before. Looking forth, we saw a mounted party enter it, at the head of which rode one whose appearance and bearing proclaimed him a leader of men. He was (the innkeeper, who had ascended to my room, informed me) the renowned guerillero, Martin Zurbano.

Soon a sergeant of cavalry came to the inn, stationed sentries at the door, and summoned all its inmates to the presence of his chief; and we all issued into the plaza, following him as directed.

The guerilla leader took my passport; upon reading which — that is, if he could have done so upside-down — he courteously addressed me, and said, that, as a foreign officer, I was exempt from further interference; then, turning to the innkeeper, he roundly abused him, and afterwards minutely questioned him as to the occurrences of the previous evening.

Returning to the inn, I went up to my room, accompanied by Pedro, to view what was going on in the plaza. Blasco had not made his appearance; and I began to fear that he had gone off with the Carlists. While speculating as to what I should do in case the one-eyed man did not soon appear, I was attracted by an unusual stir in the square below, and saw, with horror, my acquaintances of the day before, — Lieut-Col. Rafael Soler, and his wife Doña Florencia, dragged out by soldiers, and placed before the horse of the truculent chief by whom I had just been examined.

The sight of my agreeable and gentle companion of yesterday's ride confronted with one whom common report declared to be as savage and remorseless as the Pyrenean wolf struck a chill to my heart; but it was speedily followed by a desire to save her from the fearful fate that no doubt awaited her. I knew how cruel and vindictive were the combatants on both sides in this terrible civil war, in which each party massacred prisoners, and seldom granted quarter. I hastily descended to the door, and attempted to open it: but the clatter of the muskets of the two sentinels, and their crossed bayonets, admonished me that I was a prisoner within the posada; and I could only return to my post of observation.

I now saw that the poor colonel was wounded, a bloody bandage encircling his head; and was told he had also a bullet-wound in the chest, — probably a mortal one: and I do not believe that his devoted wife wished to survive him. There they were, confronted by and hopelessly in the power of the fierce guerilla, who regarded them with a look in which I could discern no gleam of mercy; while the unhappy pair returned his gaze with a proud look of courage as undaunted as his own.

After a short colloquy, consisting of abuse from Zurbano, and defiance from the officer, — the wife seeming perfectly calm and resigned, — the guerilla impatiently waved his hand, and I caught the words, "Cuatro tiros pasalos, por las armas!" ("Take two files, and shoot them!") The pair were dragged away. I could look no longer, and withdrew; but in less than two minutes the quick, short commands to a squad, the answering clank of muskets, and the sharp report of half a dozen pieces, told me that another cruel and bloody scene had been enacted in the sad drama then in progress in distracted Spain.

In the Peninsula, war assumes a personal character, and becomes the expression of petty hates and revenges rather than a general contest for great principles. Life is little valued: the prevailing indifference to it, or fatalism, the Spaniard seems to hold in common with the Moslem. All know that they owe a death to Nature, and believe that no forethought or precaution can retard or prevent it when the fatal hour arrives. Life is daily staked, and all parties conclude to stand the hazard of the die; those who win exacting the whole pound of flesh, and those who lose paying the forfeit as a matter of course. To beg for or to grant a pardon would be alike degrading, as strength is estimated by the blows struck, and not by those withheld. And thus it is in all civil wars, which are notoriously more rancorous and vindictive than hostilities between rival nations.

Martin Zurbano was a native of the neighborhood of Logroño. He early espoused the queen's cause, and fought bravely in the war. His forces occupied that town when attacked by the Carlists, and retreated at first; but, with his accustomed tenacity and energy, he returned with re-enforcements during the night, and retook the place. He was a fair type of the Spanish guerilla. He committed many horrible crimes in the progress of the war and afterwards, the story of which has been told by French and English writers. After years of guerilla warfare, he received the reward of his crimes, by a providential retribution, on the very spot where the Carlist colonel and his wife were executed, — the plaza of Logroño, — in which place his brother and his two sons had been already shot.

The next morning I had the melancholy satisfaction of assisting at the burial, in consecrated ground, of the ill-fated Solers; and made arrangements with the *cura* for prayers for their repose. Every thing had become quiet in the town, Zurbano having gone in pursuit of the retreating Carlists; and Blasco mysteriously re-appeared at the posada, telling me that he was well known to the Christino chief, and that he had kept himself secluded in fear of being recognized. He adjured me by all I held sacred to leave Logroño immediately; for, should Zurbano return and find him (Blasco), the guerilla would not fail to visit him with his vengeance, "in spite of the fact," said he, "that your worship is the ambassador to the King of France, and I your *major-domo*, and, as such, justly partaking of the sanctity of the diplomatic character."

I gladly assented to his prayer; for I longed to leave a place in which I had seen nothing but deeds of blood, and to get upon the road, hoping that, when again in the saddle, exercise and variety would dispel the gloomy memories of Logroño. Our beasts were quite rested, and had been well fed and groomed, thanks to Pedro: so we started at a gallop from the door of the inn, and were soon in the open country. Guided by Blasco, we took roads leading to the mountains, stopping only at insignificant hamlets; and, without meeting any more of the bands of the two contending parties, we arrived in due time at Pamplona.

I remained for a few days in the country of the Pyrenees; visited the pass of Roncesvalles, the breach of Rolando, and other places of interest; then, crossing the frontier, I went through Bayonne to Paris, taking Blasco with me, Pedro having been sent to the care of a friend of Blasco at Moncada, in Catalonia, with our beasts, there to await our return to Spain.

During our stay in Paris, nothing worthy of record took place. I may mention, however, that my Spanish guide, Manuel Blasco, found but little to admire in France, — not even the ladies: the practice of the *nil admirari* philosophy somewhat surprised me in so devoted a squire of dames.

He was always busy, however; but, our pursuits not being always congenial, I saw but little of him, until one day he came to tell me that he was about to "assist" at a grand exhibition given by the officers of the garrison of Paris, and at which all the best swordsmen, professors, and amateurs were expected. I attended on the evening appointed, and was much pleased with their skill in all sorts of what the French call *armes blanches*. Towards the close of the *séance* Blasco appeared, dressed in a magnificent Andalusian or *majo* costume, all silk and embroidery, that he had obtained from the Spanish embassy, and in which I could hardly recognize my quondam guide. He gave a fine display of skill with his national weapon, the sword, successfully encountering some first-rate swordsmen; also defending himself against the lance and the bayonet, and against great odds; finishing by dividing in twain the carcass of a sheep at one blow of his *toledana*. He was decidedly the hero of the exhibition.

Of all the distinguished persons I saw at this visit in the capital of France, I have preserved to this time the most agreeable remembrance of one who considered himself the most humble among them, — the poet Béranger, the Robert Burns of France.

By appointment, I proceeded at ten, A.M., to the small two-story house, No. 21 Rue Vineuse, Passy; and was ushered up stairs to a landing on the second story, where the maid opened a door, and I found myself in the presence of the author of the "Redingote Grise," "Le Violon Brisé," "Le Vieux Sergent," "Les Etoiles qui filent," &c. A little man, not more than five feet five inches in height, but solidly built, with an intellectual head, and silky white hair, arose from an easy-chair, — the only one in the room, — and forced me to take it. He had handsome features, clear black eyes, and an expression of open-hearted benevolence. He wore a rather shabby dressing-gown, and on his head a little *calotte*. I felt at once relieved from all constraint in his presence. Nothing could be more humble than his surroundings. The little room was darkened, which led me to suppose that his eyes were weak; but it was quite airy. A small bed, with plain check curtains, occupied one end of it; a writing-table with a portable desk, a few books, and only two chairs, — *voila tout!*

No pomp of literary display was needed to give interest to the first song-writer of France or his humble dwelling.

"They will tell of all his glory round the hearth for many a day."

Unversed as I was in literature, I dashed at once upon something I was familiar with, and mentioned Walter Scott. Béranger, I found, did not esteem the "Wizard of the North" a great or a correct writer. He said he had detected many blunders in his works, especially in "Quentin Durward," in which the life and character of Louis XI. had been misrepresented. He admitted, however, that his works contained many grand pictures of splendid and interesting groups; remarking, that, in the novels, the interest of the reader attaches itself naturally to some other individual rather than to the hero or heroine. He instanced "Ivanhoe," in which Rebecca is the centre of interest. This he considered a defect. With Scott's poetry he said he was not familiar, as he did not understand the English tongue.

After a conversation of half an hour, I rose to take leave; and the poet accompanied me to the stairway, and kindly shook hands at parting.

Béranger was at that time really a power in France. His *chansons* had an immense circulation, and doubtless had a mighty influence in bringing about the revolution of 1830. The *chansonnier* did not view the government of Louis Philippe with approbation, and refused every thing like favor at its hands; which conduct increased his popularity with the masses. His retirement and preference of the peaceful enjoyment of his chimney-corner (*coin de feu*) did not proceed from a cynical or misanthropic affectation, but was from the genuine desire for repose after a busy and lately not unrewarded life.

At the funeral of Lafitte the banker, which was attended

by the king and the princes, the royal coaches passed unnoticed: but, when Béranger's carriage appeared, it was welcomed with a burst of acclamation, and hundreds strove for the honor of drawing him in triumph; but he, with difficulty, persuaded them to desist.

The service upon which I had been sent having been performed, we returned to Spain by the way of Perpiñan, joined Pedro and our animals at Moncada, and continued our journey to Madrid by way of Valencia, Murcia, and Granada.

In the latter city I had an opportunity of seeing the famous *torero* Pepe (Joseph) Montes, the *preux chevalier* of the arena. This worthy was performing, or, as we should say, "starring," in the provinces; and Blasco informed me we might perhaps never again see such sport as would now be afforded us in the *plaza de toros* of Granada. Conducted by my squire, I entered the *sombra*, or shaded seats, in which were gathered representatives of the aristocracy, including the officials, two-thirds of those present being beautiful ladies; while below us raged, roared, and gesticulated the "great unwashed" of Granada.

Montes, adoptive father, it was afterwards said, of the no less celebrated Lola, was a man of wealth, and then about forty years of age, a little above the ordinary height, of grave aspect and demeanor, lithe as a serpent in his movements, and of a pale olive complexion. He was a native of Chiclana, a suburb of Cadiz. His eyes had the look of alertness I have seen in men, who, like him, often owe their lives to their instant perception of danger. No doubt the immense success of this Andalusian hero, the Bayard of his heroic profession, was due rather to his coolness and consummate knowledge of his art than to muscular strength. Blasco told me, that, as soon as Montes saw a bull, he could form an accurate judgment of the animal's character, — whether its attack would be straightforward or strategetic, whether its sight was good or bad, and whether it would be cautious or impetuous in its charge. Thanks to this sort of intuitive perception, he was always ready to meet the beast with an appropriate defence. Nevertheless, as he often pushed his temerity to foolhardiness in a spirit of bravado, he has had countless hair-breadth escapes in the arena, and bore many scars of his victorious conflicts, having on several occasions been carried grievously wounded from the ring.

On the first day I saw him his costume was magnificent, — silk and velvet, embroidered richly with gold in the most elaborate style of the *majo* dress of Andalusian dandies. Unlike most *matadores*, Pepe Montes did not content himself with simply killing the bull when the signal was given by the presiding officer. He superintended and directed the combat, going to the assistance of those *toreros* who were in danger, many of whom owed him their lives. Consequently, his *cuadrilla* were devoted to him, knowing he would never desert them; and he has often extricated *picadores* and *banderilleros* from the horns of the savage bull. He has been known to *colear*, or seize by the tail, an enraged bull, which, having disembowelled the horse, was seeking the death of the rider, sheltered by the body of the prostrate animal; and, while he turned swiftly the enraged beast three or four times, the man had time to escape amid the frantic applause of the spectators. I saw him once plant himself firmly in front of an enraged bull, and fix his eyes upon him, standing with crossed arms, while the animal stopped suddenly in his charge, and seemed subjugated by that keen and unshrinking gaze. Then came a torrent of wild applause, shouts, vociferations, screams of delight, from the fifteen thousand spectators, who stamped and danced upon their benches in wild excitement. All the ladies waved their kerchiefs, and every hat was thrown aloft; while Montes, the only cool, collected person in the vast multitude, enjoyed his triumph silently, slightly bowing with the air of a man who felt himself capable of much greater things.

O ye silvery-toned singers, ye fairy-footed dancers, all ye who flatter yourselves that you have excited popular enthusiasm! you have never heard Montes applauded by a crowded circus. Sometimes he would be *encored*; and a pretty girl near me called out to him, "Vamos, Señor Montes! vamos, Pepito!— you, who are so gallant, do something for the sake of a lady, — *una cosita*" (a small matter). Then Montes leaped lightly over the head of the bull: turning quickly, he shook his red cloak in the animal's face, and, by a rapid movement, enveloped himself in it with folds of most graceful drapery. Thus he invited the charge, which he avoided by stepping nimbly aside.

On the second day of the bull-fight at Granada, Montes received, in spite of his popularity, a rather rough proof of the impartiality of a Spanish public, and of the extent to which it pushes its love of fair play towards beasts as well as men.

A magnificent black bull of the Sierra Morena, whose grazing ground was in sight from the arena, was turned into the *plaza de toros*, entering with a dashing, defiant mien. There was a murmur of admiration among the connoisseurs. Here were all the points to be desired in a fighting bull: his horns were long, thin, and sharp; his legs small and nervous. His broad chest, heavy dewlap, and mighty shoulder, united to a symmetrical form, indicated vast strength. His fixed, staring eyes and gallant bearing gave promise of unyielding courage.

He rushed upon the *picador* nearest him; and over went horse and man, — the former dead ere he measured his length in the arena: then fell another horse; and the men had just time to save themselves by leaping over the barrier. In a quarter of an hour this bull killed seven horses. The *chulos* were frightened, and kept near the barricades, shaking their *muletas* at a respectful distance, jumping over the barricades when he approached them. Montes himself appeared disconcerted, and once placed his foot upon the ledge as if to follow them. The spectators shouted with delight, and paid the bull the most flattering compliments. Presently a new exploit of master *toro* elevated their enthusiasm to the highest pitch.

Another venturous *picador* cantered towards the bull, and, lowering his lance, pricked him in the shoulder. The latter bowed his stately head, thrust it under the horse, and with a mighty effort lifted both horse and rider, and placed his forefeet on the ledge; then by a second lift he threw both horse and man clear over the barrier into the corridor surrounding the arena. This unheard-of feat drew down thunderous bravos.

The bull was now master of the field of battle, and paraded the arena in triumph, amusing himself with tossing the dead horses. The stable was empty: there were no more horses. The *chulos* and *banderilleros* sat upon the barriers, not daring to approach the bull, and harassed him with their barbed darts. Impatient at the inaction, the people shouted, "Las banderillas, las banderillas!—Fuego al alcalde!" denouncing the alcalde because he did not order them to attack the conqueror. At last a *banderillero* advanced, and planted his little barbed weapon in the neck of the bull, and ran away quickly, pursued by the animal. In leaping the barricade his arm was grazed, and the sleeve of his gay jacket torn by the horn of the bull. The spectators again applauded "Viva, viva, bravo toro!" but, in spite of the applause, the alcalde gave the signal to despatch the bull.

Blasco informed me this was against the laws of tauromachy, which require that the bull shall receive four pairs of *banderillas* before he is left to the sword of the *matador*.

Montes now came forward amid the hooting of the vast assembly, who were not well pleased that so valorous an animal should be despatched without further baiting.

Instead of advancing, as was his wont, into the middle of the arena, the *matador* placed himself within twenty paces of the barrier, in order to be near a refuge in case of accident. He was pale, and did not indulge in the little coquetries of courage, or dalliance with danger, which have procured him the admiration of Spain as a finished knight of the bull-ring. Taking his stand firmly, he slowly unfolded the scarlet *muleta*, and levelled his Toledan blade, shaking the former at the enraged beast. The great black bull, in his turn, lowered his mighty horns, and rushed upon the man. For a brief instant the dust obscured the pair: then the bull was seen prostrate at the feet of the man, dead, as if struck by a thunderbolt. Montes stood proudly erect over his foe, holding his sword, its glittering sheen now dimmed with blood.

The keen weapon, directed by the firm hand and wrist of iron, and guided by the unerring eye of the *matador*, had entered the forehead and pierced the brain, — a thrust forbidden by tauromachian rules. The *matador* should pass his arm between the horns of the beast, and stab him in the nape of the neck, severing the nerves concentrated in the *medulla oblongata*. It is the most dangerous thrust for the man, but gives the bull a chance for his life.

Blasco instantly detected the foul stroke; and, while he was explaining it to me, a storm of indignation arose from the multitude, who had also discovered it. A hurricane of abuse and hisses was poured out upon the *matador*. Butcher, thief, brigand, assassin, executioner, were the mildest of the complimentary epithets hurled at him. "To the galleys with Montes!" "To the fire with Montes!" "To the dogs with him!" were some of the amiable ejaculations of the assembly. Not content with mere words of vituperation, some excited persons threw into the ring fans, hats, sticks, water-jars, and every other available missile.

Montes bit his lips with rage until they bled; and his pale

visage was fairly green with fury. He affected, however, to be unmoved, and leaned gracefully upon the sword, which he had cleansed from blood with the sand of the arena.

Such is popularity. The day before no one would have thought it possible that Montes, the Bayard of the ring, the consummate *torero*, would have been thus severely punished for the infraction of a rule rendered doubly necessary by the agility, vigor, and extraordinary fury of the animal with which he had to contend. Another bull was killed after this one, but was despatched by another *matador*, almost unnoticed, amid the continued indignation of the spectators.

The fight over, I wished to be introduced to the famous *torero* ; and Blasco, who knew him well, went with me to the Fonda for the purpose ; but Montes had left. Angry and half ashamed, he had hastily got into a *calesin* with his *cuadrilla*, and left the city, shaking the dust from his feet, and swearing that he never would again return to Granada.

From Madrid I returned to Gibraltar, having accomplished the mission I was ordered to perform, and rejoined my ship.

XV.

DURING my tour in the Iberian Peninsula, I was profoundly impressed by its loveliness and romantic character, even while conscious of its abasement and degeneration; and I have, both before and since that time, witnessed the progress of a similar state of things in the colonies of which Spain and Portugal are the mothers and progenitors. As I have seen with my own eyes how the policy of both her and their rulers has checked all progress, and engendered the same fatal decay in parent and offspring, I may be excused for saying a few words on that subject.

The causes of the ruin of Spain are, indeed, countless: and its history will always be one of the most instructive; for in it may be found every principle of policy and every form of administration by which a country should *not* be governed.

Throughout the country, and particularly in Estremadura, there are dreary wastes, cut up by *barrancas*, called *despoblados* (unpeopled districts); and these are the fruits of the exterminating policy pursued by the rulers who succeeded Charles V. When we reflect that their desolation is the consequence, not of invasion or conquest, but of monstrous misgovernment, and contempt for all sound principles of human policy, we are filled with wonder and commiseration.

History tell us, that, from ten millions in the time of Philip II., the population of Spain decreased to about six millions in that of Charles II., with a continuing depletive flow; and that the Cortes told the latter monarch in an address, that the nation could not prolong its existence for another half-century unless the progress of the evils that afflicted it was arrested.

Spain had already lost three millions of her most industrious inhabitants in previous reigns by the expulsion of the Moors, which was characterized by Richelieu as the most stupendous blunder ever achieved by any government, which transformed an earthly paradise into a sterile desert.

Then came the emigration to America, which carried off several millions more to gather the riches of Mexico and Peru.

All these drains upon the population caused a general neglect of agriculture and the mechanic arts, and, ultimately, beggary and famine. The writers of those times relate the most painful stories of the sufferings and death from hunger of even the highest and richest people, the royal table being scantily supplied, and the Court often going hungry. The army and navy were in a deplorable condition. Their officers were frequently seen begging in the streets with that air of proud dignity characteristic of and inseparable from the Spaniard. The nation that sent forth the Armada for the conquest of England now owned but a score of paltry, rotting hulks at Cadiz and Carthagena. Philip IV. could raise only about fifteen thousand troops for the invasion of Portugal; and consequently that country was lost to the Spanish crown.

We cease to wonder at the decadence of this great and haughty people, who once rivalled imperial Rome, when we examine some of the processes of which it was the result. One of these was the barbarous expedient of the Duke of Lerma, of debasing the coinage, under Philip III. Silver and gold coin vanished: prices rose, and large sums were paid in the debased coin, which was made a legal tender by royal edict; and the barter, the badge of barbarism, re-appeared. Not a third of the king's revenues ever came into his coffers, owing to the corrupt system of farming them to dishonest officials.

The imprudent sovereigns we have referred to, aided by the prejudices of their proud and insolent subjects, — still to be seen in the *Españolismo* of the present day, — completely extinguished the commerce, agriculture, and industry of the country. The tourist in Spain sees hardly a tree; and, asking for the reason, is told that Spaniards hate trees. But this is not the true reason for the arboreal destitution. This is a consequence of legislation, — the enactment of laws against the enclosure of fields. These laws, known as the laws of the *mesta*, protected the grazing interests at the expense of all others; and were enacted by the influence of the nobility and the great landed proprietors in order to make the kingdom an immense grazing-ground for their numerous herds of merino sheep and horned cattle, under the pretext that these animals constituted the real wealth of the country. This policy, so ruinous to small land-holders and tenants, was persisted in to the last, and exists even now in some parts of the New World. But, not satisfied with these restrictions upon agriculture, Philip II. passed a law that punished with fourteen years' exile the farmer who made bread of wheat of his own raising, or who sold it in the market.

Operating in harmony with these incredibly foolish laws, the *mayorazgos* (entails), and the statutes of mortmain, aided in the almost total extinction of agriculture. The natural result was, that Spain was supplied with grain from other countries; and, having no manufactures to exchange for breadstuffs, was annually drained of specie to the amount of more than thirty million of dollars.

Industrial pursuits fared as badly as agriculture. Every Spaniard wished to be noble; and their monarchs, fearing the rebellious spirits of mechanics, invented the *Alcabala*; which was a tax laid upon every article manufactured and sold, and which bore so heavily on some handicraftsmen, that it was cheaper for them to remain idle than to work. The natural consequence was, that industry of all kinds perished in the country; almost the only manufacture left being that of Toledo swords, which escaped destruction owing to a prejudice in favor of its supposed noblity. Even the manufacture of the famous Segovian cloths, and Cordovan and Galician leather, ceased entirely, and it became disreputable to engage in it; while the laboring-classes were regarded as pariahs, and stigmatized as *pecheros*. Moreover, to induce the Spaniards to become ennobled, the nobility were exempted from taxation; and this privilege augmented their haughtiness, and intensified their contempt for all business. It was considered beneath the dignity of a Spaniard to bargain, or to receive back change for gold in the purchase of the merest trifle; while interest for money loaned was accounted Judaism and the sum of all baseness.

Such ideas prevailing among the Spaniards, all lucrative occupations naturally fell into the hands of Jews and foreigners, who flocked into the Peninsula from every part of Europe to work for the Spaniards, who would not work for themselves. These remained long enough only to accumulate a competency, with which they hurried home, where they were not subjected to the universal contempt with which all Spaniards regarded them. All the wealth of the New World, millions upon millions, thus passed through the country, scarcely a dollar remaining in it; and year by year the Spaniards grew poorer and poorer. The proceeds of the grinding taxation of their European provinces, — Naples, Sicily, and Lombardy, — with the bullion from both the Indies, rolled into Spain in a golden current, which traversed without enriching it; and, like a worn-out profligate, she swallowed every thing, but digested nothing. There was one long holiday in the Peninsula; but though revelry, feasting, and idleness were the order of the day, the real national prosperity was gone forever.

The court, in those unthrifty times, scornfully ignored every axiom of political economy suggested to common sense by the stream of wealth poured into the country.

In former years, when the kings of Castile were elected by the barons, they told the sovereign at his coronation that they who sanctioned it were his equals, and, united, his superiors; and that they conferred upon him the regal power, and promised to obey him, *provided* he continued to respect their rights; and, if he did not, then not, "*Y, si no! no!*" But now the sovereign was worshipped by his unworthy subjects, men like himself, with a slavishness hardly less base than the reverence paid to the grand lama; and the once chivalrous house of Burgundy had degenerated so fearfully, that it was remarked by a contemporaneous historian that Charles V. was a warrior and a king, Philip II. a king only, Philip III. and Philip IV. not even kings, while Charles II. was not even a man.

The latter imbecile sovereign was a mere human machine, whose every step, word, and action were regulated by an unchangeable system of etiquette, which set at naught volition; and whose appearance, as one may still see in his portrait in Madrid, was that of hopeless idiocy, which was his real character. His costume, also strictly regulated by etiquette, consisting of a rigid black velvet dress, with the huge *golilla* (ruff) encircling his neck, — painfully suggestive of the head of John the Baptist in a charger, — strengthens his resemblance to an automaton. The irrational and impious system of king-worship was immensely popular; and the Spaniards even committed the impiety of speaking of *las dos majestades* (the two majesties), coupling the sacred host with their earthly sovereign, and thus adding sacrilege to their other national sins. In their most violent revolts the Spaniards never thought of deposing the king; always shouting " Viva el rey absoluto!" whether he was a tyrant, a knave, or an idiot. Finally their manners grew intolerable; political bigotry and fanaticism ruled the kingdom; and irreligion was so universal, that assignations were usually made in churches, even at the hour of the holy sacrifice! Crime remained unpunished, or was condoned; and the proverbial delays of the law were prolonged tenfold.

At the time of my tour, Ferdinand VII. had been dead about three years: his infant daughter, Isabel II. was the titular queen; and her mother, Maria Christina of Naples, third wife of Ferdinand, was regent of the kingdom. The old king had reigned with absolute power for more than twenty years over a population of twelve millions of Spaniards, who, almost unanimously, had hailed his accession to the throne of the Bourbons, loudly clamoring for the ancient *régime* of despotism. The *vox populi* being in full harmony with the secret wishes of the king, with the concurrence of the army and the armada (navy) he issued a decree annulling every act of the Cortes passed during his captivity in France, — which acts were exceedingly liberal, — and restoring the absolute monarchy. This measure was received with immense enthusiasm. The sight of a whole nation thus debasing itself, and eagerly riveting chains upon its own limbs, is melancholy indeed; but the fact is beyond dispute. This cowardly weakness was particularly lamentable in this instance; for Ferdinand VII. was a weak man, depraved in heart and corrupt in life, with scarcely a redeeming quality. His first wife was his cousin, Maria of Naples, — a lovely, gentle, and affectionate princess: but her brutal husband blighted her life; and she perished, as there is every reason to believe, by poison administered by his hand. He then sought a wife among Napoleon's family; but the emperor thought he could not recommend for a husband a man who had attempted the life of both his parents, and had murdered his wife: so the offer was declined; and, eight years afterwards, Ferdinand married his niece, Maria of Portugal. At the same time, his brother, Don Carlos, wedded a princess of the same royal house. Ferdinand hated his brother, and desired to shut him out from the succession. In less than one year, the queen died childless; and, a few months afterwards, the king, anxious to secure an heir, took another bride, — Maria Amelia of Saxony. Meantime insurrections, executions, imprisonment, and misery afflicted poor Spain.

For ten years the queen endured her husband, and then sank childless into the grave, leaving Ferdinand, a worn-out *débauché* of forty-five, imbecile in mind and body, but still haunted by the thought that the sceptre would pass into the hands of the hated Carlos. His last bride was Maria Christina of Naples, a frivolous girl of twenty, without conscience or moral scruples, but gifted with a considerable amount of shrewdness, which fitted her admirably for the palace intrigues in which she became so famous.

Almost her first act after marriage was to take as her lover one Muñoz, a private soldier in the king's life-guard, — a young, handsome, and vigorous man, but of the lowest extraction, manners, and deportment. She lavished wealth and titles upon this person, creating him Duke of Rianzares; and with her friends exulted in the probable success of their scheme to secure an heir to the throne, and thus to defeat the pretensions of Carlos. There was only one drawback to this little game; which was, that, should the offspring of the queen prove a female, Carlos would be still the next in succession, under the Salic law, which had prevailed in Spain for a hundred and fifty years.

While all the kingdom anxiously awaited the issue of the accouchement of the queen, the Carlist party were dismayed by the promulgation of a decree by the king, revoking the Salic law, and transmitting the crown to females in default of male heirs.

On the 10th October, 1830, a daughter — afterwards Isabel II. — was born; and, a formidable insurrection having broken out in Madrid, the king repealed his obnoxious decree, but again re-affirmed it after the crisis had passed. There is no doubt that the queen procured, by her influence over the miserable old monarch, the execution of these several decrees, and even guided his hand in signing them; for Ferdinand was a confirmed invalid, and lived secluded in his palace, entirely under his wife's influence. She thus secured a party in her favor, which she used every means to strengthen; and finally the old king, exhausted by his excesses and sickness, delegated the regal authority to his wife as a reward for her wifely care.

The two parties of Christina and Carlos now secretly prepared to appeal to arms: but their preparations were suspended upon the announcement that the queen was again about to become a mother; for, should the issue be a son, Carlos would have no claim. After a few months of hopes, fears, and doubts on all sides, the queen gave birth to another daughter, — the infanta Luisa. Finally the old king was called away, and died Sept. 29, 1833. His death-bed was the scene of quarrels, reproaches, and even blows, among his affectionate relations, who departed with malevolence in their hearts to summon their adherents on either side; and the civil war, so long deferred, at last broke out.

I frequently saw the queen-regent and her two daughters, and can vouch for their fine appearance; but, that they had much Bourbon blood in their veins, I presume no one in Madrid could be found so credulous as to maintain, expecting to be believed. The well-known fact that Doña Christina continued to increase her family after the death of Ferdinand VII., and profited by her position to acquire the means of supporting them all handsomely, may be of interest to those who ardently admire royal institutions.

Even from the foregoing meagre statement, it must appear that no nation in history was ever so entirely abandoned to the adoration of senseless eccentricities as was Spain. She appears to be isolated from the rest of the world in thought and feeling, and has been governed by passions and vices apparently most incompatible. In no other country has the monarchical principle of government obtained so much discredit. For four centuries the Spanish crown has never been worn by an enlightened sovereign devoted to the interests of his people, or deserving any better fate than historical ignominy; yet Spaniards have continued to believe in their rulers, to fight for them, to die for them, and even to prostitute their country for their interests.

What will be the end? The answer is, that Spaniards have always been fanatics in politics, and "Españolismo" has ever been their test of truth. An abandonment of that false standard must precede the disinthralment of Spain, political and intellectual. Until then, liberty will be unknown to her, and progress impossible.

XVI.

ABOUT a year after my Spanish tour, — which interval had been spent in cruising in the Mediterranean, — the ship arrived in the harbor of Algiers; and I had a short leave to visit the interior of that French colony. A British admiral compares the city of Algiers to an old main-topsail spread out on a hillside to dry : not an inapt likeness to one looking from the anchorage. Its white walls, and cross-streets in parallel lines, certainly resemble the reef-bands. The Arabs more poetically compare the city to a diamond set in emerald and sapphire, — alluding to the green hills and the blue sea around it. Here, as elsewhere, Nature is more truthfully depicted by barbarian poetry than by civilized prose.

The clear skies in its calm atmosphere reflect a dazzling light, and the sharp outlines of the mountains cut the horizon distinctly in the transparent distance; while the gentle sound of the sea-breeze and the scent of the sweetly-perfumed land transport the vision of the imagination far into the depths of the remote Atlas. On landing, these charms measurably fade ; and the city hardly answers the promise of first sight from the sea. In the Moorish quarters especially, the narrow streets and peculiar architecture of the houses, built with reference to the Mussulman's ideas of seclusion and jealousy, make the city an inextricable labyrinth, full of oddity and mystery. These streets are rough to mount, and rougher to descend, many of them being "impasses." We are agreeably surprised upon entering some of these houses, as all their comfort and elegance are reserved for the interior, wherein are freshness, coolness, and rich furniture. An inside gallery runs around a court filled with beautiful fountains, and adorned with flowers, upon which open all the apartments of the mansion; and a fine terrace forms the roof, from which the eye ranges over the sea and the lofty mountains of the Jujura. The French authorities had occupied some of these palaces of the old Algerines as government offices and quarters; and in several of them I was hospitably received. Abd-el-Kader was then still at large, and at war with the French, who indeed were masters only of the seaboard, and of the interior so far as the city of Blidah, which had succumbed not long before to their arms.

Although Algiers is chiefly known to us by tradition as the capital city of piracy, and though Shakspeare makes it the birthplace of Sycorax, the mother of the imp Caliban, still, seen in the lovely month of March, one must imagine it to be peopled by the most amiable of corsairs and sorceresses. The skies have all the smiling sweetness of Italy; and the climate is so delightful, that even the galley-slaves, as we are told, when liberated, pined to return to the scene of their captivity.

After a few hasty preparations for my trip, I mounted one of the stair-like streets leading to the casbah, which formerly was the citadel of the dey, and is now a French fortress and dépôt. I occasionally paused to view the strange sights, — the veiled and spectral forms of the Moorish women, and wild-looking, coifed Arabs in their flowing white bornouses, with here and there a Turk or a Frank. I heard the gay notes of an infantry bugle; and soon a company of French soldiers passed by on their way to relieve some post or guard in the upper part of the city. The French foot-soldier has a martial and forcible aspect, which always commands my attention and admiration, mixed, I confess, with a little envy. Their elastic step, confident air, and determined bearing, give one the assurance that those active feet will follow the path in which they may enter to the end.

Having arrived at the casbah, I was politely received by the old major in command of the dépôt, to whom I was accredited by superior authority, and introduced to the captain of the foreign legion, who was to command the detachment detailed as convoy which I had received permission to accompany. Capt. Senneval invited me to dine at the mess; and I met at their hospitable board several military men of the different corps then in the colony. Their conversation was general, frank, and open, relating principally to the war in progress; and I heard of acts of brilliant valor, and even of eccentric hardihood, spoken of without boasting or military pedantry. These African heroes told only of what they had seen, not what they had done; and I was convinced of the truth of their stories by the simplicity of the narrators.

There were about a dozen officers at the table, which was plentifully supplied, and handsomely decorated with flowers; the waiters being fine-looking Maltese women, under the management of an old steward; also a Maltese, who, as I was informed, had been a pirate. Among these officers I saw representatives of nearly every nation in Europe. The old major had cast off his shabby blouse, and the blue spectacles he wore in his bureau, and appeared in all the glory of the epaulets of his rank, cross of the legion, and *pantalons garance*, which he wore with the ease and grace of an old soldier.

The officers, I was told, were of two classes; those who served with the legion as *étrangers*, — free lances, who had taken service under the French flag, having left their native lands under untoward circumstances, — and of French volunteers sent to serve in that corps to attain promotion. To the latter class belonged Capt. Senneval and a regular *vieux moustache* near whom I sat, and who rejoiced in the *nom de guerre* of Capt. Eylau, — so called from a habit he had of talking continually about that great battle, in which he served as a drummer-boy; his present rank being that of captain of "zephyrs," as they are called in the African battalions.

Coffee and cigars having ended the meal, I rose from table, and entertained myself for a while with the new and strange sights around me.

At that time Blidah, now only a few hours of peaceful travel by railway from Algiers, was a garrisoned post in an enemy's country, surrounded by tribes of stealthy, wandering Kabyles; and our expedition was sent to convoy stores for the use of the garrison. It was composed of two companies of infantry, — one of zephyrs, and one of the foreign legion, and a squadron of spahis, — native cavalry; the whole under command of Capt. Senneval.

Although this officer was quite a young man, his commission was older than that of Capt. Eylau; which gave him the command.

Our little column — with the exception of the cavalry — started at early daybreak in order to arrive at a certain bivouac not very far from Blidah at an early hour, provided we were not interrupted by the Kabyles. This was not improbable, for stores were much coveted by them, especially ammunition; and there were always spies in Algiers to give intelligence of any important movement. It was rumored that the emir himself was known to be far from the plain, or table-land, of Algiers: and the quiet attitude of the neighboring tribes confirmed that opinion; for they were very uneasy when their great chief was near or among them.

In hope of a quiet march, Capt. Senneval had directed the troop of spahis not to mount and follow our column until the infantry and wagons had been two hours on the road; knowing that it is very fatiguing to cavalry to regulate its march by that of infantry, and *vice versâ*. After quitting Algiers, we rode leisurely across a level plain by a well-worn road through a country in which we saw a few Moorish houses surrounded by high walls, all having the same mute and lugubrious appearance. Soon even these disappeared; and only a few fig, aloe, and dwarf-palm trees were to be seen. The country was known to be inhabited by the wild tribes; but we saw not a human creature, nor even a domestic animal.

The way was so monotonous, that I began to yawn from weariness; when suddenly Capt. Senneval, who rode near me, in the centre of the column, put spurs to his horse, and dashed to its head. Looking for the cause of his movement, I saw a light-blue smoke curling up in the cool mountain-air far ahead. It was evident that this aerial spectre, clearly drawn upon the deep blue of the sky, was a signal of some sort; for the officers knew that there were no villages or lodges, even of the temporary sort called "gourbis," in that direction. Old Eylau was called to the front, and a rapid conference ensued, a party of *éclaireurs* being detailed to scour the country in the advance; and we proceeded about a league farther.

The sun was now getting powerful; and the soldiers marched along with their great-coats open, their muskets *en bandoulière*, and long walking-sticks in their hands,— a peculiarity of African troops, who use them also as tent-poles. As the sun became hotter, the road-song — *chanson de route* — died away; and no sounds were heard save the tinkling of the mess-pans and accoutrements of the troops, slung to the goat-skin knapsacks, in which the French soldier carries his whole worldly wealth.

Suddenly arriving at a place where the ground was somewhat broken, we heard shots from the *éclaireurs*. The aide-major of the command halted, and closed up the wagons; the bugles sounded the "rally," which brought in the skirmishers to the main body; and the troops deployed from column to line of battle. The enemy was in force in our front, at no great distance, determined to dispute our progress; their main body being masked by a cloud of Arab horsemen galloping swiftly about, their white bornouses floating in the air, shouting, and firing their long Turkish guns, or brandishing them at arm's length. Behind them were the dark masses of Kabyle infantry.

Capt. Senneval approached; and I saw, by his intrepid air and bearing, that our safety was in good hands. The soldiers of the legion betrayed at once all their national characteristics. The Spaniard was disdainfully grave; the eyes of the Pole grew bright, and his color heightened; while all the mustaches, brown, red, or black, bristled up at the very idea of a fight, giving me, a neutral spectator, the agreeable assurance that I was under excellent protection. The "zephyrs" entered into the spirit of the thing with the customary gayety of the *gamins* of Paris, from which class their ranks were mainly recruited, and with the laughing philosophy in the hour of danger for which they are distinguished. These *enfants perdus* are generally well commanded; and their officers, being taken from the regiments of the line, show their soldiers an example of intrepidity, allied to habits of discipline, which proves to them that all the military virtues may be united. The officers identify themselves with their soldiers in action, decide rapidly, and act quickly.

Just such an officer was Capt. Balment, commonly called Eylau, who had spent his whole life under the French colors.

The wagons and ambulances of the convoy were massed in the rear of the line of battle, and the action was becoming warm; when I saw an old non-commissioned officer brought to the rear for treatment, and I addressed him. He was already in the hands of the surgeon, and submitted himself with cool imperturbability. Withdrawing his pipe for a moment from his mouth, " Ah ! " said he, " they have among them some prominent officer of Abd-el-Kader, if not the emir himself. I see it by the boldness with which their cavalry attack our line. They are sustained by a strong force of infantry."

The situation was, indeed, becoming serious; and I began to repent having wished to see something of the country beyond the walls of Algiers. Men were falling; and a soldier in front of me was killed by a bullet, slightly spattering me with blood and brain. A band of the Kabyles, led by a chief of large stature, advanced towards our line at the charge, directing themselves upon the "zephyr" company commanded by Eylau. The captain drew his sabre, sheathed till now, took his *brule gueule* from his mouth, and placed himself in front of his covering sergeant, on the right of his company. The enemy, howling and gesticulating, charged the "zephyrs;" but they endured the shock steadily, receiving the horsemen on their sabre bayonets, many of which were impurpled. Then Capt. Eylau, passing from defence to attack, threw his company — dressed as if on parade — upon the Kabyles. I saw his sabre plunged into the body of the tall chief, who fell like lead; and, quick as lightning, a zephyr, rummaging among his white vestments, drew forth his watch, and secured his arms. So skilfully was this done, that I thought the dexterity of the *gamin* must have been acquired in a different field.

Eylau was triumphant, driving the enemy far from the wagons; but they outnumbered us, and, despite the well-sustained fire of the French troops, re-enforced their front line, and renewed the action, as if determined on victory. I saw in the faces of Capt. Senneval and others that the crisis had arrived, and that they were wishing for any, even the smallest re-enforcement, when a movement took place in the enemy's line: their fire became hesitating, and then ceased. They broke, and ran; and we knew that they were charged in flank by French cavalry.

We saw the red bornouses and white turbans of the spahis,

their flashing sabres above their heads, dashing upon the Kabyles, whose rout was completed by a charge of our infantry; and the field was won. The squadron of spahis had left Algiers, as ordered, two hours after our departure, and were leisurely following our trail, when, hearing the din of battle, they had galloped up just in time to decide the combat. The enemy were now in full retreat, pursued by the spahis, who mercilessly cut them down as they ran.

Our tired and exhausted soldiers were then marched to a pleasant bivouac near by; and, with the readiness peculiar to Frenchmen, the whole force was soon under shelter from the burning sun. Fires were kindled, and cooking began; while the soldiers divested themselves of their arms and accoutrements, and lay around in groups under the trees, or near the water. Soon the spahis were seen returning from the pursuit in a cool, sauntering manner, contrasting strongly with their former impetuosity, and unlike the eager, talkative Gaul. They sat solemn and straight upon their saddles, silent and almost motionless, many of them being Mussulmans. Every spahi bore some spoil of war, — Kabyle "flissos," yatagans, guns, pistols, and trinkets of different kinds.

These doughty cavaliers were headed by their officer, — a slender, blonde young man, who was evidently one of the *jeunesse dorée*, although attired in the costume of an Oriental Frenchman. The Vicomte de Bertrand could never have been mistaken for a Turk, notwithstanding his dress; for his air, actions, and gestures instantly betrayed his nationality. On his head was a snowy turban of irreproachable twist, rolled around a "checia," placed far back on his head, like those of the "Turcos;" and his blonde mustache hung down from the corners of his mouth, of a shape and length equally forbidden to true believers. Although his garments were of the regulation color of the spahi uniform, his red vest was embroidered with gold in fantastic designs unknown to the *ordonnance;* and his light-blue trousers terminated in red morocco boots, that would not have been out of place at Franconi's. He bestrode a fine sorrel-horse, lithe and slender like himself, showily caparisoned *à la Turque,* and which seemed to partake of his rider's disposition, as the pair advanced towards the bivouac curvetting and prancing, horse and rider on excellent terms with each other. Notwithstanding his dramatic and exaggerated Orientalism, I was informed that the vicomte was an excellent officer, and a man of brilliant and generous qualities; which report I had an opportunity of verifying before we parted.

I strolled towards the spahis, who were now mingling with their comrades; when suddenly I heard a salutation in Spanish in a well-remembered voice, "Ah! mi teniente que alegria de verle!" and, could it be — yes, it certainly was — my old friend and trusty squire here in Africa, — Manuel Blasco y Gusman?

Blasco was mounted upon a spirited Arab, a red bornouse hanging from his shoulders instead of the *capa parda,* on his head the spahi turban in place of his *montera,* and from the pommel of his saddle there dangled by the *mahomet* — a long lock of hair left by all Osmanlees to hoist them into paradise — a grisly human head. We had much to say to each other at this unexpected meeting; for Blasco was as garrulous and declamatory as ever. We rested all night at this bivouac without further adventure, and next day arrived at Blidah.

This city was celebrated under the Turkish rule as a sojourn of pleasure, and known as the "voluptuous." It always had a large population, and is famed for the excellence of its oranges and lemons. It was taken by the French army under Marshal Clausel in 1830. The foot hills of the Atlas range approach its walls quite nearly; and it overlooks the fertile plain of the Metidja, and commands the passes of those mountains. The surrounding country is remarkable for the beauty of its landscapes, the richness of its soil, the salubrity of its atmosphere, and the abundance of its waters.

The city is charmingly ensconced in a perfumed forest of oranges, limes, mulberry, figs, jujubes, dates, and other African trees. These rich groves are watered by the Oned Kebir, the sources of which are not far from the city. I was the guest of the colonel commanding the garrison, and his amiable lady, in a luxurious palace which had once belonged to a rich Moslem. I made some excursions in the neighborhood in company with the French officers, so far as was prudent on account of the lurking Kabyles.

After several days passed in a most agreeable manner, I returned to Algiers and to the ship under the protection of the spahis, gratefully acknowledging the hospitality of my friends. I left Manuel Blasco in Algiers; that worthy informing me that he had decided to take up his residence in that city after the termination of his enlistment, or even before that time if he could obtain his discharge. I rather doubted his purpose, until he introduced me to a portly Mahonese lady, who kept a hotel and baths, and appeared to possess a fair portion of this world's goods and a fine run of custom. She was a widow whom he had won by his blandishments, and who — I afterwards heard — consented to marry him; and Blasco became very popular in his capacity of landlord.

XVII.

AFTER returning from the Mediterranean, I was almost immediately ordered to join the squadron of Com. George C. Read, and with it made a cruise of circumnavigation.

Stopping at Madeira and the cape on our outward voyage, we entered the Mozambique Channel, and anchored at Zanzibar, then under the government of the imâm, Syeed Syeed bin Sultan of Muscat.

This prince was a Mussulman of the strictest sect; and, although more liberal than most Eastern despots, had attained supreme power by the usual stages of crime, among which were the murders of several of his nearest relatives. Having gained the object of his ambition, he adopted a conciliatory domestic policy, and was tolerant, even generous, to foreigners; so that, in time, he became the most popular of Asiatic rulers. He also greatly extended his dominions, and added to the hereditary possessions of his house nearly the whole coast of Africa, from Cape Guardafui south to the Portuguese settlements, with which nation he was thus brought into collision. The imâm was at Zanzibar on our arrival, and received us hospitably, insisting on furnishing the whole crew with provisions during our stay.

Visiting the imâm at his palace at Mtony, we found him a handsome middle-aged man, of fine personal appearance, evidently a full-blooded Arab, with the slender form, clear olive skin, regular and handsome features, and small delicate extremities, of that race. In his deportment he was a perfectly well-bred gentleman; and his manners far surpassed in courtesy and grace the most refined European standard.

His son, who was present at the interview, was of the same type as his father. Among others of his suite was a tall, stalwart negro, conspicuous by his costly dress, and who was acting then as vizier, being a man of uncommon intellect for one of his race, in spite, as it seemed, of the cruelty which had deprived him of his manhood; for he was a eunuch. Having turned Mussulman while a slave of the imâm, he had been manumitted in conformity with the laws of the Wahabee sect of Islam, which forbid the enslavement of a believer in the Prophet. I was told a singular story of this eunuch; and, as it illustrates the peculiar military policy of the prince, I will repeat it.

Ahmed had been from boyhood the personal attendant of Syeed. He became attached to his master, served him with affectionate fidelity, and was his chief agent in the accomplishment of the crimes by which that prince mounted to his throne.

When the imâm began his wars for conquest, he coveted possession of the town of Mombas, on the mainland of Africa, not far from Zanzibar. He accordingly blockaded that seaport with his fleet, having a land force on board his ships; but the Portuguese had no idea of surrendering as long as they could hold the castle. This castle is situated upon an island in the mouth of the harbor, commands the entrance, and is the key to the place.

The troops of the imâm, as is customary in Arabia, consisted of his own black slaves, naked, and armed with a long straight sword, and a small target, or buckler, of rhinoceros-hide, in the use of which they are very skilful.

Finding the garrison obstinate in spite of his blockade, the imâm hit upon an original and ingenious expedient to gain the castle. Taking advantage of a dark night, he manned all his boats, and put into them five hundred picked men commanded by Ahmed.

Rowing in close to the beach with muffled oars, this forlorn hope was landed on the island as near the walls as possible; and then the imâm addressed them in low tones.

After appealing to their courage and fidelity, he threw his blood-red flag to the intrepid eunuch in command of the storming party, and said, "I am determined to possess that castle by to-morrow morning; and I command you to hoist that flag upon its highest tower before the dawn. Should you remain where you now are, the enemy will probably exterminate you at dawn; but should he foolishly spare you, and I do not see my flag flying from the castle at daylight, I shall then open the fire of my ships, not upon the walls of the fort, but upon *you*." The imâm then coolly left the bewildered negroes to their *kismet* (fate), and regained his ship. How many of the devoted band were slain, I know not; but, when the first gray light of approaching day fell upon the walls of the Castle of Mombas, it revealed that red flag streaming from its battlements: the garrison had passed under the edge of the sword, and the town and its dependencies capitulated to the imâm, who anchored his ships in the harbor, and took possession.

Our cruise extended to the Red Sea, Muscat, the ports of the Persian Gulf, and Surat; and we finally anchored in the harbor of Bombay, where the squadron rendezvoused.

The war with Cabul broke out about this time; and a large army, destined to act against that country, was united from the three presidencies of British India at Bombay under the command of Lord Keane. The subsequent operations and disastrous defeat of a part of this army have been told by Lady Florence Sale, wife of Sir Robert Sale, who was in the campaign with her husband, and taken prisoner by the emir, Dost Mahomet.

The presence of so many officers made Bombay quite a gay city while we lay there; and, shortly before we sailed, I witnessed the march of the army, — a most curious military spectacle.

The host of fifty thousand combatants was encamped on the wide glacis of the walled and fortified city, which extends in a semicircular form about one and a half miles towards the populous surrounding suburbs.

In the centre of this fine esplanade we were stationed near the statue of Lord Cornwallis, which commands a view of the whole area.

The troops had all gathered at their respective camps, and the regimental parades were succeeded by a rest in place; when, at the sound of the sunset-gun from the fortress, every tent was struck, disappearing as if by the wand of an enchanter.

At the same time the band struck up the fine old English air, —

"Don't you hear your general say,
Strike your tents, and march away?" —

and the leading regiment, followed by all the other corps in column of companies, took up the march, which, in India, is nearly always at night, in order to avoid the heat.

First came several regiments of European infantry, all stalwart, well-drilled men, evidently superior in physique to the natives; then some fine field-batteries, escorted by the British regular light-cavalry, hussars, and lancers; then more batteries of native artillery, followed by several thousand native irregulars, mounted on Persian horses, and presenting a somewhat mediæval appearance, being clad in shirts of glittering mail, with steel helms and shields, armed with matchlocks, javelins, and even bows and arrows.

These troops were more picturesque than efficient, I should suppose: for there was little uniformity among them; each man owning his horse, as I was told, and furnishing his own arms.

After these came the Sepoy infantry, twenty thousand strong, — a noble-looking body of men. The siege-train, escorted by native cavalry, closed the long procession of regular troops.

Then followed a crowd of people unknown to European armies, but who in India greatly outnumber the regular soldiers, — the camp-followers; a cosmopolitan throng of men and women, in all the varied costumes of the East, — Europeans, Persians, Mahometans, Gentoos, Parsees, on horseback and on foot, in vehicles of all sorts, drawn by horses, bullocks, asses, and mules, — some borne in palanquins, some riding bullocks, and a few on camels, mingled with the *syces* (grooms) of the officers, with their beautiful led horses; while at intervals in the long array might be seen the stately movement of the colossal elephant.

This motley crowd were all talking and hallooing amid the rout and dust, in strange contrast to the silence of the disciplined masses that preceded them.

Having visited the celebrated cave-temples, and seen the other objects of curiosity in this part of India, we sailed, and, after touching at Goa, arrived at Colombo, in Ceylon. While at this port we heard of several acts of piracy committed by the Malays of Sumatra, and sailed for that island to punish them. To detail all the events that took place during our stay here would hardly interest the general reader, so long a time has elapsed since their occurrence. I will therefore content myself with saying that we remained about three months on the coast of Sumatra, engaged alternately in threatening, negotiating, and fighting the Malays. One town, Muckie, we entirely destroyed, as an example to the rest, — *pour encourager les autres*, — some of its people having taken the American bark " Eclipse " of Salem, murdered the captain and others, and plundered the vessel of a large sum. Exposure and hardship on the Sumatrian coast introduced the cholera and dysentery among our crews. The squadron was compelled to quit the coast; and March, 1839, saw us at anchor at Singapore.

From Singapore we went to China, and remained there for some months, engaged in attending to American interests; and then sailed for the Sandwich Islands, where we arrived in due season, after having experienced a terrible typhoon in the China Sea while passing through the Bashee Passage into the great Southern Ocean.

After visiting several of the most prominent island-groups of this ocean more or less frequented by navigators, we hove to off the tiny island known as Pitcairn's. This mere point in the great Pacific Ocean is well known as the home of the descendants of the mutineers of "The Bounty," — children of Englishmen by Tahitian women, and immortalized by Byron in the beautiful poem "The Island."

After the mutiny, and the arrival of Capt. Bligh in England, — before which he endured incredible hardships, and crossed the broad Pacific in the launch of "The Bounty," in which he and his officers were set adrift, — the British Government sought assiduously but vainly to discover the refuge of the mutineers. They were found at last, accidentally, by an American whaleship, upon Pitcairn's Island, which had always been supposed to be uninhabited. The ringleaders of the mutiny having nearly all died, and time having weakened the government's resolution to inflict vengeance upon the poor remnant, the king took the islanders under his protection; and, Pitcairn's being considered too small for its increased population, the inhabitants were removed to Norfolk Island. But they were so unhappy in their new abode, that they were soon remanded to their original and native home, in which, for more than forty years, they had been secluded from the rest of the world, and ignorant of any other of that world's empires.

There were originally five couples of English and Tahitians; and from these had descended the population of the island — three hundred and more — at the time of our visit. The widow of Fletcher Christian, the ringleader of the mutiny of "The Bounty," was still living. There were also three Englishmen landed on the island since its rediscovery with their children by island wives.

Although the increase had been great in the population of the little islet, — for it is no more than an islet, and one can row all round it in a boat in three or four hours, — there were yet no persons among them over fifty; which was considered a great age, and about the usual limit of human life, as I discovered in conversing with the people. The increase of the population, then, was due, not to longevity but to their practice of early marriage, and consequent fruitfulness.

What evidence of a general law are we to deduce from this state of things?

Christian and his companions, with their Tahitian wives, landed at Pitcairn's in 1789; and in 1840 there were but ten survivors of the first generation, the children of the mutineers, although these islanders came into the world under circumstances apparently favorable to longevity. Why this premature decay? Not hereditary disposition; for the Tahitians are a long-lived race, and there never were epidemics on the island. Neither could they complain of too monotonous or insufficient nourishment; for the land was very productive. I can truly say, I never beheld a more athletic and admirably-formed people, or one seemingly more free from any signs of physical inferiority. It could not arise from intermarriage, the effect of which would be visible in mental and physical degeneration as well as abridgment of life. On the other hand, we know, that in some countries, — the Alps and Norway, for example, — cousins constantly marry each other for long-continued generations, from necessity; and nowhere can be seen more robust or long-lived people.

There must be some other cause; and this I find in their isolated condition.

A state of monotonous peace and contentment, preserved by careful vigilance or absence of temptation, is not the normal state of man, nor one in which his energies have the healthy play which insures durability of constitution. The average man of our modern civilization, even in the United States, — where his labors are greater, perhaps, than in any other country, with his burden of cares and passions, his wasting exertions amid earnest competitions, — has no cause to believe in a general shortening of the span of life allotted to him. Neither is a savage liable to this complaint; for, should he escape the casualties of quarrels and war and epidemics, he is likely to live long.

The wild tension of his energies and passions, the sharp spur given to his faculties by their constant exercise in the service of the instinct of self preservation, all tend to maintain the vigor of his powers, and to counterbalance the effects of habitual sloth and frequent excesses. But, when the constitution lacks one or the other of these stimuli, there seems to be a tendency to early decay. It is not intellectual exercise that is wanting, or that given by education; neither is it bodily exercise, — for Pitcairners have enough of both, — but it is the exercise of other mixed powers implanted within us, — the passions of hope and fear, the desire of achievement, and the triumph of success. The mere animal enjoyment of life, for a while, may be a substitute for these in early youth; but it cannot outlast natural growth; and, in the mechanical prolongation of it which follows, the faculties seem to wane in a gentle decline. This is not a wild conclusion from an insulated and peculiar case; for the same phenomena may be witnessed elsewhere, as in the Sandwich Islands, the Tonga, the Navigator, and Samoan groups, and, in fact, in most of the Pacific islands.

At the termination of this cruise I remained but a few months on shore, and, having been ordered to the corvette "St. Louis," sailed for the old cruising-ground in the West Indies.

We were among the Windward Islands, westward from St. Thomas, one day, when I had charge of the deck under a clear, pleasant sky; and, as the regular trade-wind of the tropics was blowing, the ship was running along free, under all sail, when the lookout cried from the masthead, "Breakers ahead!" I knew by the reckoning that we were several hundred miles distant from land, but immediately shortened sail; while the captain, officers, and crew, startled by the cry, came running on deck.

Then occurred a remarkable event. The ship headed westerly, with the wind, which had died almost to a calm, on the starboard quarter. On the lee-beam the ocean seemed much agitated; and soon a huge "comber" appeared, extending to the horizon on either end, and apparently over thirty feet in height above the sea-level. All hands were called; and we wore ship to the southward, and brought by the wind on the port tack, while carpenters were battening down the hatches fore and aft.

As the ship came by the wind, it suddenly fell calm; but she now headed the great wave, which rushed onwards with a terrible roar and irresistible momentum. It struck her; and her bows were raised high in the air, almost bringing her deck perpendicular, and throwing every man off his feet who had not secured himself to something in anticipation of the expected shock.

She was one of the deep-waisted class of sloops-of-war, with heavy bulwarks full seven feet from the deck to the hammock-nettings,—of all vessels the worst to be boarded by a heavy sea. Fortunately, the ports were all out; which proved our salvation. For about two minutes, I suppose,—

it seemed a much longer time, — the ship, her crew, and every thing about the deck, were completely submerged. At my post on the poop I felt the good ship tremble through all her timbers under the weight of water on her deck, and clung to the mizzen-rigging, in which I had lashed myself. She then came up slowly to the surface, the water pouring from her port-holes in torrents; while the great wave, or bore, was seen and heard far beyond her, steadily moving with great velocity on its mysterious course. Three other waves followed the first, but greatly diminished in size and volume; then the surface of the ocean resumed its natural appearance, and the trade-winds again set in. The ship sustained little harm; and, although a few men were badly bruised, there was no serious damage to life or limb. A great many articles were washed overboard, however; and, for months after, every thing lost was laid to the great sea bore.

It is my belief, that had this disaster occurred at night, or had the ship received the shock anywhere but on her bows, she must have gone down, and left not a soul to tell the tale of how or when she disappeared, as has happened to many others, — "The Hornet" and "Albany," for instance, whose fate remains a mystery to this day.

These sudden and mysterious disappearances are not very uncommon. I well remember that of the British sloop-of-war, "Clio," in the Grecian Archipelago. She sailed from the Gulf of Salamis, bound to Malta, but never reached her destined port. Some days after her departure, a violent explosion was seen and heard from the Island of Milo — which is the residence of the Archipelago pilots — in the midst of a terrible squall of thunder and lightning. The experienced men who saw this declared that the explosion was not caused by the elements; and, as the ship was to have touched at Milo in order to land her Archipelago pilot, it was concluded that an electric flash must have fired her magazine, in an instant sending ship, crew, Greek pilot, and all, into eternity.

These "bores" — which, happily, are seldom encountered — are, I believe, attributed to volcanic disturbance of the ocean-bed; an opinion I think erroneous. They are due, I believe, like earthquakes, to the subtle and omnipresent electric fluid which pervades all Nature, and even the whole stellar system; the sun being now well ascertained to be in electric communication and sympathy with the earth. But to enter upon this subject would be not only out of place here, but would render my little memoranda of service too diffuse and voluminous.

XVIII.

IN 1845 I sailed from the Chesapeake in a corvette destined to re-enforce our squadron in the Pacific, and arrived in due season at Mazatlan, in which port we found the fleet assembled under the command of Com. Sloat. My ship was shortly after ordered to the coast of California, then an insignificant Mexican province, in which but little interest was taken by the world, and the population of which was but a few thousand.

As the details of my experience in California, during that cruise, have already been published in "A Tour of Duty in California," printed in 1849, I will only advert here to such events as are necessary to preserve the continuity of my narrative, and, resuming the thread of my story at the end of that book, pass to those of succeeding years in the order they occurred; thus furnishing a sequel to that little volume.

The 14th of June, 1846, must be regarded as a memorable day in the history of California; for then her "manifest destiny" became apparent, impelling her to "gravitate" towards the Union. The movement was inaugurated at the little town of Sonoma, the scene of the ancient mission of San Francisco Solano; the Mexican flag having been struck, and what was known as the "bear-flag" substituted for it; while a provisional government was established, countenanced, and authorized by Frémont, under instructions from Washington. Soon afterwards the whole United-States squadron arrived at Monterey; and on the 7th of July, 1846, Com. Sloat issued his proclamation, taking formal possession of the Californias in the name of the United States, landing his forces at the same time, and hoisting the American flag. By previous arrangement, the flag was also raised, and the proclamation read and promulgated, at Yerba Buena, now San Francisco, and other principal localities. In command of a party from the ship, I had the honor to hoist the flag at Sonoma; and, in less than a week, all Upper California was in our possession.

It is a significant fact, that only the day after taking possession, and even before the excitement of that event had subsided, her Majesty's ship "Cornwallis," Admiral Sir Michael Seymour, arrived at Monterey with orders like Com. Sloat's, — to take possession of the country as security for British holders of Mexican bonds. Admiral Seymour's orders, however, were conditional; and seeing the stars and stripes at the flagstaff on shore, and learning what had taken place, he soon sailed away.

Alta California, thus seized in consequence of the war between the United States and Mexico, was held until the new year; when a revolt broke out at the Pueblo de los Angeles, and Lieut. Gillespie of the marines, commanding the garrison, was forced to retreat to San Pedro, where he embarked.

In a subsequent attempt to recover the Pueblo by Capt. Mervine of the frigate "Savannah," his force was repulsed; whereupon Com. Stockton — who had succeeded Sloat — assembled all the naval force at San Diego, while Frémont marched by land, to attempt its recapture, it being regarded as the capital of Upper California.

The squadron made their rendezvous at San Diego; and Stockton immediately set about preparing a force to march upon the Pueblo, while Frémont was approaching the same point from the north. Just at this time, Brig.-Gen. Stephen W. Kearney arrived in California by the overland route from Sante Fé. He was attacked by a party of Californians under Andres Pico at San Bernardino: several of the officers and soldiers of his escort were killed and wounded, and his baggage and a field-piece fell into the enemy's hands. Kit Carson, who was with the general, brought the news of his arrival to San Diego; and he was safely brought into our garrison by a party sent for the purpose.

Com. Stockton, having completed his preparations, set forth towards the Pueblo at the head of four hundred seamen, sixty dismounted dragoons of Kearney's escort, fifty California volunteers, and a light battery. He first encountered the enemy — about five hundred cavalry, with artillery — at the ford of the River San Gabriel, not far from the Angelic capital, on the 8th of January, and celebrated the day by a spirited little fight. Having forced the passage of the San Gabriel, our little column debouched upon the "Mesa," a table-land some four leagues in extent, through which runs the road from San Diego to the Pueblo de los Angeles. As we came in sight of its white walls in the afternoon, we saw a long procession of horsemen issuing from the town, and directing their march towards us. It soon became evident they meant to oppose our progress; and our jolly tars were in high spirits as they formed in square, the artillery at the angles, to receive them. The ground was a perfectly level, treeless plain, and thus admirably fitted for the evolutions of both infantry and cavalry. The enemy's cavaliers were about two thousand strong, principally *rancheros*, and the best horsemen, probably, in the world. They were dressed in the Mexican costume, in gay *serapes* of all colors, and divided into bands, or squadrons, each of which had some kind of music, — trumpets, bugles, and even guitars and fiddles. They were armed with the *escopeta* (a clumsy carbine), a few with pistols and rifles, and some with sabres and *machetes;* but by far the larger part had only a short lance, with a long blade, that could be used with one hand. Many flags streamed over the column; some troopers having gayly-colored handkerchiefs fixed to their lances, which, fluttering in the breeze, gave a festal aspect to the concourse. Confidently approaching our little force, they sent their led horses to the rear under charge of their *vaqueros,* and began their dispositions for an assured victory, forming in two columns with a squadron front, opposed to two faces of our square.

Meanwhile our men stood firm, as it had been thought best to withhold our fire until the charge was made. Orders were issued to wait until the enemy came within pistol-shot; but our sailors, seeing a tumultuous, noisy crowd of men and horses rushing upon them with cries and waving flags, opened fire at half-musket range rather prematurely. Our cartridges, being an ounce ball and three buck-shot, proved very destructive. Men and horses tumbled over in considerable numbers, and the six-pound field-guns completed their discomfiture. They retired, however, in tolerable order, carrying off the wounded, — those who had lost their horses hanging by the stirrups of the more fortunate, — and again formed for another charge. Three times they essayed to shake our square; but, being steadily met with the same withering fire, they at last desisted, and rode off towards the mountains, leaving open to us the road to their capital, which we entered on the same evening.

The force which attacked us on this occasion consisted of native Californians, superior to Mexicans in physical power and military spirit, and far better horsemen; while all the conditions of the action were favorable for cavalry in attacking infantry. These men were not only finely mounted on well-trained horses, but had also remounts on the field. Yet not one of them got within twenty yards of our square, in the face of that steady rolling file-firing; nor was a single bayonet or lance, on either side, reddened with the blood of horse or man. It was a fair test of the respective merits of fiery and chivalrous cavalry opposed to steady and disciplined infantry; and the former was, as sportsmen say, "nowhere."

Their leader, Flores, attacked our sailor battalion in preference to the volunteer force of Frémont, which had the *prestige* of long frontier experience, which had habituated them to Indian warfare, and made them unerring marksmen. I think he committed a serious blunder; and that, had he engaged Frémont's force, — which had no knowledge of infantry drill or discipline, and no bayonets, — he must have been successful.

This affair ended the struggle for the possession of Upper California; and our squadron sailed soon after for the coast of Mexico, where part of it was employed in blockading Mazatlan and San Blas, while my ship was sent with the frigate "Congress" to Guaymas. We summoned that town to surrender; but, receiving a defiant answer, opened our batteries the next morning, and soon reduced it to a heap of ruins. Meanwhile Mazatlan was taken possession of, and also the important town of San José: at Cape San Lucas and La Paz the American flag was hoisted, and the province of Lower California occupied.

The operations in the Pacific thus resulted in giving us full possession of both the Californias, and military occupation of two of the enemy's most important seaports.

My ship now started on her long and tedious voyage home by way of Cape Horn, touching at Valparaiso. It was an uneventful voyage, and ended with our arrival at Boston in June, 1848.

To the inmates of a cruising-ship, months, and even years, seem a short period in the retrospect, so few incidents occur by which to mark the time. One day is like another; and, while the dim vista of the future stretches vast before us, we wonder at the nothingness of the past as the sands of the present drop unnoticed away. Thousands of miles are traversed, marked by scarcely a change in our habits of thought or action. We are conscious of no novelty save the variations of climate, by which we are alternately "scorched in the tropics, and frozen at the pole."

After making Boston light with a southerly breeze, we were all thinking of a speedy arrival in harbor, and an early meeting with friends, when — presto! the wind changed, and flung a cloud over our bright anticipations. At midnight a north-east gale roared in fury; and

> "A heavy sea ran mountains high,
> And drenched the toiling crew:
> I thought of home, I heaved a sigh;
> Our good ship — she heaves *to*."

I cannot conclude this account of my first visit to California without recording my impressions of one spot, whose features will ever linger pleasantly in my memory. I have seen most parts of the habitable world; and, as I now recall their respective beauties and advantages, I am forced to the conclusion, that in climate, fertility, and healthful conditions, three regions have been specially favored by Nature, — the Valley of Mexico, Eastern Syria, and Southern Alta California. At first thought, it may seem strange that the claims of this last-named region have had so feeble recognition; but it should be remembered, that, thus far, California enterprise has demanded immediate results and has ignored all opportunities, however promising, that did not offer them. The resources of Southern Alta California have been lost sight of in the hot search for instant profit. This feverish haste in the race for wealth is now subsiding; and the eyes of practical calculating wisdom have been turned to this hitherto-neglected section of the State.

Although the picture of San Diego, seen as I sailed into its harbor (the finest, except that of San Francisco, in California), is still vivid in my memory, I shall not-attempt to reproduce it, or to give any detailed account of a place which has been so accurately described by Mr. Dana in "Two Years before the Mast;" but the statement of a few facts touching the situation and material advantages of San Diego, toward which emigration is now tending in considerable volume, may be of service to those who seek information about it as a field of commercial operations.

San Diego is the seaport of Southern California. "It stands," in the language of Rev. Walter Colton, in his book published in 1850, "on the border-line of Alta California, and opens upon a land-locked bay of surpassing beauty. The climate is soft and mild the year round, the sky brilliant, and the atmosphere free of those mists which the cold currents throw on the northern coast: the sea-breeze cools the heat of summer; and the great ocean herself modulates into the same temperature the rough airs of winter. . . . Before the eyes that fall on these pages are under death's shadow, San Diego will have become the queen of the south in California, encircled with vineyards and fields of golden grain, and gathering into her bosom the flowing commerce of the Colorado and Gila."

This prophecy has not yet been verified; but the realization of the visions is only delayed. At the present time San Diego contains thirty five hundred inhabitants, twenty to thirty stores, a fine flouring-mill, several churches, free schools, &c. Its population is unlike that of most California cities, being permanent, and possessing, in a remarkable degree, the culture of the Eastern States. The city is the natural commercial centre of a vast extent of country fertile and rich in minerals, including all Southern California, Southern Nevada, Arizona, New Mexico, and Northern Mexico. On the completion of the Transcontinental Railway, — which is to be built *viâ*

Marshall, Tex., — San Diego, which will be its coast terminus, will become an important point of trans-shipment in the trade with China and Japan, and will compete not unsuccessfully with San Francisco for the commerce of the Orient. It is well known to mariners that vessels plying between Oriental ports and San Francisco invariably pass down the California coast till they reach or pass the thirty-second parallel, in order to avail themselves of the trade-winds. This practice virtually places San Diego between San Francisco and the Orient, and gives her an advantage over any northern port of several hundred miles of travel.

In view of the unquestionable superiority of San Diego in geographical situation, agricultural and commercial resources, and climatic charms, and especially of the tide of emigration now tending thither, there is little hazard in adopting Mr. Colton's prediction, with a reasonable extension of the limits he fixed for its verification.

XIX.

A FEW months after my arrival in the United States I received orders from the navy department to proceed to California as government agent, for the protection of live-oak and other naval timber on the public lands in that Territory; and sailed in a merchant-vessel for my destination *viâ* the Isthmus of Panama. Since my return home, gold had been discovered at Sutter's Fort on the Sacramento, and the tide of emigration had set in towards the new "Dorado," that, less than one year ago, had come under the rule of the United States.

Landing at Chagres, I found that ancient and dilapidated seaport crowded with adventurers from New Orleans of all races and nations, insanely eager to reach the land of gold, in which they expected to reap an easy harvest. Since the time of Morgan and his bold buccaneers, the little seaport had never contained such a shaggy, unkempt, and reckless crowd of dare-devils as now occupied it. Every available "bungay," bateau, skiff, and canoe had been secured for the navigation of the river to Cruces; and the boatmen were rejoicing in the sudden advance in the price of their services. Being able — unlike most of these emigrants — to speak Spanish, I soon procured the aid of two river-men, and a fine canoe with a *toldo* (awning), large enough for two persons to sleep under; and, having put our luggage into her, prepared chocolate with a spirit-lamp of our own. *En passant*, let me recommend chocolate prepared in the Spanish fashion, whenever it can be had at any price, as the best *provant* for all weary travellers. It contains within the smallest compass more nourishment than any other comestible. It restores the losses of the body, corrects the lassitude common to wayfarers, is agreeable to the palate, never palls, and is easily digested. It is also highly sedative in its effects.

Our boatmen, with the propensity to procrastinate characteristic of their race and calling, left us on some slight excuse to return to the *pulperias* (grog-shops) of Chagres, having received an instalment of their promised compensation. Having finished our frugal meal, we lit our pipes, and were contemplating the dark river and the distant lights of the town (for it was now nightfall), when we were hailed from a canoe near our own. The speaker was a fellow-passenger from New York, bound to California, with a corps of butchers and meat-packers to exploit that peculiar industry, and well known as "Baron" Steinbergen. The baron was a jovial, handsome man, tall, stout, with a Rubens head and complexion. He spoke not a word of Spanish, and was consequently at the mercy of his boatmen.

These fellows had fitted him to a hair's-breadth with a little dug-out, which might have served him admirably for a coffin, but which was not roomy enough for a boat, and in which he dared not turn himself over for fear of a capsize. Having thus secured him, the rascals had decamped, taking with them their paddles, — an unnecessary precaution; for the poor man could have made no use of them, nor even bestir himself sufficiently to get up the anchor by which the boat was moored.

We lost no time in relieving our friend from his uncomfortable position; hauling his craft alongside our own, and refreshing his inner man. About midnight, our boatmen and the baron's returned, our friend unwillingly took possession of his fairy skiff, and we began our voyage up the dismal Chagres

River. After two days and nights on this sluggish stream, amid almost incessant rain, the nights made hideous by the drinking and gambling of our black crews, we at last reached Gorgona. Here the villains, landing our baggage, left us in the lurch, having been bribed by a party who came along just then to carry them to Cruces. In this miserable village I was compelled to remain a whole week, while the advancing wave of emigration swept by it in every description of floating craft; several vessels having arrived at Chagres since our departure, crowded with passengers.

Eager, excited, and with minds intent upon prospective nuggets, these poor fellows deemed no exertion too arduous, no expense too great, as the price of their speedy arrival in the gold regions. Most of them, unused to hardship, instead of wealth found disease and death (as I afterwards learned) in El Dorado.

Every horse and mule in Gorgona had been employed to carry men or baggage to Panama; and, unable to get away, I amused myself in shooting some of the game that abounded in the neighborhood. Many a duck of brilliant plumage, snowy ibis, gorgeous flamingo, chattering parrot, and fat *chichalaka* (tropical pheasant), went down before my gun: but I paid dearly for my sport; for I awoke one morning with a pain in the back, a furred tongue, and aching head, and knew at once that the insidious isthmus fever was upon me. I instantly determined to start for Panama before the disease had wholly overpowered me; for to be sick at Gorgona, without friends, medicines, or doctors, was certain death. So I sallied forth, took the road on foot, and, by great good luck, met an *arriero* returning, with two pack-mules, which I secured at once.

We left Gorgona at mid-day, taking the rough bridle-path, which was a difficult scramble for the whole distance. The journey seemed to me a real Inferno, — the dark road through a dense tropical forest, the snakes, and monkeys gibbering at me from the gnarled trees and lianas. That night I spent in the hut of a poor woman on the edge of a prairie; and the next day, being unable to sit upon my saddle, her two sons carried me in a rude litter to Panama. This poor woman knew that I had a large sum of money in gold, which she carefully guarded until all was ready, when she put it under my head, and, telling her sons to carry me gently, bade me God speed. This is not the only time, when, in countries called uncivilized, my life has been saved and my property secured by the influence of poor women: and I have therefore gratefully put this fact on record; for, under the like circumstances in my own country, I should have been murdered without hesitation or remorse. I will add, that these disinterested poor women have invariably been pious Catholics.

At Panama I fortunately encountered in the streets an acquaintance, Don Diego Feria; and in the fine airy mansion of this good Samaritan I went through the various stages of the *calentura* of the isthmus, attended by the surgeon of a British ship-of-war.

At last "The California," the first steamer of the line, arrived, and we who had tickets repaired on board. She was loaded to the guards with passengers, and sailed, leaving hundreds unable to get away. These last groped their way up the coast in all kinds of vessels; one party of seven persons actually starting for San Francisco in a half-decked launch, and arriving at their destination in a hundred and thirty days, after encountering incredible hardships and dangers.

We passed through the Golden Gate on the 28th February, 1849; and, landing, I saw with astonishment the great change that had come over San Francisco. The little idle place I had left, with its three or four houses and some twenty-five inhabitants, was now, by the potent power of gold, metamorphosed into a canvas city of several thousand people: the beach, where only the year before I had shot snipe and curlew, was thronged with immigrants from every part of the world; and the harbor, formerly only visited once a year by a trader in hides or an occasional whaler, was now crowded with merchantmen from every seaport in Europe, the United States, and South America. Their cargoes had been landed and covered with sails, or were still on board in charge of the officers, the crews having deserted and gone to the mines. Lots were staked off, and had already reached fabulous sums; and the thoroughfares were filled with a rough, armed, and unshorn crowd of fellows, who had returned with nuggets and dust from the "placer."

As I passed through a street between some shanties, I was hailed by an old shipmate of "The Portsmouth" sloop-of-war, who had been discharged on the coast before the ship sailed for home. With a beard that reached his waist, a sunburnt visage, and long hair over his shoulders, a red shirt, buckskin unmentionables, and a revolver stuck in his waistband, the trig, neat man-o'war's-man was not easily recognizable. Jack was now a millionnaire in his own estimation, and therefore on terms of complete social equality with his former officer. He turned up the corner of a sail that covered a lot of elegant furniture, piled in the street, the "venture" of some European merchant; hauled out an elegant fauteuil of crimson velvet, respectfully forcing me into it; and then crossed over to a shanty, whence he returned, bringing a whole basket of champagne. He then beheaded bottle after bottle, draining each in succession; in which agreeable employment he was politely aided, upon invitation, by some thirty thirsty bystanders. Then, in the excess of his delight at meeting me, which he said no words could express, he successively demolished the bottles, the glasses, and the superb chair, by way of venting his superfluous enthusiasm. Jack then drew forth a long buckskin purse filled with dust, and magnanimously paid the shot; and we left the scene of his strange triumph under a salute of three cheers from his invited guests.

This was but one of the rare sights of those days in San Francisco. A few shrewd fellows who landed from "The California" without a dime, as they confessed to me on board before leaving, became rich in twenty-four hours by purchasing town-lots or goods, and selling immediately to others at an advance before consummating the first bargain. Every business negotiation was conducted on a cash basis of gold-dust, no credit being allowed or demanded; and thus the game of speculation went on without promissory-notes, books, or banks. Coined money was at a premium of fifty per cent; and loans of dust, by weight, at ten per cent per month on good security. To give an adequate idea of the state of society, the wonderful vicissitudes of individuals, the tragical and the amusing incidents that frequently occurred, is a task to which my powers of description are unequal.

Gen. P. F. Smith of the United-States army came out with us to take command of the military department of the Pacific, accompanied by some staff-officers, and Mrs. Smith, who had a quite engaging Irish maid. Only two days after they had landed, I called on Mrs. Smith, and found her in despair, her maid, her chief dependence and only domestic, having left her service.

I expressed my regret that the promise of high wages should have induced the girl to abandon her allegiance to so deserving a lady.

"But, my dear sir," said Mrs. Smith, "it is not a question of wages that has separated us. Mary is engaged to be married to a gentleman of large fortune; and the ceremony will be performed as soon as permitted by the rules of the church."

There was nothing more to be said.

Like the rest, I felt the necessity of being a laborer in this vineyard, in which none were idle, and, with Baron Steinbergen and his " retainers," started for San Rafael, where we proposed to inaugurate measures for supplying provisions to the hungry crowd suddenly thrown upon these shores, instead of following the diggers to the mines.

XX.

IN October, 1846, while in command of the military post of Sonoma, I purchased the estate of San Geronimo, consisting of two square leagues (*dos sitios de ganada mayor*), about five miles from the old mission of San Rafael, in what is now called Marin County.

The *Cañada* (hollow, or vale) of San Geronimo is one of the loveliest valleys in California, shut in by lofty hills, the sides of which are covered with red-wood forests, and pines of several kinds, and interspersed with many flowering trees and shrubs peculiar to the country. Through it flows a copious stream, fed by the mountain-brooks; and the soil in the bottom-lands is so prolific, that a hundred bushels of wheat to the acre can be raised with the rudest cultivation, and other crops in corresponding abundance.

While hunting elk in that neighborhood, I had come upon this beautiful valley, and determined to possess it, if possible; and in due time I acquired the property, and stocked it with horned cattle and mares in the usual fashion of making a settlement in California.

In my absence the cattle had increased to about five hundred head of animals of all kinds, which roamed at will in a state of nature over my domain, the *mayor-domo* engaged to take charge of them having left the place, and gone off to the *bonanza* (corruption of *abundancia*), a few months before my arrival.

I laid in a stock of tools, farming-utensils, &c., and arrived at the mission of San Rafael, where I was hospitably received by my old friend — mentioned in the "Tour of Duty" — Don Timoteo Murphy. Here we sojourned for several weeks; but, finding it impossible to engage in any regular pursuit in consequence of the unsettled state of the country, I concluded to follow the current setting towards the "placer." A party was formed of my neighbors the rancheros, who, with their Indian servants and *vaqueros*, made a company of some thirty persons. We had a *caballada* (herd of horses) of a hundred head, and drove with us over two hundred head of beef cattle, collected from the herds that ranged over our lands, whch we intended to sell in the mining country.

The cattle, being perfectly wild, were always driven on the full run, so that a day's drive was quite wearisome; the cattle seizing every opportunity to escape, bolting suddenly from the column in order to return to their *acarencias* (grazing-grounds). At the end of each day's march, or run, we were all too happy to rest, to wash if possible, and to cook and eat our suppers of beef, often without bread or salt; such was the scarcity of articles usually considered necessaries, but which we should have ranked among luxuries. Before dawn we were astir, after passing the night on the hard ground, with nothing between us and it save our saddle-leathers, the saddle-trees being our pillows, and *serapes* (blankets) our only covering: then, after a hurried breakfast of beef, we collected the scattered herd, and began another day's hot and dusty ride.

Good pasture-fed California beef broiled on the coals of a wood-fire, with plenty of spring-water, was our diet; and very good fare it was. My health was never better, my physical powers never greater, than when I was a *ranchero* in that glorious country. Constant exercise, and sleeping in the open air, — no hardship in that pure, dry atmosphere, — hardened my body, invigorated my constitution, and induced an elevation of spirits, and confidence in my ability to endure privation, that I have never felt before or since. I would recommend such a course of training to an invalid as better than all the nostrums of the faculty.

Arriving at the dry diggings, our party separated; and for two months we "prospected" in the vicinity, changing our ground as we saw a chance to dig, trade cattle, swap horses, or to barter our little stock of goods for "dust." I also made a trip in a dug-out to San Francisco on account of partners and self, and returned in a larger boat to our camp on Feather River, laden with dry-goods, groceries, crockery, and hardware. We sold all off at enormous prices, — butcher-knives fetching twenty dollars apiece, common iron spoons five dollars, and ordinary wash-bowls and meaner vessels fifteen dollars. Labor was so high in the diggings, that it was difficult to compute its value. Some Mexicans, encamped near us, paid their camp-keeper a hundred dollars per day for his services and for cooking; and, even at that price, they were most unwillingly rendered. These fellows averaged much more than that sum daily in digging and picking up nuggets, or occasionally washing the dirt of the gulches.

I sold all the flour I brought up, which came from Chili, in bags of four arrobas (twenty-five pounds to the arroba), at a hundred dollars the sack. Several dozens of common calico shirts, bought for the use of our company, were snapped up at twenty dollars each, unwashed, after my partners had worn them for a week; and a digger taking a fancy to my Mexican spurs, worth about three dollars, did not think them dear at twenty-five. Gold was then found everywhere, — on the surface, in the clefts and hollows of rocks, in the brooks, and upon and beneath the soil.

All nations were represented in the Sacramento dry diggings; but the luckiest miners were always the Mexicans and South-Americans. They possesed all the qualities which insure success, — skill in prospecting, quick eyes for gold-bearing formations, rapidity in extracting or washing the auriferous earth, and great industry and patience, — although lazy, and indeed useless in other employments. Honesty pervaded the little community; for the Botany-bay men had not yet arrived in California.

After a stay of several weeks, we returned to our homes, bearing with us the fruits of our industry; and I set to work at San Geronimo with about a score of Indians; and having scratched up with the rude ploughs of the country about fifteen acres of ground, and enclosed it with a brush fence, I set out for San Francisco to procure seed for planting.

Many vessels had arrived since my last visit; and the cry was, "Still they come." Their crews would scarcely wait long enough to furl sails after their arrival, so impatient were they to leave for the diggings. Most of these ships had brought over emigrants from Europe, in a sorry plight after their long voyage. Among them were young and energetic men, some hopeful, others sad and despairing; old men and women, who had followed those they loved to this distant land, only to lay their bones in it; mothers, accompanying their children to an unknown destiny; and all expecting to reap in California the harvest denied to them at home. Let Europeans say what they please of our country: to a great part of their population it is a paradise. In Europe all cannot have bread and work. Their governments and social constitutions leave them to suffer in silence; and their more fortunate fellows give them nothing but advice, — to be resigned. They are like pegs driven into the ground, and must be content to occupy the same places in the social organization from birth till death. Of course all do not find America the land of promise they expected; but they may have land and liberty, and that is all the Almighty gave Adam and Eve. It is then, for them, a paradise. The emigrant comes to America, and is received with an affectation of generosity: but it cannot be denied, that, in giving this welcome, we obey our own interest quite as much as the dictates of charity; and our reception of him is not unmixed with ostentation.

After all, we are *parvenus;* good, without being tender or polished. We distribute to the emigrant tools and seeds; apportion to him, with a significant gesture, a portion of the soil; and go about our affairs, saying to him in effect, "Here you are; fix yourself; I am busy." Thus those who receive this curt hospitality are not oppressed with a load of obligation: they work, take root, and are soon occupied in conquering a position for themselves, and seeking rights denied them elsewhere. They are not mendicants gratefully obliged, but poor men who become citizens.

Among the ships in the harbor, I found an old friend of other days in command of a brig from Honolulu, sitting in solitary state in his cabin, his crew having left him. From him I obtained a few barrels of potatoes which he had among his stores, — poor and small, it is true, but the only ones to be had; and, with this prize seed, I returned to San Geronimo, where I planted the precious seed in the enclosure.

I then left the place in charge of my Indian servants, and addressed myself to the duties of my office as timber-inspector.

In the intervals of these duties I piloted several vessels up the Sacramento River, among which was a bark from Peru, with a company of miners on board, organized at an immense expense, and with whom I remained for several weeks.

While these Peruvians were working in the diggings, I observed that they consumed much less provisions than other miners, while doing the same amount of work, or even more; and that they also seemed better able to endure exposure to the heat of the sun and the dews of night. Asking their director, a German, the reason of this, I was told that it was owing to the use of "coca," an herb indigenous to Peru. They had brought the coca with them, — dried, olive-shaped leaves, of a dark-green color, and packed in sacks of matting of about an arroba (twenty-five pounds) each. Each miner had a small leather pouch for coca, and a small gourd filled with pulverized lime. Three or four times daily they suspended their labors to masticate coca in the following manner: —

First they selected the leaves, and carefully removed the stalks, which they threw away. They then rolled the leaves into a small ball, or quid, called an *acullico*, which they placed in the mouth; and thrusting a little stick into the gourd of lime, its end being moistened, they drew it out, and punched the *acullico* repeatedly with it. The lime soon mixed with the coca in the process of mastication, and caused an abundant flow of saliva, which was partly expectorated, and partly swallowed. The strength of the quid having been exhausted, it was thrown away, and a fresh one substituted. The coca is prepared and used like the betel-nut of the Malays; but, unlike it, it does not stain the teeth black. I found, upon trial, that coca has a pleasant, aromatic flavor something like tea-leaves; but my lips and gums were somewhat cauterized by the lime. The average consumption by these miners was said to be from one to one ounce and a half daily.

When excessively used, coca is said to cause a bad breath, to color the gums, and to make the lips pallid. Sugar is sometimes used with the *acullico*. The inveterate *coquero* (coca-eater) finds it difficult to abandon the habit when once acquired, and returns to it frequently after successive discontinuances like the confirmed opium-eater. Thus parties of *coqueros* often meet clandestinely in Peru to enjoy their peculiar dissipation. Coca is raised and cured in the mountainous districts of Peru on the flanks of the Cordillera, whence it is sent to other parts of the country. It is prophylactic, and slightly aperient;

and an infusion of its leaves makes an agreeable and strengthening drink. The price in Lima is about an ounce (sixteen dollars) the arroba.

The moderate *coquero* goes through much toil with apparent ease, and, as I have already said, consumes much less food than those who do not use coca. I have been told wonderful things by military officers serving in Peru, — of long marches made by the soldiers of that country using coca on quarter rations. No doubt this plant, so little known to other nations, is one of Nature's inestimable blessings; for, like others of her gifts, it is not detrimental except when abused. It supports the bodily strength, prevents muscular waste, and is said to make one gay in spirits and long-winded.

My attention was drawn to one of the miners mentioned above, named Pedro Beltran. I knew this man to labor hard at "panning" dirt for a whole week on one scanty meal of flour-cakes daily; and he slept only two or three hours at night. He need not have worked so hard; but he told me that he came to the *bonanza* to get money, and in the shortest possible time. He made, that week, a little over eleven hundred dollars, half of which went to the company by the terms of his contract. The week after, he accompanied the director and myself on foot on a prospecting tour lasting three days, easily keeping up with our horses, although we travelled at least thirty miles a day. He returned, seemingly not at all fatigued by his long march, and resumed his labors.

I left him in the diggings working hard as ever "on his own hook;" for this company, like all the rest, soon broke up, and Pedro went vigorously to washing gold-earth, stopping only for his *chacchar* (quid, or chew). He was sixty years old, and told me he had never been ill in his life. He was married, and his wife had reared a family of eight sons and five daughters.

XXI.

MY crops turned out beyond my most sanguine expectations; and I had the satisfaction of reaping a splendid harvest, which was disposed of at high prices. Agriculture, even the grazing interest, at that time the leading one of California, had been entirely lost sight of, the whole population having been busily engaged in securing the dazzling dust and nuggets; and food of all kinds was held at enormous prices.

Every article of breadstuffs was brought from abroad, while the emigration of 1849 probably amounted to a hundred thousand persons. The small seed-potatoes, not larger than a walnut, which I planted, produced at least twenty-fold; and the improvement in quality over the seed was really wonderful. The virgin soil, of pure vegetable *humus*, so nourished and stimulated their growth, that I had several hundred bushels of potatoes in the crop, each of which weighed ten pounds avoirdupois, or over; and the average of the rest would not fall below a pound. The sale of this crop at one real (twelve and a half cents) per pound, which was the market price, fully repaid the expense and trouble of planting.

San Francisco had become a city of some forty thousand people, and was the business centre of the rising State. With the increase of population, the irregular placer-mining became obsolete, or practised by those only for whom its adventurous character had a peculiar charm; while rude machinery, dams, conduits, canals, and sluice-ways, began to be constructed in the mining regions.

Certain branches of industry, indispensable to the new state of things and to the development of the country, were exploited; and saw-mills, lime and brick kilns, and stone-quarries, were established at favorable points; while with the acquisition of wealth came the desire of enjoyment and comfort: fine houses were built, and mechanics of all kinds found employment at high wages. The *bonanza* no longer absorbed all the laborers, many of whom, indeed, from choice, abandoned the search for gold, tired of the exposures, hardships, and self-denial which attended it.

The proverbial adaptation of the Yankee to every condition of life was illustrated on every side; but foreigners were not behind him in bettering their fortunes in the new cities springing up all over the country. Meanwhile, keeping pace with the emigration from beyond the seas, a hardy though rude population flocked into California from our Western States, and, spreading themselves over the country in the rural districts, settled down on "squatted" or purchased farms, and set manfully to work to plough and sow.

The industrious and orderly, however, did not constitute the only addition to the population; for, following the law of civilization, in their train came those who seem born only to prey upon their fellows: and as "where the carcass is, there will the eagles be gathered," New York sent out its "roughs," and Australia its "ticket-of-leave men;" and desperadoes of all kinds, finding a congenial field for their operations, effected a regular organization, with ramifications all over the State. A little later the people were aroused from their apathetic tolerance of these villains, who corrupted the very source and fountains of justice; and that sharp cure, the vigilance committees, took them in charge with excellent results. The original simplicity of California, as it was when we took military possession, its patriarchal institutions and benevolent customs, as I have endeavored to portray them in the "Tour of Duty," had all vanished forever.

At the end of the rainy season, and the advent of the delightful California spring, my little party of neighbors again visited the mining regions, finding every thing changed in the operations, which were now carried on in the neighborhood of the water-courses. What I saw was hardly calculated to give one an elevated idea of human nature. These scenes were at once curious and sad to a thoughtful student of human nature. I had been among tribes of barbarians, and on the islands of the Pacific peopled with naked savages; but here I found that man is more of a savage when he has once lived in a civilized condition, and retrogresses, than when born in barbarism. The denizens of the mining region were indeed clothed, poorly enough to be sure, but with some regard to decency; but, morally, they were utterly naked. The robes of hypocrisy which clothe humanity elsewhere were thrown aside, and neither virtue nor modesty had any respect. "These seekers after gold," thought I, "are in a hurry: they have no time to lose, and, casting off all restraint, return to natural brutality. California is to them a sort of chrysalis, from which they expect to emerge furnished with new and gorgeous wings. It is a neutral ground; and they arrive here from an obscure past, in order to wrest from it the elements of a purifying future."

"Auri sacra fames," I said, passing near a group earnestly engaged with tin pan and "long tom" washing the auriferous dirt. A young man looked up from his pan knowingly, but without quitting his occupation. "Sir," said he, with a touch of irony in his tone, "you will gain little here by selling quotations. Had it been possible to live by such a trade, I should not now be here; for I have studied the 'humanities,' carried off prizes, and learned by rote all that has been said against money-getting. Had I time, I would answer you with Seneca;

but we will adjourn that pleasure until we meet in New York. In reply to your three words of Virgil, I will answer you with Ovid, 'Effodiuntur opes, irritamenta malorum:' I will then lie back in my chair, and cry with Catullus, 'Me mea paupertas;' with Horace, 'Aurea mediocritas;' and with Juvenal, 'Obscena pecunia.' Now, my dear sir, I am too poor to console myself with such trifles. 'Non in pane solo vivit homo,' says the Scripture in our vulgate. And it is true: dry bread is insipid. The meagre fortune I possessed did not permit me to add to my daily crust the good wines and succulent meats I coveted, as many horses as I liked to use, and the sum of love necessary to my existence: so I came here courageously to increase my resources. Should Fortune not smile upon me, I will step into some druggist's shop, and choose among the infernal distillations of death a remedy for all ills."

"My dear sir," said I, "my little remark, or quotation, was made without allusion to yourself or any individual; and I am sorry to have offended you."

"Oh! no offence, sir, in the least," he returned: "your exclamation produced a slight irritation; that is all."

A shade of melancholy here passed over the young man's face, replacing the feverish gayety with which he had just spoken.

"Here," said he, offering me a small nugget: "put that on your vest-chain. When you look at it, you will call to mind a poor devil you met in the placer, who knew Latin, and who was unhappy. After all," said the young man cheerfully, "Juvenal is the only one who has the right expression, — 'Obscena pecunia.'"

Being interested in the youth, and inclined to serve him, I proposed to him, on leaving the placer, that he should accompany me.

"Thanks," said he. "But what would you do with me?

You cannot give me twenty thousand a year, can you? I will not accept a humble position : and I have only one card left to play; that is myself. I will wait for the smiles of Fortune. For those I brave fevers, Indian arrows, Yankee bowie-knives, cholera, and wild beasts. Apparently you have enough and to spare; and you had better leave this. You excite jealousy and anger among us; you are independent and happy; your presence here is a reflection upon us all; and it will be an act of charity on your part to disappear. Curiosity is abuse for the prisoners one visits in a jail; and we are the convicts, sent here by an unknown code. We undergo our punishment in this limbo, from which few escape alive. Depart, then! Is it such a fine spectacle to see men dispute each other's right to a few square yards of soil impregnated with yellow dust? to see them murder each other for a look? to refuse the water that cleanses, the adieu which consoles, the tomb even, which, perchance, is denied them after death? Here the corpses are left to rot on the surface. Digging is to take out gold; but to dig a grave would seem sacrilege. We dig, we play, we die. The expense of supporting life follows the same progression as other expenses. A poor laborer may earn here twenty dollars a day; and the pulsations of our arteries are multiplied in unison. Time passes not for us as for you. You are more than a stranger to us : in fact, you are a monster.

"Go, then, sir! Were you a doctor, now, you might serve us; for any chance barber coming this way visits the sick at an ounce of gold a visit. Even then he wearies out Nature by his treatment. Ah, sir! you have, somewhere, a patrimony, a family : go and find them again. I will not advise you to keep your fortune; for, should I find one, I shall probably spend it all in a few years. I merely say that you had better return to civilized lands; to a happy country, in which men are still men; where the heart may complain of suffering, and where all you have to combat is civilized egotism.

Adieu!" said my philosopher with a smile, "Æternumque vale."

Returning to our ranchos with a fair share of profits in the autumn, we began the usual routine of work, holding a *herradura* (branding cattle) every week in succession on the different ranchos in accordance with the custom, and with the not as yet obsolete laws of the *mesta*. Crops of vegetables were not as remunerative as the year before, so many cultivators having entered the field, tempted by the high prices; and the business was overdone.

I built a new house on my place, and projected other improvements; and my neighbors, stimulated at last to enterprise in that direction, began to bestir themselves. But we were all annoyed by the incursions of the "Gentiles," — as the wild Indians are called in contradistinction to the "Christians," or tame Indians, — who came stealthily upon our lands to steal horses. The rogues always selected these animals, as they could run them in a single night beyond all possible successful pursuit.

At last, in self-defence, we organized an expedition to suppress these frays, and at the same time to indemnify ourselves, by securing some of these "Gentiles," intending to keep them as hostages, and to use them, meanwhile, as laborers. A council of rancheros was accordingly summoned at the "Baulinas," — a rancho on the sea-coast belonging to Don Juan Briones, — at which I assisted with several others; and a plan of operation was formed.

XXII.

FIVE rancheros, each with five to ten Indian *vaqueros*, assembled at the rendezvous at the appointed time with a *caballada* of some fifty excellent horses. The tame or Christian Indians enter into the spirit of these *razzias* with great zest, and take keen delight in entrapping their wild relatives. At the trysting-place Don Jose Armenteros was unanimously chosen leader of our party, whom we were to obey until the termination of the expedition. He was the major-domo of the ranchero Rafael Garcia, and noted as the best rider, the most skilful *riatero* (thrower of the lasso), and the most accomplished in all the sports of the campo : he had also the advantage of experience in similar expeditions. At the rendezvous we began preparations for the expedition by a grand feast on the supplies brought or sent there by the provident wives of the rancheros, consuming all our stores in one night; and then, like Hernan Cortes after he had burnt his ships, we were ready to push into the wild regions before us, unencumbered with whiskey or other groceries, and depending solely on the rifle or the *riata*, for our subsistence. We carried with us a few trinkets for trading.

At daylight we rose from the ground, and, taking a northerly route, set forth into the wilderness at full gallop, the *caballada* in advance, with all the *vaqueros*. headed by Armenteros. Encamping in the woods north of Bodega the first night, we resumed the march at early dawn, and rode all day through a beautiful and fertile country, more like a gentleman's park than a primeval forest. The trees were superb, the *Palo Colorado* (red wood), a kind of cedar; *Wellingtonia gigantea*, coeval possibly with the Deluge; the *pinabete* (a pine of great size, hard and tough as oak); the *madron*, an orange-colored wood, laurels, and bays, mixed with live-oak, *alamos*, and *alamitos* (poplars); while the red berries of the *mansanito*, gleaming in the undergrowth, formed a picture of arboreal splendor nowhere else to be seen.

Now we ascended the spur of some mountain-range commanding a view of the sea on our left; then plunged into a dense forest; and anon crossed a broad and smiling savanna, enamelled with beautiful flowers of every hue and delightful perfume, *romero* (rosemary) being in great abundance. There shone the lily of the valley, poppies, and tulips of every tint, the aromatic anise-seed, the butterfly-flower, which is indigenous, dancing on its long stem, an almost perfect counterpart of the insect from which it takes its name; here the humble *canchalagua*, a febrifuge, and the *yerba del tos*, a specific for pulmonary and catarrhal complaints.

We killed a deer in the afternoon; and, while selecting a place for a bivouac, Armenteros lassoed a bear, on the savory paws of which, a *bonne bouche* with hunters, we supped heartily.

We were now in the Gentile country: so the next morning a place of security for our *caballada*, abounding in grass and water, was selected on a point of land projecting into the sea; and old Juan Briones, with two *vaqueros*, left to guard the neck which connected it with the mainland. The rest of our party continued their route.

Don Pepe, as Señor Armenteros was called, was now in his element, and recounted many anecdotes of former raids. He led our small but well-armed and mounted party in an easterly direction until about noon, when we halted in a dense wood;

and he set out with one man, my Antonio, whom he selected for his intelligence and courage, to seek an Indian village or rancheria. Meanwhile we picketed our horses, and beguiled the time with smoking and *monte* (Spanish game of cards).

At daylight Don Pepe and Antonio returned with an ally in the person of a naked Indian, with shaggy, unkempt hair, and a horrible squint. This worthy bore a wooden bow ingeniously strengthened on the back with deer-sinews; and under his arm, as the Devil in the song is said to have carried his tail, he carried a quiver made of the skin of a cub bear, filled with arrows tipped with obsidian, or volcanic glass, which abounds here.

Don Pepe introduced his new ally as an old acquaintance; and we returned with him to his rancheria, he being, according to our chief, *muy bravo*, and crafty as brave. We found the rancheria in a valley near the sea, which was not visible from our bivouac, but which we could distinctly smell, in a most ancient and fish-like odor. Not wishing to share the lodges of this untutored and unsavory race, we remained in a grove on the outskirts of the village; the Indians contributing to our frugal evening meal some excellent salmon, and melons from their *milpa* (garden).

Next morning we collected a few beads and light goods, and invited the men to visit our camp: ladies are not allowed that privilege among the Gentiles.

The eyes of the strabismic unfortunate grew more fixed to the tip of his nose than ever at sight of our wonderful treasures; and I feared they would "shoot madly from their spheres," so distended were they in admiration of the many-colored beads, great needles, awls, mirrors, and knives displayed in our camp. Encouraged by the cupidity of our visitors, our spokesman began cautiously to approach the subject of our mission into their country; but he found the wary Gentiles better diplomatists than he imagined.

For two mortal hours the keen encounter of wits endured. Don Pepe endeavored to induce the Indians to send men from their rancheria to accompany us home, promising them good cheer in plenty and a generous reward. But all his eloquence was in vain: so we broke up the conference, and prepared to pass the day in quiet by ourselves, consulting about future movements, cleaning our arms, and recruiting our horses. In the afternoon we were called upon by our cross-eyed friend and another chief, and informed that we should have their assistance in getting all the help we wanted, if we would be guided by their advice, and grant their exorbitant demands. It was plain that a council had been held, and that our allies wanted to get rid of us, after obtaining certain articles they coveted, especially fish-hooks, at the sight of which in the forenoon they had greatly marvelled, never before having seen steel or iron hooks. They also feared that we should forcibly compel them to furnish the help we asked for: so, like skilful diplomatists, they resolved to divert our military prowess from themselves to their enemies. Accordingly an harangue was addressed to Don Pepe, who understood the Indian language, abounding in gestures and gutturals; which he was desired to expound to us in good Castilian.

The whole story was to the effect that our hosts (as they might have been termed) were a much-abused and long-suffering people, honest and above horse-stealing; while a neighboring community some ten leagues away were vile oppressors and bloody-minded villains, horse-thieves by profession, whom it would be both just and creditable to capture and enslave, in which laudable enterprise they would cheerfully aid us. While still deliberating, our conference was suddenly broken off by the appearance of Juan Briones and his *vaqueros*, who brought the astounding intelligence that our whole *caballada* had been stampeded and carried off by unknown Indians. Briones himself and a *vaquero* were wounded by arrows; and the other boy dragged along at the end of his lasso an Indian of dogged and sullen aspect.

While we were listening to the story of Briones, one of our servants came up, and told us that every Indian in the rancheria hard by had vanished. As these Indians instantly kill and eat their stolen horses on reaching a place of security, our indignation was at once aroused; and we prepared to follow the trail, and rescue our *caballada* of over forty fine, well-trained steeds, amongst which were many especial pets of every individual of our party. Rafael Garcia particularly lamented a gallant *pinto* (spotted horse), threatening to cut his *pedazos* (morsels) out of the ugly maw of any Gentile who had eaten him; and all our party of rancheros imagined their noble steeds cut, slashed, and carbonadoed to make a banquet for thieving and graceless heathens.

Luckily Don Pepe had secured the persons of the two chiefs, at Briones' first intimation of our loss, before they could escape; and instant death was now denounced upon them if our horses were not recovered by the morning's light. Making a virtue of necessity, these worthies communicated with their subordinates, who had taken refuge in the inaccessible undergrowth hard by, and collected a party of twenty braves of their rancheria, armed with clubs, wooden spears, and bows and arrows. The big chief was lashed securely to a *vaquero* of our party as a hostage; and the whole party started for the hills.

We soon struck the trail of our horses; and it was so broad and plain, that we pursued it at full speed, our Indian allies stopping occasionally to verify it, while the moon shone in unclouded brilliancy after the short twilight had passed away. Don Pepe rode far ahead of the main body with his *vaqueros*, keeping a sharp lookout on the Indian runners, who out-travelled our horses, and seemed to enjoy the sport of tracking their fellow-men and brothers quite as well as we did. I have often observed this peculiarity among savages when backed by whites. .

About midnight we noticed that the hoof-tracks were quite fresh in the moist ground, and by other signs we knew we were not far in the rear of our *caballada* and their abductors. We now relaxed our speed, and proceeded cautiously, in order not to alarm the Indian camp, upon which we might come at any moment. At last it was reported near at hand; and we dismounted, leaving our horses under charge of our *vaqueros*, while we silently and stealthily approached the village on foot.

The little rancheria of lodges built of slender sticks, wattled with grass and mud, huddled around the usual *temascal* (sweat-house), indispensable in every place of the kind, lay in the gorge of a *cañon* (gulley); while the hills rose steep around it on every side, save that by which we approached.

No sound broke the solemn stillness of the night, and the whole scene was brightly illuminated by the moon and twinkling stars.

These Indians had no domestic animals whatever, not even dogs; which lack accounted for the silence, which remained unbroken, until, on a nearer approach, we heard the stamping of our captured horses from a rude corral near the sweat-house. Don Pepe instantly formed his plan. We withdrew again to our cover, each of us being assigned his place. The plan was explained to the Indians, the main body of whom, led by Don Pepe, making a *détour* round the village, climbed the hillside, and took up a position at the head of the *cañon* in order to cut off the retreat of men and horses to the hills. The rest of us were to attack in front on signal from our leader, and simultaneously with his party.

At two o'clock the moon had set, and the village was but faintly illuminated by the stars; when a group of Indians, asleep until then, aroused themselves under our very eyes from their first nap, and gathered around a fire, whose embers they raked into activity, and began cooking, eating, and gambling, often wrangling with each other as they tossed the bones. We could even smell the savory horsemeat as it spluttered on the coals; and Rafael Garcia felt a bitter pang at the reflection that it might be a part of his inestimable *pinto*, for which he had refused five hundred dollars.

We waited in silence for an hour or more, until the first faint, gray streaks of dawn appeared in the east; when the Indians of the rancheria gradually ceased from gambling, and sank again in sleep.

The gray tints now became ashes-of-rose color, and the radiance of the stars was slightly dimmed, when from the head of the *cañon* came the cry of the *coyote* — the small wolf of the country — thrice repeated. This was the signal for mounting before the onset.

We all bestrode our horses, and a few minutes passed in breathless expectation: then, from the same quarter, came the old Spanish war-cry "Santiago" from the deep chest of Don Pepe Armenteros, followed by the shrill war-whoop of our Indian allies. This ancient war-cry is still used by the descendants of those heroes from whose lips it aroused the echoes of many a bloody field in bygone ages. It was the signal for the charge of mail-clad knights against Moor and Saracen, against Mexican and Peruvian, in later times; and now we heard repeated in these untrodden wilds the battle-cry of the Cid, of Ferdinand of Aragon, of Gonsalvo de Cordova, Don John of Austria, Pizarro, Cortes, and Almagro, — "Santiago y cierra España" ("Santiago and close Spain").

We instantly moved up, and, intervening between the fire and the corral, stood guard to prevent the horse-thieves from stampeding our imprisoned animals, to which they instinctively rushed when aroused from their sleep. The Indian horde, thus meeting our levelled fire-arms and lances, faced instantly in the opposite direction, but were intercepted by our leader and his party, and turned again on us, using war-clubs, spears, and bows, while a crowd of squaws in their rear hurled stones and sticks at us over their heads.

The *mêlée* became general, and shot after shot was heard; while sabres, lances, and fire-arms met the ruder Indian weapons in a hand-to-hand conflict. Some of the Indians, diving under the bellies of our horses, succeeded in breaking down the corral; but our *vaqueros* secured the breach before the animals could escape, and the enterprise was not renewed. The contest ceased at last, the Indians sulkily retiring out of harm's way when convinced that they had no chance of success; and their head men sullenly informed us that they wanted peace.

It was granted as soon as asked for: our object was attained; and we recovered all the horses, save one that had been devoured, without the loss of a man, although most of our party were badly bruised by the shillelahs of the Indians, and several received arrow and spear wounds.

Fortunately these horse cannibals had selected for their feast an animal more fit for eating than for his other qualities.

We now prepared to inspect and adjudge the *spolia opima* of our vanquished foe; but there being but little *matériel*, and that little having been appropriated by our Indian allies in their way, we hesitated not to seize the *personnel* we had legitimately acquired, according to the notions prevalent at that time in California. The prisoners thus pressed into our service were divided equally among our party, submitting resignedly and even joyfully to their fate: they selected those of their squaws and children whom they wished to accompany them; and we all left for home, after rewarding our Indian allies. Arriving at our respective ranchos, our captives were soon domiciled, and supplied with full rations of beef; and, having finished their task of making *adobes* (sun-dried bricks) for building-purposes, they were permitted to depart, laden with good shirts and blankets.

Two of the "bucks" remained with me, preferring good living and kind treatment to their precarious, half-starved condition in their native wilds; and, from savage and graceless "Gentiles," were converted into decent and respectable "Christianos."

I remained at San Geronimo, attending to my duties both public and private; but, near the end of the year 1849, I resigned my commission as lieutenant in the United-States navy, hopeless of promotion after twenty years of service, yet reluctant to abandon my profession.

XXIII.

AMONG my guests at San Geronimo during this rainy season was one Sandy (or Alexander) McGregor, a Kentuckian born of Scotch parents; and, large as has been my acquaintance with mankind, really the most remarkable man I ever met, albeit utterly unknown to fame.

The most gifted persons, I have long ago ascertained, are by no means the most celebrated or notorious; and I have known several instances of those in the humbler walks of life, of the finest natural ability, and even of deep erudition, who have never aspired to rise in the social scale by means of their talents or learning, improbable as this may seem.

Of this sort was Sandy McGregor. His *physique* instantly commanded attention, especially his high frontal bones, rising almost into deformity, crowned with red hair and shaggy brows, beneath which his piercing gray eyes seemed to glow with real fire. He was slightly above the medium height, lank and raw-boned; and his sinewy arms were as long as Scott has told us were his clansman Rob Roy's, who could tie his garters below the knee without stooping. He was a good rider, an unerring shot; and his muscular strength was herculean.

His character was as remarkable as his physical organization. I have never met with any man of such truly heroic attributes as this obscure Kentuckian, who was destined to go through the world without an opportunity of displaying them on a stage commensurate with their importance. His courage was of the lofty kind usually found among Kentuckians; added to which he had an imperturbable *sang-froid* that was equal to any emergency, not only in situations of personal peril, but also in financial or business operations where great daring and quick calculation were essential to success.

He acted promptly and decided quickly, like most frontiersmen accustomed to a life of constant danger; and carried his decisions into effect with a power of will as fixed and inevitable as the fabled Nemesis.

This man's intellect was of the highest order: he had a power of combination I have never seen equalled; and his memory was so remarkable, that he could relate even the most minute transaction of his life with perfect distinctness.

He was obstinate, — mulish even; and his opinions once formed were unchangeable: but he was generous to a fault; and, without being impulsive, was a true and reliable friend.

In this sententiousness he had reason; for his estimate of men and their acts was generally as correct as a geometrical problem. By some process of ratiocination which I never could comprehend, and of which he himself could give no lucid explanation, McGregor could at once resolve the most intricate arithmetical questions that might be proposed.

With all his wonderful genius, this singular being had received no education, being entirely ignorant of letters: he could not write a line of intelligible English, or even sign his own name. True, he did make certain marks with a pen that looked like it, as he was sometimes called upon to authenticate a document by his signature; but it could hardly be taken for what it purported to be, had the scrawl not been attested by an intricate *rubrica* (flourish) in the Spanish manner.

McGregor was a man of wealth, possessed of real estate and stock of different kinds: he not only had investments in the principal cities of the United States, but had also dealings with bankers in the European commercial centres; and his paper was good in all. His large property was intrusted to agents of his own selection, who were accountable to him alone, while he picked up amanuenses wherever he might be for his correspondence.

The parents of McGregor died of the cholera in 1832: and he had not a relative in the world, as he told me; for he was a bachelor.

He had left his home at eleven years of age; since when he had roamed over the continent, having adopted the wild, free, and independent life of a trapper and fur-trader. In this capacity he passed many years without seeing a white face, and was a chief in some Indian tribes.

Having accumulated a pecuniary nucleus by that traffic, he increased his capital by judicious speculations. Sandy had been converted to the Catholic faith by Father De Smets, the celebrated Jesuit missionary to the tribes of the Rocky Mountains: and I was sometimes astonished to hear this unlettered demi-savage talk about the abstruse theological discussions he had entered into with learned persons of other denominations; for, whatever he attempted to learn, he mastered thoroughly.

With all these, and higher qualities I need not describe, McGregor had his failings. He could hardly be called intemperate; for, although he often indulged in potations "pottle deep," I never knew his reason to be clouded, or his motions unsteady: he betrayed his "elevation" only by his Scotch fondness for argument on such occasions. But his besetting sin was play. He was the most inveterate gamester I ever knew; and I have known many.

All games of chance were familiar to him: but poker, brag, and euchre were his favorites; and he frequently sat at these games for several consecutive days and nights, his adversaries relieving each other when exhausted; but there never was a sign of weariness in his iron frame and tenacious spirit. He would play for any amount, great or small, and with any one who would play with him: he preferred gentlemen, if he could have them, and high stakes; but, if no others offered, I have known him to sit down with a poor Mexican or Indian, and play for *clacos*.

One night, when I was sitting with McGregor, a neighbor came to my house with the intelligence that a ship had been wrecked at the Punta de los Reyes, a bold promontory stretching into the Pacific about four or five leagues from San Geronimo, and that the whole rural population was in motion for the scene of the disaster. At daylight we also started with our *vaqueros*, arriving quite early at the rancho of Rafael Garcia, which was the only inhabited place in the vicinity of the wreck.

The vessel proved to be a large bark from Bremen, as we were informed by her captain, who had landed safely with his crew and passengers; the latter having immediately left for the gold diggings. He had mistaken the mouth of the Estero de los Tamales for the harbor of San Francisco; and, attempting to enter it, his vessel had struck upon a reef, and almost immediately broken up. The shores of the estuary were covered with pipes, hogsheads, casks, barrels, and boxes of merchandise of every description; the ship having been laden with an assorted cargo of European goods. Many residents of the surrounding region had already arrived, and were helping themselves to these articles, to which their "right there was none to dispute;" while the jolly proprietor of the soil dreamed not of asserting his rights of "flotsam and jetsam."

There were cases of the finest wines and liquors, sardines and sweetmeats, all unknown to the primitive rancheros: and the men were securing these; while the women were breaking open cases of silk and woollen fabrics of delicate texture and gorgeous dyes, disdaining the commoner cotton prints, which they left for their Indian servants. These lighter articles having been appropriated *galore*, the multitude turned their attention to the plethoric casks and barrels which were thumping in the surf, as if they, too, were desirous of being assisted up high and dry on the beach, to share the fate of their more buoyant shipmates. The wind, blowing directly into the estuary, drove the whole cargo, or as much of it as would float, right on the beach, where it could be secured: so the people had only to help themselves.

The lord of the manor, Don Rafael, and his hospitable family, quickly converted the occasion into one of festivity; and the poor rancho resembled the mansion of Magnus Troil on the night of the ball. The long, low, one-storied house, with its spreading eaves, was profusely illuminated with the best wax-candles in bronze or plated candelabra of artistic patterns, adorned with artificial flowers of every hue; while the rugged walls were concealed with framed engravings: and beneath them was arrayed elegant furniture in buhl and *marquetrie*, on which stood crowds of bottles, from which the company regaled themselves with unlimited champagne, and the delicate wines of the Rhine and Burgundy, and toasted old Father Neptune in gratitude for his beneficence.

Instead of *tortillas* — the national griddle-cake — we had soda, wine, and captain's biscuits; and *paté de foie gras* took the place of beefsteaks broiled on the coals, — called *carne asado*.

The rancheros, who had brought their guitars and fiddles strapped on their backs, soon struck up merry tunes; and the light-hearted Spanish girls and their cavaliers danced the *jarabe*, the waltz, and other national dances, all night long; while the elders sat about amusing themselves with monte and euchre.

Fat muttons and beeves were slaughtered by Don Rafael; and the *cocina* was alive with women preparing the various dishes affected by native Californians, seasoned with the condiments saved from the wreck. Wearied at last, I went forth to enjoy the fresh air, and found myself in the presence of a strange scene. Those guests who were, like myself, tired of dancing, or were desirous of sleep from other reasons, lay around the house on the grass under the trees (no hardship in this lovely climate), rolled in their gay *serapes;* or were lounging in groups, smoking the eternal cigarette.

I even fancied there were some couples improving the occasion to enjoy each other's society while their parents were absorbed in cards, or who snored, oblivious of their children and all the world besides.

The next morning I was early afoot, but found all the guests already risen, and awaiting their *desayuna,* which they took *al fresco,* there being no room within-doors, nor tables enough to hold a hundredth part of the company. It was the jolliest *merienda* (picnic) I ever attended, and was kept up for a whole week.

In the daytime we had exhibitions of skill with the lasso, the game of *colear,* — in which a party on horseback chase a wild bull, and try to upset him by his tail, — cavaliers trying to unhorse each other; and one day a large grisly bear was tied to a fierce bull with a riata, and both turned into a corral to fight. The bull was victorious, — *viva el toro,* — killing the bear, although dreadfully lacerated; after which feat he was magnanimously liberated to rejoin his harem in the wild woods.

The captain of the lost bark made a trip to San Francisco and returned before the festivities were over; and the novel spectacle pleased him much; although, poor man, he told us he had lost his little all, and would have to begin life anew, with the disadvantage of this misfortune upon him. Still, he said, he was in a country where, above all others, there were opportunities to retrieve his losses.

Before he left us, he accompanied McGregor and myself to

the wreck in a canoe. The ship had drifted or been forced over the reef into still water under its lee. The captain told us that in the run, under the floor of the cabin, was a little iron safe, containing a small sum of money, some valuable articles, and a lot of papers; which last he was exceedingly desirous to recover. He said that if we could get these papers for him, even if wet, we were welcome to the remainder of the contents of the safe, which would well repay us for our trouble; and having received his address, and promising to mention the subject to no other parties, we separated.

We could do nothing at the time of our visit to recover this safe, as the quarter-deck was several fathoms under the surface of the water, and operating from a rickety canoe was impossible. The great fandango having come to an end at last, the merry party separated, returning to their homes with their valuable acquisitions, and with the consciousness of a well-spent holiday, whose pleasures no untoward circumstance had occurred to mar.

McGregor and I returned to San Geronimo, and set about concocting a plan to recover the captain's iron safe. Our preparations being completed, we set out for the estuary, but avoided the house of Garcia, preferring to keep our business to ourselves. We encamped in a well-sheltered and concealed nook on a beach between two headlands, and came prepared to spend a week if necessary. Our first step was to send an Indian boy to get the canoe we had used before, and which was the only boat in the Estero de los Tamales. Then we made a raft, under my directions, of the empty casks and driftwood, of which there was plenty in the neighborhood, lashing its parts securely with some small manila cordage I had brought with me.

This raft we towed off to the wreck at slack-water early in the morning before the wind had risen, and brought it over the quarter-deck of the submerged vessel. I had secured the services of a native of the Sandwich Islands, who was a skilful diver, like all his countrymen; and from the raft he went down upon the ship's deck, and, after considerable exertion, succeeded in getting the companion-way detached from its place on the quarter-deck. The cabin was now open to us. Our diver next pried off the scuttle in the cabin-floor leading to the run, and, finding the iron safe directly beneath it, made ropes fast to it; and we suspended it to the raft.

We then towed the raft back to the beach, and soon landed the safe. This we blew open with gunpowder, and found its valuable contents uninjured. We gave the captain his papers and half the money: the other half and the jewelry we divided between us.

As we could work only when the sea was calm, our operations lasted nearly a week; but our time just then was of little account.

XXIV.

IN the month of September, 1851, my friend McGregor and myself planned a voyage from San Francisco to the coast of Mexico, and purchased together the brigantine "La Golondrina," a clipper of two hundred tons burthen, built in Ferrol, Spain, from a Baltimore model. She had a Spanish register, and, consequently, sailed under Spanish colors. Taking command of this little vessel, I shipped a crew of twenty men, and fitted her for sea. Our crew was as cosmopolitan as San Francisco itself. My chief mate was a Yankee from Truro on Cape Cod, the best man on board; the second officer a hardy Dane; and the boatswain was my old shipmate whom I have mentioned as receiving me with such lavish hospitality when I landed in California from the steamer. The crew consisted of four Dutchmen and a Finn, two Italians, one Frenchman, two Spaniards, and five Kanakas. The cook was a North-Carolina darky named Job.

Having been a packet, "The Golondrina" had superior accommodations. She carried two twelve-pound carronades, or howitzers, in the waist, one on each side, and a long nine-pound pivot-gun of bronze on the forecastle, with the necessary ammunition and small-arms.

Sandy McGregor knocked two berths into one to accommodate his long legs; and, as supercargo, purchased, and stowed away under hatches, a notable cargo of Chinese goods for the market to which we were bound. We made a good run down the coast, and, having disposed of our cargo to advantage, took in a return freight, which was landed in due season at San Francisco.

The business proving remunerative, we soon started on a second trip, touching at Cape St. Lucas, thence to La Paz, Loreto, and Mulege, ports of the Sea of Cortes, and to Guaymas, where we remained for some weeks; then, having finished our business, we continued our voyage down the eastern shore of the Gulf of California. The tract of country lying between the *embouchures* of the Hiaqui and Mayo Rivers is peopled with a race of fierce and intractable Indians, with whom the Spaniards have had much trouble since the days of Cortes, who gives them the same warlike character in the account of his voyage of discovery to this sea, which bears his name. Their territory, however, is claimed, under certain grants, by some Mexican proprietors, who have possession in some places, the inhabitants of which pay them a sort of feudal tribute. Most of the tribes live in independent communities, and are very warlike. Large tracts are owned and peopled in this way by the two rival families of Iñigo and Gandara, who keep the State of Sonora in constant turmoil with their conflicting pretensions; being, indeed, the Guelphs and Ghibellines of the country. The object of their contentions is, as usual in like cases, political, — the filling of the offices, and consequent power of laying imposts and taxes, and receipt of the customs.

In passing this part of the coast a day or two after leaving Guaymas, running before the trade-wind, we espied a vessel ashore on the beach; and, feeling our way with the lead, stood in as close as was prudent. She proved to be a polacca-brig high and dry on the beach. Her bows were nearest the shore, her stern being seaward, and her crew were crowded together aft; while a swarm of naked Indians on the beach were shooting their arrows and hurling spears at them, occasionally trying to board over the bows. As soon as this state of affairs was understood, I ordered the anchor let go, hoisted out and manned the launch and two whale-boats, putting one of the carronades into the former, and, with nearly my whole crew in the boats, pulled for the wreck. Nearing her, I saw that boarding would be dangerous in the state of the sea : so, consulting with McGregor, I resolved to disperse the Indians first, and then attempt the rescue of the people on the brig. The Indians were frantic at the prospect of a rescue, and redoubled their efforts to board; so that the crew had their hands full in repelling them.

McGregor and the second mate, with eighteen of my men, armed with muskets and bayonets, in the two whale-boats, now landed through the high surf that was running on the beach; while I, in the launch, brought the gun to bear upon the Indian rout, having let go my grapnel over the stern, thus anchoring the launch just outside the surf. As soon as I saw the whale-boats land, I fired the carronade, loaded with grape, into the crowd; and at the same time McGregor charged them with the bayonet, after a volley. The Indian mob opened and admitted our sailors, closing upon their rear; and I feared, for a moment, that they must be surrounded and all killed or taken prisoners : but a second shot from my carronade caused the Indians to waver; and I saw McGregor and his men re-appear, maintaining an effective fire. Sandy himself seemed to clear his way with his long and keen sabre wherever he moved; and the sheen of its blade was dimmed by blood. Our men kept together, back to back, in two small groups, as they had been instructed, like what is called a Prussian or light-infantry square, which enabled me to fire an occasional shot at the Indians without hurting my own fellows. The Indians at last were convinced, that, with their inferior weapons, they could not successfully oppose us, and that mere numbers would not give them the victory; for they had not injured a single man of our force, while many of them had bit the dust. So they began to scatter, retreating a short distance, apparently to hold a council.

I had no desire to see the combat renewed, and, sending a round shot at the enemy, sounded the recall, and my boats came alongside the launch. The casualties were few: four men had broken heads, and three had spear and arrow wounds; while McGregor reported six bodies of the enemy left on the field, of which he grimly exhibited the scalps. He had acquired the Indian habit of preserving trophies of his victory. He said that they had carried off many dead and wounded in their retreat, and would not trouble us again; in which opinion I fully agreed with him.

We now turned our attention to the crew of the brig; and veering a line to them from the windward, out of the launch, thus established communication. We then brought them one by one — seventeen men and one lady — aboard the launch, together with some wearing apparel and a few articles of value, returned to "The Golondrina," and gained the offing. We lay off and on during the night, and stood in on the next morning, at the solicitation of the captain, intending to recover some of the lading of the brig if it were possible. She had, however, broken in two during the night; and the Indians swarmed in such numbers on the beach, that I abandoned the plan, and continued our voyage. The brig was "The Hermosa Gaditana" of Cadiz, on a trading voyage. Her passengers and crew were profuse in their expressions of gratitude to us for saving them from death, which assuredly would have been their fate at the hands of the savage Hiaquis.

Touching at Altata, in a few days I landed them all safely at Mazatlan; for which I have since received substantial acknowledgments from the Spanish Government and others.

Vessels arriving at Mexican ports with merchandise are commonly admitted to discharge their cargoes only after a tedious negotiation with the *administrador* (collector), and much bargaining with the underlings of the customs as to the scale of duties to be paid, which leads to tiresome delays; and do not usually anchor in the port until the negotiation is concluded. The *arancel* (tariff) is seldom adhered to, or even taken as a guide: so that you never know how much or how little duty you will have to pay.

This state of things produces frightful corruption and bribery, and encourages smuggling, which is connived at by the officials, who do not scruple to make out of their official positions as much money as they can.

In our case, finding we could come to no satisfactory agreement with the *resguardo* of Mazatlan, after anchoring I sent McGregor in a boat to San Blas; whence he returned in a few days with the announcement that our goods would be admitted at that port on much more reasonable terms than at Mazatlan. San Blas, also, had the advantage of proximity to the interior lines of travel and transportation. "The Golondrina" was always ready for sea: so Sandy and myself went ashore to the counting-house of a merchant who had accepted the draft of our consignee in Guaymas for thirty thousand dollars; which amount was paid in golden ounces, and taken charge of by my partner, who secured it round his waist in a handkerchief.

The Mexican laws are very severe against the exportation of bullion under any circumstances; and it is necessary to smuggle it out of the country at great risk, heightened by the promise to informers of one-half the forfeited amount. The officials, consequently, have sharp eyes for smugglers. Sandy determined to take the chances; and together we walked leisurely down to the quay, past the custom-house, with its lounging officials, and entered our whale-boat, and shoved off. Whether my partner had put on too bold an air as he passed this group, marching with his head in the air and regarding them defiantly, or whether his gait betrayed his secret burden, I know not; but we had scarcely got a boat's length from the quay when an inspector came running down from the custom-house, shouting to us to return. The guard, loading their pieces, followed him, under command of a sergeant.

My partner and I exchanged glances without speaking, and instantly understood that we must keep all the advantage we had, and continue our course to the vessel. I therefore called upon the men to stretch to their oars, and give way with a will; and the light whale-boat flew through the water. We had about two miles to row; but, when we had made about half the distance, we saw the captain of the port's gig in full chase, and rapidly gaining on us. "Now," said I, "Mac, throw the money overboard; for, if it is found on us, we shall have twenty years of presidio." — "No," said he coolly: "wait."

Not knowing what his plans were, but confiding in his resources, I kept silence. Our boat ran alongside "The Golondrina," and we went up the side. McGregor went forward; while I remained on the quarter-deck to receive the captain of the port, who soon reached the vessel.

In the expression of his face I saw at once that he knew all about the money; and he told me politely, but firmly, that he came to take possession of the vessel. Though strongly tempted to pitch him overboard, I restrained myself, and stood quiet while he summoned from his boat his most skilful detectives, and began to ransack the little vessel. They were evidently old hands at the business, and searched everywhere for two mortal hours; when they ceased. The bland captain then took his leave, giving me to understand that he should return soon; and, if the money was not forthcoming, he should unship the rudder, and unbend my sails. The vessel would be libelled in the court of admiralty; and, meanwhile, he should leave an officer on board until he returned.

Although my partner was present during our conversation, his conduct was an enigma to me; for he never lost his *sang-froid*, and did nothing but smile at the threats of the official or my own misgivings: but when dinner was served in the cabin, after the departure of the port-captain, his composure was accounted for. Honest Job brought his capacious iron pot into the pantry, as usual, to dish up the meal, and from its depths fished out Sandy's pongee handkerchief, containing the gold which had been so diligently sought for by the myrmidons of the customs. My partner then told me, that, while coming alongside in the boat, he had caught sight of Job's ebon visage, busy near his galley-fire, and, by a gleam of inspiration, conceived the idea of hiding his treasure by popping it into the cook's kettle; which he lost no time in doing, telling Job to continue his avocation with an appearance of indifference.

Our merriment over the successful result of his ruse, however, was suddenly cut short by the darkening of the cabin skylight; and, looking up, we saw the head of the officer whom Capt. Horn had left on board at his departure, and who could not restrain a Spanish exclamation at sight of the treasure lying before us.

The situation now called for prompt measures. The angry inspector was quickly bundled into a boat, and transferred to a small vessel near us; our anchor was tripped, and sail made; and, in less than twenty minutes, we were gliding towards the entrance of the harbor. We soon gained an offing: but, as usual in this latitude, the wind fell towards night; and the next morning the high peak of Creston, marking the port, was still in sight. We were in good spirits, however, as we had outwitted the custom-house officials, and at sea with our ship and cargo under us. Just after breakfast, looking toward Mazatlan, we saw with the glass two large *balandras* (large launches) and a man-of-war's boat coming out of the harbor;

and, as they approached us, we saw that the former, besides their usual crews at the oars, were crowded with Mexican soldiers, while we knew at once that the man-of-war boat was from the British frigate "Constance."

We had no alternative but to prepare for action immediately; knowing that, if we yielded, imprisonment and confiscation of ship and cargo would inevitably follow: so we got the long nine up on the forecastle, fixed it on its pivot, cast loose and shotted the carronades, and laid muskets, pistols, cutlasses, and boarding-pikes in readiness for use; while the men collected at their quarters, delighted at the prospect of a row with the "greasers."

As the boats came nearer, the Spanish flag was run up to the peak; and I hailed them through the trumpet, telling them to keep off, and training the guns upon them, with lighted port-fires.

The English boat kept farther off than the others: and I concluded she would take no part in the combat, if one ensued; although she had a small boat-gun in her bow, and ten armed and red-coated marines in her stern-sheets. It is the practice of British ships of war abroad to mix up with the quarrels of others, — I suppose, under instructions from home; and they seem to be a sort of self-constituted ocean-police for all nations.

Any active interference with my vessel would have come with exceeding ill grace at that time; for "The Constance" was well known to be full of contraband bullion, her boats having been engaged in smuggling *plata piña* (brute silver) ever since the ship had been on the coast: but perhaps the captain thought he had a monopoly of the business, and was inclined to use his force and the *prestige* of the British navy to prevent others from sharing it, under the specious pretext of vindicating the Mexican laws.

My hail was answered by Capt. Horn, from one of the *ba-*

landras, with a summons to surrender. To this I answered that my vessel was at sea, more than a marine league from Creston, and consequently out of the Mexican jurisdiction; that my duty compelled me to maintain my maritime rights and those of other interested parties; that he had better give up the idea of meddling with me; and finally, to cut the matter short, that, if he attempted to invade my vessel, I should treat him as a pirate. As this speech — shouted through the trumpet in Spanish, *ore rotundo* — concluded, my men gave a loud and defiant cheer. The three boats then drew together, apparently to concert a plan of attack; and, a light air springing up, we hauled by the wind on the starboard tack, hauled up the foresail, and braced the maintopsail aback, to show we did not fear them, nor wished to use our heels — which we might easily have done — to escape.

The *balandras* then separated; one pulling ahead of the vessel to board over the bows, while the other made for the starboard gangway. The English boat remained in reserve, attempting no demonstration.

Hans Petersen, the second mate, stood at his gun in the starboard waist, port-fire in hand; and, when the second *balandra* was within pistol-shot, a soldier fired his piece at me, standing on the poop, the ball whistling harmlessly through the mainsail. Instantly I gave the order, "Fire!" Bang went the carronade right into the bows of the boat! The sea was freckled with grape; and, in an instant, Horn and his whole crew were struggling in the water, which was tinged with blood. The other *balandra*, which was pulling toward the bows, seeing the saucy "Golondrina" coming toward her with a "bone in her mouth," — for I had filled away with the intention of running her down, — rowed across our course to avoid collision; and we passed on, tacked, and came towards the boats on the port tack again.

They had had enough, however; for the cry of "*Misericordia*" was raised on our approach: and leaving them to assist the sunken boat, and rescue her crew, I wore ship, and bore away for San Blas.

XXV.

WE did not touch at San Blas, as we knew the report of our affair at Mazatlan would soon reach there; and, preferring to keep out of the way for some time until the memory of it had blown over, we kept on our southerly course for a few days, and anchored at last in the Bay of Manzanilla.

Colima is the most secluded of all the Mexican States; the roads leading to it being exceedingly rough, and its capital difficult of access by land; while its commerce is very insignificant, although the harbor of Manzanilla is a commodious and excellent one. We found no vessels at this port, nor had any visited it for a long time; so that our advent was warmly welcomed. The customs-people were exceedingly accommodating; and we found them very open to the smallest *gratificacioncita* in expediting our little *comercio* with the towns and villages of the neighborhood. We were soon welcome guests everywhere; and the little *contretemps* at Mazatlan, although soon made known to them, with its attendant loss of life, proved rather a recommendation than a disadvantage, if we could judge from the hospitality with which we were everywhere received.

In company with a party, among whom was a European gentleman of scientific attainments, I visited that great natural curiosity, the volcanic mountain of Colima, which, were Mexico better provided with accommodations for travellers, hundreds would visit. Having seen the most gigantic of all the volcanoes, Mouna Loa, and those in the Mediterranean, South America, and the East Indies, as well as the Central-American burning-mountains, I do not hesitate to say, that to a geologist, and observer of natural phenomena, the volcano of Colima surpasses them all in interest.

The city of Colima itself is a great curiosity, and reminded me a little of Blidah "the voluptuous," in Algeria, being situated in the midst of a dense grove of waving palm-trees. These almost conceal the one-story adobe houses. The people are better off than those of other Mexican towns, fewer "leperos" and beggars being seen among them. The city stands in a fertile valley thirty leagues from Manzanilla, its nearest seaport, and twenty leagues from the original crater of the volcano. The superior prosperity of the people is probably owing to their separation from the rest of the world by deep and almost impassable *barrancas*. This region produces the best coffee raised in the republic: none of it is exported beyond the city's walls; and it commands a price of sixty cents to a dollar a pound. Wheat, rice, maize, and indigo of very superior quality, are also produced in the vicinity. The climate is perfect, and the country rich in metallic deposits. Although twenty leagues from the crater, Colima is built upon the lower edge of the extended slope of the mountain, and may be said to be in daily, hourly, danger of being overwhelmed, — a contingency that would impart some excitement to its residents, were they not Mexicans.

Proceeding on horseback towards the cone, we arrived at the little town of Zapilon, near which several new craters had been formed, and stopped for the night. After dark the scene was magnificent. From the old crater at the summit of the mountain, and from two new ones in sight, vast volumes of seething, hissing crimson matter shot upwards, carrying with them great stones, which dropped, and burst, apparently, with a tremendous noise; while streams of liquid lava rolled down the sides like molten iron from the furnace.

Mount Colima is a porphyritic mountain, twelve thousand feet above the sea-level, insulated in an immense plain, and nearly a perfect cone, with the grand crater at the apex. It stands alone in its solitude; and its aspect is barren, terrible, and threatening. No birds or other living things make their homes on its adamantine sides; nor is there a tree, or shrub even, to be seen.

We did not undertake the ascent of the mountain; for certain death would have followed the attempt. Even at Zapilon we were closer to the crater than was quite prudent; for the town was overhung by an enormous avalanche of volcanic matter, which threatened to overwhelm it at any moment.

From the mountain we went to examine the great *barranca*, which may be considered a natural fosse, or military ditch, separating this stupendous mountain-fortress system from the rest of Mexico. It is thirteen miles in length, and, from parapet to counterscarp, three miles in breadth; the sides of the fearful gorge being nearly perpendicular, and three thousand five hundred feet in height. It is one of the great wonders of Mexico. This fearful gorge bears evidence that it was torn out of the solid earth at some remote period by a current of lava flowing from the main crater of the mountain. There are six other *barrancas* intervening between this and the town of Zapotlan, which is the frontier-town of the neighboring State of Jalisco. The whole region is subject to earthquake-shocks. The lava, both old and new, is a reddish-brown basaltic rock porphyry, very jagged and rough when cooled. The volcano is seventy miles from that of Jorullo, which suddenly rose from the earth on the night of Sept. 29, 1759, amid extraordinary convulsions of Nature; thousands of acres of valuable land having been devastated, and a river swallowed up.

This narrow strip, extending from sea to sea, has always been interesting to the student who is content to study Nature's operations, instead of striving to invent new theories about them. It is well known that a connection exists between the volcanoes I have mentioned and those of the Valley of Mexico, extending as far east as that of Tuxtla. During the past century, it has been noticed, that, when any disturbance takes place in the latter, a sympathetic movement manifests itself along the whole chain.

The inhabitants of this region are convinced of this; and they even go so far as to predict that the shocks periodically felt all the way from Vera Cruz to Colima, from east to west, transversely across the continent, will result some day in a grand cataclysm, that will rend the continent asunder, so that the waters of the Atlantic will mingle with those of the Pacific through the gap.

Having disposed of a large portion of our cargo of fine silk-goods at Colima, we sailed up the coast again to San Blas, where, having made a satisfactory arrangement with the *resguardo*, we landed the rest of our goods. McGregor contracted with an *arriero* for mules, and accompanied them to Tepic, where they were stored temporarily. This course became necessary in consequence of our selling "The Golondrina" to British parties, who arrived at San Blas at the same time with ourselves.

Australia had been discovered about this time to be a land of gold; and thither these parties were bound, having taken the route through Mexico. The transfer was made at San José, in Lower California; and, returning thence, I rejoined my partner at Tepic. It was now the last of October; and we decided to carry our goods to the great annual fair, held in November at the town of San Juan de los Lagos, which is resorted to by the whole mercantile community of the republic, and is the chief indigo mart of the country. We had still on hand an attractive invoice, chiefly of Chinese goods, which were scarce and high at that time, although a drug in San Francisco; and the great fair presented a chance for high prices not to be missed.

A long train of heavily-laden mules accordingly issued early one morning from the city of Tepic; and in its rear might be seen a score or more of well-armed Americans and Europeans, amongst whom, mounted on prancing and curvetting steeds, gayly caparisoned in Mexican fashion, rode Sandy McGregor and the reader's humble servant. Passing through Istlan, Madalena, and Plan de Barrancas, we arrived on the second day at Guadalajara. From this gay city, the second in importance of the republic, and capital of the State of Jalisco, my partner pushed on towards San Juan, while I remained for a few days to attend to some business. Having finished this, I followed him in company with a Prussian gentleman and his servant. We had arrived in sight of the lofty towers of the Cathedral of St. John, the loftiest on the American continent, when in the early morning we suddenly became aware that farther progress was prevented by a barricade across the road, made of a cart and some other obstructions. We were, then, in presence of the much-talked-of *salteadores* (foot-pads), who infest the roads to intercept those bound to the fair, and make them pay tribute.

The Prussian was an old cavalry soldier; and drawing his sabre, and shouting a Spanish ejaculation I dare not repeat, he spurred his horse toward the obstacle in front; and I had no option but to follow him. We easily leaped the tongue of the cart, and were in safety on the other side of the barrier; but, in our ardor, we had forgotten our valet, who followed us with our valises on a sumpter mule, and who was immediately seized by the robbers. They soon "went through" our luggage; but finding little of value, as our money was secured on our persons, they shouted to us that they intended to kill our *mozo* unless a handsome ransom were instantly forthcoming. After a long palaver with the rascals, — who, no doubt, were rancheros of the neighborhood, — they were appeased by the payment of a considerable sum; and poor Eusebio was permitted to join us.

We found San Juan crowded to repletion; while the surrounding hillsides were covered with tents and *jacals* (huts made of matting and small sticks), and seemed a populous suburb. With characteristic foresight, my partner had constructed a temporary lodging of this kind, in which our goods were stored; and, in addition, he had found room enough to shelter the family of the keeper of the *meson* (Mexican tavern), who had turned out of their house to accommodate lodgers.

This was a respectable and honest family; and, as they became interesting in connection with subsequent events, I may be pardoned for naming them particularly. They were Nicolas Herrera, his wife Francisca, their son Martin, and their niece Catalina Vargas.

The morning after my arrival I walked forth to see the fair, and was well repaid for the trouble. A vast amount of rich goods from every part of the world was attractively displayed; and there was a complete museum of Mexican manufactures, amongst which I admired most the magnificent saddlery. Trade seemed very lively; and McGregor informed me that the fair would eclipse any of its predecessors for several years, and that the population of San Juan, ordinarily but five thousand, was augmented to near two hundred thousand. As the mercantile transactions were exclusively carried on by my partner, I had little to do save to amuse myself with the novel sights of the great fair, of which I wearied in about a week; and, to pass the time, cultivated the society of the Herreras. One day, when sitting smoking with the head of the family, his hostler, an idiot named Pancho, passed by; and I made some inquiries concerning him. He informed me, that some twenty years before, a poor family from the State of Guerrero had received his hospitality at the *meson ;* and, on the morning after their departure, an infant was discovered lying upon the litter of the stable, in which their beasts had been kept. The wayfarers were of a despised race, the *pintos,* or spotted people of that State, who somewhat resemble the lepers of old, or the pariahs of the East. In Christian charity, the worthy couple had the child baptized; and Doña Francisca gave him her name on the occasion. (Pancho is the nickname of Francisco.) The infant was put to nurse, and, when old enough, ran about the great court of the *meson* amongst the *arrieros* and their mules until he was of sufficient stature and strength to work, when he became a useful servant in the inn. He was a robust youth, with a rough shock of reddish hair, dull, stupid face, and lack-lustre eyes, the frightfully mottled skin of his race, a rounded back, and shambling gait. Passing for an idiot, he only answered questions by awkward gestures; but could imperfectly articulate a few words when he chose to do so. He seemed to be affected by neither kindness nor harshness, and nearly insensible to both.

After a week or two, I observed that there was one object in the world that had made some impression on his obtuse intellect. This was the niece Catalina, or Chapita as she was usually called, an orphan, who had been adopted by the Herreras as their daughter. Whenever she approached, Pancho, involuntarily as it seemed, expressed the pleasure he felt in seeing her by pantomimic gestures. Chapita, who was very beautiful, fascinated others besides the poor stable-boy; but the admiration of those was deepened by a sentiment of respect for her discretion; and I once heard one of her countrymen, accustomed to think lightly of female virtue, say of her, in his figurative language, " that she sowed at every step seeds of love which were destined never to germinate." Martin, the son of the house, had arrived to attend the fair from the presidio of Altar in Sonora, where he owned a large estate which his father had given him.

The young *hacendado*, a tall, slender youth of fine personal appearance, set off by his handsome national dress, was an accomplished cavalier, and an adept in the exercises of the *campo* and the *mesta*.

I could not help musing on the miserable destiny of poor Pancho whenever I saw him pass, bereft as he was of every thing that solaces the lives of other men on life's journey. Poor devil! what had he to hope or live for? He existed merely by that instinct of self-preservation with which Providence has endowed animals, and even the vegetable kingdom; and yet in the breast of this wretched idiot a warm and delightful passion had grown up, which cast a vivid light over his vacant intellect and hopeless life.

The fair of San Juan drew to a close; the extempore habitations vanished from its suburbs; the busy crowd dissolved; and the roads were filled with travellers returning to their several homes, leaving the little town to its usual stagnation. We had disposed satisfactorily of our merchandise, and shared the profits; and as McGregor was desirous of visiting the mining country near the city of Chihuahua, in which he had important interests, I resolved to accompany him.

It would take too much space to give in detail the story of our journey northwards: so I will merely say that our route was by the way of Parras and Mapimi. The season was propitious; and our road lay through grand and striking scenery, but for a part of the way was infested by hostile Indians, for whom we were compelled to keep a sharp lookout.

At length, after twenty days of dust, heat, and drought, as many nights among fleas and other vermin; after many weary leagues ridden with our hands literally upon our weapons, and eyes weary with watching; after traversing mountain-passes, fit ambuscades for lurking savages, and lined with crosses, which indicated the fate of unfortunate travellers; after starving for hours, and arriving at *haciendas* only to find them deserted, — we at last came in sight of the steeples of the Cathedral of Chihuahua.

XXVI.

THE Bolson de Mapimi, and that part of the State of Coahuila which contains the abandoned mines of Santa Rosa, constitute what is probably the richest silver-mining region in the whole world. All the mines of this section of country have been worked for many years, and immense treasures have been taken from them: still it remains almost a *terra incognita*. This is because the whole district is overrun by the Apaches. The mines are either altogether abandoned, or are worked only spasmodically by companies with insufficient capital to organize mining on a scale large enough to insure a certain return for their investment within a reasonable time.

But it will be asked, " Why does not the required capital flow in this direction?" I answer, that I have heard every reason except the true one given among these people, who do not like to hear unpalatable truths any more than others. The true reason is, that the political condition of the nation is so bad, that no confidence can be felt in the security of an investment in any one thing in this country; and until another and stronger race controls the government, and gives protection to capital, and encouragement to enterprise, the riches of the country will remain undeveloped. The miserable population of this district dig out silver only for their present wants, or to supply that craving after fortune which appears to enter into the nature of every Mexican. They take enough silver out of Nature's strong box to serve for a few nights' gaming; and, when that is lost, return to get a little more.

Our first call upon the argentiferous deposits was made at Santa Eulalia, about thirteen miles from Chihuahua, which are the *crême de la crême* of all the mines of this richest district in Mexico, the very mountains being of silver. The *haciendas* of San José, Santa Rita, and La Parcionera, near the Real of Santa Eulalia, are worked in the rudest manner. Only the soft clay "pockets" of the galleries of these mines are worked, as the miners can scoop out the rich ore with — tell it not at the École des Mines or at Freyburg — hornspoons; and the limestone, which is not difficult of reduction, will yield from forty to a hundred and fifty dollars per ton. The deeper workings prove that the richest ores have not yet been reached. In the presence of all this great wealth, needing intelligence and capital to bring it to the surface, the native population are wretchedly impoverished, and merely idle away the time between the cradle and the grave, craving nothing but their bare sustenance, and occasional means of diversion of the most pitiful sort.

The prudent capitalists, even those reared in the country, never dream of investing their funds in mining operations, for the reasons I have just stated; and having visited the region, and examined its resources, I felt less inclined than ever before to enter into a speculation requiring, to protect explorations, many millions of associated capital, and a stable form of government such as is not to be had in Mexico.

While in this wild region, I halted for a day at a solitary *hacienda*, which, indeed, was like all of them, — a kind of walled and fortified dwelling, — to wait for my companion, who had gone to a mine not far off. The *intendente* ("land steward") of this place informed me that in a *laguna* not far away were plenty of wild ducks and geese; and I resolved to try to make a bag of some of them.

He said it was well; but that I must keep a sharp look-out for Indians, whose war-parties sometimes raided in that part of the country. I had heard so much talk of Indians since leaving San Juan, that I had become quite incredulous about them: so I strolled forth afoot with my gun, and soon reached the *laguna*. While poking about in the rushes to get a shot at some ducks, I observed in the soft mud the hoof-marks of horses, ridden by somebody, as was evident by the order in which they followed each other in two parallel lines. I happened to know that the horses of the *hacienda* were in another direction, guarded in a valley; and, calling to mind the warning of the old *intendente*, I concluded not to awake the echoes just then with my gun, but to beat a hasty retreat.

It was two or three miles to the *hacienda*, over an arid plain, dotted here and there with clumps of chaparral; and, luckily for me, the soil was what is called in Mexico a *pedral*, covered with stones as hard as flint, and leaving no trail from horse or man. A smart walk brought me about a mile from where I had seen the hoof-marks; and although I kept on, *la barbe sur l'épaule,* I was congratulating myself that I should soon reach a place of security, when I heard in my rear the sound of hoofs echoing from the flinty ground. Instantly, regardless of scratches, I took cover in a thick clump of bushes; having previously slipped a buckshot cartridge into each barrel of my gun, cocked it, and silently awaited events. Scarcely had I settled myself in my fortress when the leader of an Apache war-party came in sight. Having no mercy to hope for if found, I covered him and each succeeding warrior in succession as they passed in perfect silence, the ground hardly reporting the tread of their unshodden horses. Each brave rode a travelling palfrey, and led in a leash by his side his gayly-bedecked war-horse. All were perfectly naked except the breech-clout, but profusely painted in the Devil's colors,—red and black. They were armed alike with lances, the blades of which had once been Toledo swords, decorated with feathers like the round shields they bore, and bows and arrows. They sat straight and motionless on their horses, like spectres; the only evidence of animation in them being their incessantly rolling eye-balls, which keenly examined every object along their route. I held my breath as the ghost-like band passed me within their spear's length in Indian file; and, though they numbered only eleven warriors, it seemed to me as if an army was going by.

All the stories about the unerring sagacity of these savages came at once into my mind; and I distinctly recollect how I was disturbed by a solitary vulture that hovered above me, from whose movements I feared some of the rascals would be led to suspect my presence. So fixed was my attention, that I could afterwards have told every minute peculiarity that distinguished one individual of this war-party from another: and I could swear that the foremost Indian wore a single eagle's feather in his scalp-lock, while each of the rest had three; why, I know not.

I also know that the war-horse of the last youthful brave was an elegant and graceful *pinto*, the possession of which I coveted as soon as I saw him.

I was in no hurry to resume my route after the Indians had passed; nor did I relax my vigilance until I had arrived at the gates of the *hacienda*, which were immediately closed after I had made my report, and all the garrison — six men and nine women with four babies — enclosed in the *patio*. The old *intendente* addressed himself immediately to his defences: but the mysterious war-party never appeared; and, as they came like shadows, so they departed.

The next day the *vaqueros* found the remains of a bullock, on which the savages had supped, a league or two off; and we heard that a man had been killed, some houses robbed, and a woman carried off from a *hacienda*, about thirty miles from our refuge, by a party answering in description to the one I had seen.

This is one of the beauties of life in these northern districts for which I have little admiration; and these raids of the Apaches affect property to such a degree, that the extensive and fertile grazing estate of which I have spoken could have been purchased for less than a quarter part of the value of the horses and cattle roaming over the eight *sitios de gana do mayor* (square leagues, or about thirty thousand acres).

These war-parties, I was told, are undertaken for plunder, murder, rape, and sometimes abduction, in pursuance of a vow, or in performance of a penance imposed by their chief.

While on a war-party, the warriors must eat but one meal a day, and are allowed but four hours of sleep in the twenty-four. They are not permitted to converse with each other, and are obliged to perform certain diabolical rites. They must implicitly obey the orders of the warrior designated to command them, who may put them to death if he pleases. As is well known, their incursions are carried far into Mexico, spreading terror everywhere; for they are conducted with remorseless cruelty. I had now seen one of these famous war-parties, but had no desire to repeat the sight; although I drew an instructive conclusion from this, as from all other of the experiences of life, — that the Apaches and other wild Indians were in the possession and practice of some sound military principles, not confined, as I had fondly imagined, to civilized society, and as old as those Greeks and Romans of whose existence they had never heard.

At Chihuahua, McGregor and myself separated, — he to return to the United States by the way of Texas, while I took the road to San Juan de los Lagos. I parted from him with regret, and the hope of again seeing him: for our connection had been a pleasant one; and through all its vicissitudes I had ever found him honest and loyal, while his business tact and natural talents had successfully carried us through difficulties that might otherwise have occasioned failure. In our journeys by land, the place of leader had always been conceded to him, experienced as he was in frontier-life; and I may say, that, more than once, the lives and fortunes of his associates were saved by his cool courage and unerring judgment. My wish to meet again was never realized; for, two years after our separation, he met his death at the hand of an assassin in New Mexico.

I shrink from recording the details of his murder; for it was perpetrated in a cowardly manner by one who would never have dared to meet him face to face, and the miscreant went scathless from the scene. It was one of those crimes that go unwhipt of justice in frontier society, to its eternal disgrace.

My first halt was at the city of Durango, where I staid a short time, awaiting a party, who, like myself, were bound southward. In the sierra, not far from this city, lives a singular Indian community, who still reject the teachings of Christianity, adhering to the paganism of their barbarous ancestors. They hold themselves proudly aloof from familiar social intercourse and intermarriage, not only with those of Spanish or mixed descent, but also with those of their own race who have adopted the religion and manners of their conquerors, and who constitute the bulk of the Mexican proletarians. These independent communities are found in other parts of Mexico, and are similar in customs and manners. Representatives of them may sometimes be seen in the streets of the towns, distinguished by their long plaited hair, and the Aztec features seen in the statuary and sculpture of that ancient people. They make baskets and other articles for sale, and are noted for the manufacture of a very superior kind of gayly striped woollen blankets, so finely woven that they hold water. In the secluded village of which I have spoken, I saw an exhibition of natural magic which would have been a creditable performance at any *séance* of the most celebrated clairvoyants, or spiritists, of our high civilization. Spirits were summoned from the vasty deep; and, unlike Hotspur's, they came, communed orally with us, and did other tricks identical with those practised by the charlatans of our own spiritual circles. At one of these *séances*, held in a mud hovel, the spirit of an aged chief communicated to the assembly some facts about my life, of which I am certain no person present could have been aware, and gave other proofs of supernatural power, which must have convinced me, had I not previously possessed convictions that could not be shaken.

Returning to Durango, I related what I had seen to an intelligent countryman settled there as a physician. He replied that the Indians of the sierra were commonly believed by the people of the country to be not only idolaters, but sorcerers; and he related the following tale by way of illustration:—

XXVII.

"SOME years since, in one of those revolutions which so often disturb this unhappy country, shortly after my arrival here, this city was occupied by a general of some notoriety, whose wars had been only of a partisan and predatory character. He was of a cruel and vindictive disposition, like most of his type, and tyrannical over all who fell under his power. For some fancied peccadillo, this person imprisoned a small party of the Sierra Indians who came into the town on a bartering expedition, among whom were a chief and his daughter. This chief was of the sacerdotal caste, who are believed to possess supernatural gifts; and the daughter was a girl of remarkable intelligence and beauty.

"Don Alvaro Lopez, although an old man, had grown gray in a career of war and rapine, which he had begun as a soldier during the war of revolution which separated Mexico from Spain; and since, when there was a lack of employment in an organized force, had been a brigand. He was licentious too; and, seeing the beauty of the girl, resolved to possess her; but, in accomplishing his wicked purpose, slew the aged chief, her father. A successful rival soon after supplanted Lopez, who was driven from the city, escaping with a small band of his followers, who not long after deserted him.

"His successor, no longer fearing him, knowing that he had lost his power and influence, and feeling himself secure from further interference, permitted Lopez to return to his home in this city, and reside under *surveillance*. Shortly after, Don Alvaro fell sick; and I was summoned to attend him.

"Meanwhile the girl — Bartola as she was called, though that was not her real name — remained in Durango, as she had no other refuge; for her kinsfolk would have destroyed her, despoiled of her chastity. She was absorbed in grief for the death of her father, and her own misfortunes, and lived upon the charity of those who pitied her sorrows; such happily being always found among us. She occupied a poor *jacal* in the suburbs, and appeared to have no other occupation than to brood over her misery.

"She would occasionally meet Don Alvaro in the city, and at such times would be heard to mutter some sounds in her dialect that seemed like denunciations, as she bent fierce glances upon him from under her tattered *reboso*. As to my patient, his case baffled my skill, and defied my remedies. His disorder appeared to be of a nervous character, accompanied with chills of a peculiar kind. Having been summoned to a neighboring *hacienda* to attend another patient, I was absent for several weeks; and, when I returned, I found Don Alvaro looking ten years older than when I had seen him last, wan, and with that peculiarly ashen-gray hue of feature which denotes mortal sickness; although his physical strength normally herculean, was not much impaired.

"'It seems to me, doctor,' said he, 'that, when my paroxysms come on, I am seized with emotions of fear and tremors, which I confess I never before in my life experienced. I cannot say there is any reason for this sentiment, that I am aware of; but, on these occasions, another personality appears to have usurped my own, and I am no longer myself. I suffer without apparent cause: my faculties are on the stretch; but I cannot perceive any tangible thing to combat. Then come sharp pains, each distinct from the other, repeated successively as if by a sharp weapon. These seem to pierce my heart and the very marrow of my bones with sudden pricks or pangs, accompanied by a benumbing sensation, and then gradually subside, leaving me in a state of extreme weakness. By a presentiment I cannot describe to you, I can tell the approach of these attacks, which soon arrive, and I become aware of a persisting, implacable assault, as it were, upon my person: my reason gives way; and I fall a prey to terror and apprehension. I am sure some one hates me, and is persecuting me by virtue of some evil influence, against which I am powerless to defend myself. Ah, doctor,' cried the unhappy man just then, 'it is coming! Great God! what do I suffer!'

"The poor devil at this juncture writhed horribly in a fearful nervous paroxysm, which I tried in vain to assuage.

"'General,' said I after the crisis had passed, 'know you of any bitter enemy who has reason to persecute you; any one whom you may have injured, and who may wish for revenge; any one you have slain?'

"'Oh!' returned Don Alvaro, '"los muertos son muy muertos"' ("The dead are dead indeed"). 'No: the dead do not torment me. My enemy lives; and she will kill me yet. It is that Indian girl whose father I killed: I see her at the very moment I suffer, — see her distinctly, with her clinched fist extended toward me, while she stands in an attitude and with a gesture of hatred, directing at my very heart the unseen arrows of her vengeance.'

"After some further conversation, I rose and left the house. The case is unique in my practice; which, however, does not prove that such cases do not sometimes exist, and are caused, perhaps, by electric or magnetic influences directed against the patient. But I am stoutly opposed to empiricism; and the whole case is enveloped in such deep mystery, that I forbear giving a positive opinion, from — I shame not to say it — sheer ignorance as to whether the patient was afflicted by remorse for his crimes, or the determined hatred of some enemy. I can give no explanation; but relate the facts of the case, leaving you to draw your own inferences.

"After leaving the house of Don Alvaro, I walked musingly towards the suburbs, and unwittingly took the direction of Bartola's lowly abode. Approaching it, I saw a light burning in the hovel; and, it being dark, my presence was undiscovered. I resolved to ascertain what I could from the girl herself, and whether there was any ground for believing that the annoyance proceeded from her, as asserted by Don Alvaro. I went to the one window, and looked in. Bartola was on her knees before a rude stool, the only piece of furniture besides the pallet which the hut contained; propped upon which was a rough statuette of clay a few inches long, in the lineaments of which might be traced a grotesque resemblance to the marked features of Don Alvaro Lopez. Had I any doubt as to the actual existence of this resemblance, it would have been dispelled by the poor imitation of a uniform that clothed the figure, bearing the insignia of the general's rank. In the region of the heart of the statuette a long needle was fixed. Bartola was so intent upon what she was doing, that she did not see or hear me, and sat Indian-fashion on her heels, naked but for her petticoat and the *reboso* around her head, her hair dishevelled, and her features pinched and haggard; while the perspiration rolled in drops from her face and shoulders.

"She rocked herself to and fro, with eyes steadily fixed upon the figure; never once withdrawing them while repeating some inarticulate syllables in a low tone, marvellously like an incantation. Sometimes she raised herself erect, and retreated a step or two; then darted towards the figure, regarding it with an intense gaze, and sometimes menacing it with outstretched arm and clinched hand. At last she seized the needle, and stabbed the image: at the same moment her limbs seemed to stiffen, and she fell backwards, with a long-drawn sigh, upon the floor.

"There was something terrible in the scene; and I felt rooted to the spot. As she fell, I recovered my equanimity; and, pushing against the door of the miserable dwelling, it yielded, and I entered its only room. I raised the prostrate form of the girl, who was too exhausted to resist, and placed her upon the poor bed; applied a restorative to her nostrils; and in a few moments she opened her eyes, and gazed at me.

"'Bartola,' said I, 'you know me?' She gave a sign of recognition. 'You are a sorceress, and practise the black-art! You especially direct your evil practices against the life of Don Alvaro Lopez.' She smiled triumphantly.

"'I will kill him!' said she.

"'Take care!' I said. 'You will have to do with the laws: you will be imprisoned if you do not stop your evil practices.'

"'That will not stop them,' she said proudly. 'Meddle not with my vengeance, and look to yourself!'

"'But, Bartola, you will kill yourself, miserable being that you are!'

"She made a gesture of indifference. 'Will you cease your criminal machinations?'—'No!' said Bartola; and resolutely turned her face to the wall, vouchsafing me not another word.

"Finding her obdurate, I retired, taking with me the clay figure, which I destroyed. The next morning I visited my patient, finding him easy for the moment, and related as much of my interview as was prudent to tell him. 'Ah, doctor!' said he, 'I suffered last evening more than ever. It seemed to me as if I was repeatedly stabbed by that Indian witch. What infernal power has enabled her to torment me so?' I told him I would do my best to deliver him from her, and proceeded to the military governor. I stated the case of the old sinner, and received permission to send the Indian girl, upon a certificate of insanity, to a village twenty leagues from here. I thought, that, if the fatal influence she exerted was magnetic, it would be stopped, or at least weakened, by her removal to a distance; and, wishing to act conscientiously towards both her and my patient, I resolved to try this solution of the case. Thought I, 'The unfortunate girl is not absolutely mad; but she has the fatal belief that she possesses the power of injuring him; and it is possible that her hallucination may be dangerous to herself as well as to him.'

"Bartola was accordingly removed, and placed in charge of a person selected for the purpose; and for a few days the old reprobate experienced a sensible relief from his sufferings. In less than a week, however, the nervous agitation returned, and wild delirium was exhibited during the paroxysms; and I was again called in. At the same time came a messenger from the person having charge of Bartola, who informed me that the nervous crises which had ceased with her departure hence had again set in, the attacks on her part being more energetic, more decidedly hostile, if I may say so, than before. Nevertheless, I was told, each time they occurred, they left her much weaker. 'So,' thought I, 'I will immediately see my patient, and counsel him to resist courageously and with all his force: perhaps the one who remains physically the stronger will be the victor. It is a duel *à la mort* between them.'

"I found the old brigand with a terrified expression of countenance, and nearly speechless: he beat the air with his hands, as if trying to parry a mortal thrust; he gasped in agony, and finally expired before my eyes in less than an hour after I entered the room.

"I returned home; and on the next morning the same messenger came from the village with the intelligence that Bartola, too, had passed away, after a prolonged crisis, just half an hour, by my computation, after the death of Alvaro Lopez.

" Her last words to those around her were, in Spanish, "Soy vengado!" ("I am avenged!") It is needless to say to you that science cannot explain this act of mysterious retribution, proceeding not from the action of justice, according to our lights, but which, it is evident, is permitted by the inscrutable decree of a higher than mortal power."

XXVIII.

IN less than three months from the time of my departure, I re-entered the little town of San Juan de los Lagos, and rode directly to the *meson* kept by the Herreras.

The gate was wide open : a crowd of gayly-attired people occupied the court; while from within came the tinkling of guitars and the small Mexican harp. The inn was *en fête*. Pancho alone, in his ordinary dress, came forth from the stables with his usual indifferent manner and shambling gait to take our horses. "Ah, Pancho!" said I, "what is going on? Is it a wedding?" The idiot grinned, and answered me by a forward butt of his ugly head. "And who are the happy couple? Any of the family?" Second grin, and butt with the head. "Is it La Chapita?" Third grin and butt.

This news from the lugubriously jolly mortal puzzled me: for I could not see why Pancho should smile at the idea of Chapita's marriage, unless he was to be the bridegroom; and that was too absurd an idea to be entertained for an instant.

"Perhaps," I thought, "he rejoices, in his stupid ignorance, because she whom he loves is about to be made happy; which, in a sensible person, would be prodigious self-abnegation indeed."

"Tell me, Pancho, who is to be the bridegroom?" The half-witted youth answered me by pantomimic gestures simulating a nurse carrying an infant; then bestrode an imaginary horse, and twirled round his shock pate an ideal lasso; after which performance he burst into a convulsive fit of merriment, clinging meanwhile to the cantle of my saddle.

I comprehended at once that Martin, the son of the house, was the bridegroom; and dismounted, and retired to my chamber. A little later I went to the apartments of the innkeeper's family, paid my respects to the affianced pair, and received an invitation to attend the wedding festivities. Tio Nicolas and Tia Francisco were supremely happy at the prospect of the match between their niece and son.

The lovely maid of the inn was radiant in her bridal dress, bestowing tender glances upon Martin Herrera, whose slender and graceful form was displayed to great advantage in his brand-new costume of a *haciendado*, gorgeous with sky-blue velvet facings, rich embroidery, and dangling silver buttons.

I will spare the reader an account of the excellence of the cookery in Mexican fashion, the jests, *double entendres*, songs, and other details of the somewhat gross gayety of the *fête*. Every thing went "merry as a marriage-bell," the jollity of the occasion ascending *in crescendo* until the end of the feast drew near. But at the very moment when Tio Nicolas began to cut the bridal cake, announcing its conclusion, the beautiful head of the bride dropped upon the table; her arms fell inertly to her side; and in an instant she was in a profound and deathlike sleep. This was the signal for a reproduction of the preceding pleasantries, mingled with "Bravi" and clapping of hands from the guests.

Singular circumstance! All the noise did not awaken the bride from her trance! Her mother and several matrons of the company surrounded the fair somnambula, patted her hands, put vinegar and burnt feathers under her nostrils, inundated her with cold water, and used other restoratives; but still she slept.

Nature appeared to exert herself to resist some soporific influence, and to throw it off; for there was an occasional nervous tremor: but she again relapsed into sleep. These symptoms of reviving became fainter; and the bride was carried off to bed.

The wedding-feast thus interrupted, the tables were finally abandoned; and the guests departed from the *meson,* in which silence now reigned in place of the recent joy and merriment.

The bridegroom staid near the bride as long as the least hope of returning consciousness remained; but, when she was carried off by the women, I saw him wipe away a tear: then his face assumed a suspicious and wrathful aspect, and he issued forth into the *patio.*

Following and meeting him there, he politely asked me if I sought any one; and, when I said that I was looking for Pancho, he rejoined, "I also seek him," and disappeared in the direction of the stables. We could not find Pancho, and re-entered the inn. It was a gloomy night at the *meson* of San Juan. The unaccountable sleep of the fair maid continued in spite of all the restoratives lavished on her by tenderness, aided by excellent medical skill.

At the break of day her respiration stopped, the heart ceased to beat, and lamentations filled the house. The fair bride was dead! I attended the funeral after a few days, during which I endeavored ineffectually to console poor Martin Herrera, whose deep grief was manifested only by a moody silence.

Pancho had disappeared; and I could not help secretly connecting his absence with the tragedy, but just in what manner I could not understand. On the evening after the obsequies, the mystery was partially explained. The corpse of La Chapita had been disinterred, and lay near the empty grave from which it had been sacrilegiously digged in the cemetery; while at a distance of fifty feet near the wall was found the dead body of the idiot Pancho, the skull cloven by a pick-axe which lay near it.

The gossips all hastened to the cemetery as the news

spread; and my informant wished to enlarge upon the hideous details : but, cutting short her ghastly story, I bade my attendants prepare to leave the town, as I had already finished my business, and merely hastened my journey. We mounted, starting from the *meson* at a gallop; and in less than two hours lost sight of the sky-kissing towers of San Juan.

The tragedy enacted in the little town made quite a noise in the country for a time, until something else as startling happened. Every one had his theory of the incidents of the catastrophe, and vigorously defended it. The prefect of the department, aroused to action, and the alcalde of San Juan, with other *hombres buenos*, bothered their brains for several months about the mystery, without arriving at any reasonable solution. At last it was given up as insoluble, and denounced in Mexican fashion as a contrivance of the Devil, and decreed in the book of fate.

From Guanajuato I set out for the city of Mexico. Arriving without any noteworthy experience, I alighted at the Hotel de Iturbide, the proprietor of which, at that time, was Don Anselmo Zurutuza, a large capitalist and well-known citizen, and a gentleman to whose memory I desire to pay my little tribute of respect.

Hon. Robert F. Letcher filled the post of American minister at that time in Mexico; and to him I was indebted for an introduction to the society of the capital, in which he was much respected and beloved. After having passed several years among rude and uncultivated persons thrown accidentally together, or with people of primitive simplicity, with an occasional alternated taste of barbarism, the change to a refined social circle, in which were many persons of education and accomplishments, was most agreeable; and I enjoyed it to the fullest extent.

Thanks to Mr. Letcher, I soon became acquainted with the president of the republic as well as other official persons. Don Mariano Arista, at that time incumbent of the presidential chair, is well known as a general and civil functionary, and distinguished for the mild forbearance of his rule, — a trait insufficiently appreciated among his countrymen. In person he was tall and well-formed, with good and regular features; and, in hair and complexion, what Mexicans call a *guero* (blonde).

The late war with the United States had almost utterly disorganized the Mexican army, and the artillery especially had suffered from neglect. The president, aware of these deficiencies, was endeavoring to re-establish the national forces on an improved basis, in which enterprise he pursued a liberal policy. He had set his heart upon organizing the artillery, and placing it in a state of efficiency never before known in Mexico; having constantly in mind the splendid field-batteries of the United States, which had contributed so much to our success in the war.

From consultations on this subject with the president (who sometimes asked my advice) grew an offer from him of a military position in the Mexican army, which I accepted; and I became a member of his staff, with the rank of lieutenant-colonel. I was immediately charged with the work of organizing and drilling four light batteries; giving, at the same time, instruction to a class of officers twice a week in pyrotechny, dynamics, and the science of projectiles, illustrated by target-practice, and work in the laboratory.

My duties were rendered the more agreeable by the fact that all my orders and instructions came directly from the president as commander-in-chief. When disengaged, I was expected to take my turn of duty with other staff-officers at the national palace; which was an agreeable relaxation from more onerous labors, and carried with it the advantage of free quarters and personal attendance upon my genial chief on public and private occasions. My horses and servants were also provided for at the public expense; and I had the satisfaction of soon acquiring the confidence of the first man in the republic.

In February, 1852, the whole of the *plana mayor* (general staff) received orders to accompany the president on a journey; upon which we started at the appointed time, and, after a brief stay at Queretaro, proceeded to Guanajuato.

In this great mining city we remained about a week, the president being much occupied in inspecting the principal mint of the nation; and I improved the opportunity to examine the great mines and *haciendas* of this famous district. On the Sunday before leaving Guanajuato, I accompanied my chief to high mass in the cathedral with the rest of the staff, and, during the service, recognized among the ecclesiastics who officiated at the altar a well-remembered face. It was that of Father Ipolito, who filled the cure of San Juan de los Lagos. This venerable and excellent man was a Frenchman of high character and learning, who had once exercised the sacred ministry in the United States, and was universally respected by all who knew him in both countries. After the service was over, I accompanied the suite to the door of the church; then returned, and entered the sacristy. Father Ipolito received me with much apparent pleasure, and immediately acceded to my request for an interview with him that evening, making an appointment which we were both exact in keeping.

XXIX.

SINCE the affair of the *meson* of San Juan, my thoughts perpetually recurred to the sad events which had partly induced me to leave that town on the morning of the discovery of the bodies of Chapita and the idiot Pancho in the cemetery.

The faces of the actors in the tragedy frequently came before my mind's eye; and I felt that my uneasiness could not be removed until the mysterious veil, that hid either a horrible crime or a fearful misfortune, was drawn aside.

One evening, how or *à propos* of what I do not remember, an idea flashed into my mind, and a train of circumstances that led to a tragical end stretched out like a path of light before me. The vial of Lethe! On my last trip to San Francisco in "The Golondrina," the fatigue and anxiety had affected my nervous system so materially, that I could not sleep; and, after tossing all night on a feverish bed, I went through the days in an unquiet, somnolent, and absent frame of mind, which not only unfitted me for business, but which exhausted my mental and bodily forces.

I had consulted several medical men, and tried their remedies without avail, when I accidentally met an old acquaintance, a veteran sea-captain whom I had last seen in the East Indies. He was a Dutchman, and, when I knew him, commanded an Indiaman trading between Holland and Java. Like most of his calling, this old man had been forced to act sometimes in the capacity of a physician; and he had qualified himself in no mean degree for such service. He had, indeed, quite a taste for medical practice, and carried with him an infinite store of odd recipes and sovereign cures for all the ills "that flesh is heir to," together with the Bunsby-like propensity for giving advice to all who needed it. Learning of my inability to sleep, and the attendant symptoms of my case, this "ancient mariner" had prescribed, as a sure panacea for my relief, what I afterwards called the "vial of Lethe."

It was a small cube of crystal, closed with a ground-glass stopper; its sides inscribed with gilt Eastern characters, and containing about a dozen pastilles of a pasty, chocolate-colored substance, each enveloped in gold-leaf. The composition of the medicine I never knew; but it was probably a preparation of Indian hemp and opium, as he told me he had obtained the drug, with other articles of great value, from a Javanese prince, for whom he had performed some important service. The captain accompanied his gift with serious and positive instructions, warning me against violating them; as, he said, the vial contained sufficient medicine to make one sleep for a hundred years. I had only to take a very small particle of one of these pastilles on the point of a needle, dissolve it in a glass of *eau sucrée,* and drink it on retiring at night.

I found it an efficient remedy. An hour or so after its administration, total forgetfulness of all mundane things, perfect repose of body and mind, ensued, and calm, refreshing, and strengthening sleep succeeded, lasting all night; after which I arose completely restored. After being cured of my first attack by the use of this specific, I kept the vial constantly at hand; and this it was that I drew from my pocket at the instant when — like a vision — the revelation I spoke of came into my head. I then recalled to mind that one night shortly after I had arrived at San Juan, feeling ill at ease, I had ordered Pancho to bring sugar and water for my dose; and, much to his wonder and amazement, prepared, in his presence, the draught.

With rude pantomime and uncouth sounds the idiot endeavored to inquire why I had thus medicated the water I was about to drink. I told him that I could not sleep; and that, after I had drank the potion, sleep would come. Pancho then asked what quantity of the drug was necessary to produce the desired result, handled the vial curiously, and shaking his head, as if it was something entirely beyond the range of his comprehension, left me to slumber.

I gave this incident no further thought at the time, but went out in haste the next morning, leaving the vial near my bedside, where I found it apparently untouched at my return.

It was the remembrance of this circumstance that made my heart beat as the questions of the idiot came into my mind.

I examined the vial closely, counted the pastilles, estimated those I had consumed, and was convinced that one of them had been abstracted. I meditated long on the circumstances of the complicated drama. I considered the characters of its personages, the revelation of Tio Nicolas regarding the birth of the idiot boy, the ill-concealed violence of his passion for Chapita, the anxiety of Martin Herrera at the nuptial feast, and the subsequent fate of the bride.

Pancho! I was convinced that the "vial of Lethe" was, in some way, the agent of the catastrophe; but I could advance no farther towards a full solution of the mystery. Making a full statement of all the facts in my possession to Father Ipolito, I concluded by asking his advice, saying that it would ease my mind to hear his opinion of the matter.

The good father reflected profoundly for a few minutes, and then asked me if I remembered Dario.

This Dario was an Indian of the Maricopa tribe, a captive who had been brought to San Juan, and had become a convert to Christianity; after which conversion he had been taught to assist in the services of the church, and had charge of the cemetery, performing his duties with exemplary patience and punctuality, although somewhat in years.

I instantly understood then, by the question of the reverend priest, that Dario knew more than he, at first, wished to reveal; for he had been examined at the judicial investigation of the deaths, though nothing could be drawn from him except vague and insignificant replies to the questions asked. It was with a feeling of relief that I heard the question of the excellent ecclesiastic; and, having answered in the affirmative, Father Ipolito entered upon the following narrative: —

"It is my sacred duty as well as pleasure, my son, to do all I can to alleviate the troubles common to suffering humanity; and it is a happy reflection that I can do so in your case without violating confidences which have come to my knowledge under the seal of confession. Six months after the discovery of the bodies in the cemetery, — of which incident you are aware, — I learned that Dario possessed a painful secret. At last he came to me for advice. He said he had not told the judges all he knew, because of his belief that all idiots were the natural and favored children of the Supreme Being. I remembered the superstitious respect of all savage tribes for those who are either wholly or partially deprived of reason. It was evident that Dario had not yet entirely divested himself of his old pagan notions; but, waiving this morsel of heterodoxy, I encouraged him to proceed.

"He then told me, that, on the evening of the interment, he was in his hut in the cemetery, on his knees before the cross, and offering up a simple prayer for the soul of the defunct, when he heard sounds, and looked forth into the cemetery.

"It was late at night; and, by the light of the moon, he saw a man enter the burial-ground, approach the new-made grave and kneel upon it, kissing the earth as if it had really been his mother. Dario crept silently from the hut; and, concealing himself behind a tomb, recognized in the intruder the idiot Pancho, who had brought a shovel and pick-axe with him, and began industriously to throw up the earth that covered the coffin.

"He worked vigorously, and soon disclosed the coffin, which he broke open. Dario did not interfere with his labors; for, soon after Pancho had begun his work, he became aware that there was another witness of the disinterment.

"This was Martin Herrera, who had cautiously followed Pancho, and stood watching him in the perpetration of his sacrilege; but, when the work was done, he rushed upon Pancho, crying out 'Sacrilege!'

"The terrified idiot fled towards the wall of the cemetery, Martin pursuing him, armed with the pick-axe.

"Pancho tried to climb the wall; but the avenger overtook him, and buried the pick-axe deep in his skull.

"For a moment the young man stood contemplating the body of his victim; then stirred it with his foot as if to ascertain that it was really lifeless, and returned to the grave, lifting his hands to heaven as if deprecating its wrath. But at this moment Dario saw the corpse of the girl sitting erect, and endeavoring to divest itself of its cerements, and, terrified at the sight, could no longer restrain an exclamation; at the sound of which, Martin, casting a lingering glance at his beloved, withdrew slowly from the cemetery, — as Dario thought, to fetch assistance.

"As you had left San Juan, as you tell me, on the same day, probably you have not heard that Martin disappeared from the town at the same time, going alone to the presidio of Altar, to his *hacienda;* and is now at the placer in California, having left Mexico, I suppose, until the remembrance of the tragic affair has died away.

"Inquiring of Dario why he had not in the first place seized the idiot in the act of profanation, and, above all, why he had not interfered at the last to save the woman, — who, doubtless, had been restored to consciousness by the action of the cool night air, but, unassisted, had sunk again into the arms of death, — the poor ignorant creature replied, that 'the child of Heaven,' as he called the idiot, had resuscitated the dead by his power derived from above; and that, in her second death, he recognized Heaven's vengeance for the murder of its child.

"I did not then attempt to enlighten the ignorance, and overthrow the superstition, of the poor Indian; but afterwards, I hope successfully, I explained to him the true attributes of our heavenly Father, and his ineffable goodness to the meanest of his children."

Here ended the recital of Father Ipolito. The mystery was explained at last. One of my pastilles had been stolen by Pancho, and part of it dissolved in a cup of chocolate, which I remembered hearing that she had drank just before the wedding-feast. The potion must have been a powerful one, but not necessarily fatal; for my medicine was slow in its operation, although its effects lasted for a long time.

The mutual confidences of the good father and myself were properly authenticated, at his request. And thus ends the sad story of the Fair Maid of the Inn.

XXX.

ON our return to the capital, a military expedition was prepared to march against those rebellious chiefs who had organized armed resistance to the authority of the government in the State of Michoacan.

This force consisted of some two thousand infantry, fifteen hundred cavalry, and two batteries, of which the president assumed the command.

The cavalry and infantry began their march at midnight, and were already far on their road, the artillery still parked in the grand square before the national palace, when, at early dawn, we were awakened from sleep by fifty trumpets and cornets in the court, sounding the inspiriting strains of the Diana. I immediately mounted, and put my guns in motion; and, when we halted for our *desayuna* at the garita of Belen, the column was overtaken by the president and his staff. We bivouacked that night at Quajimalpa, a poor village; and next day arrived at Toluca, one of the most beautiful as well as one of the most ancient of the cities of Mexico. The mountain of Tutucuitlalpico rises above the city fifteen thousand feet; and upon its very summit is a lake of clear, ice-cold water. Continuing our march, we halted the next day at La Gabia, a *hacienda* belonging to the Count of Regla, thirty square leagues in extent. This vast estate shares the peculiarities of nearly every climate, from hot to cold, and yields their several products. In its area may be found flourishing, according to the different elevations of the soil, wheat, maize, and the fruits of the temperate zone; and, not far off, sugar-cane, coffee, palms, and olives, and all the rich and luscious varieties of tropical fruits. The State of Michoacan, or Morelia, has been considered since the times of the Montezumas the most fertile as well as the loveliest district of Mexico, and is entitled to the appellation of the Garden of the Valley.

Our little army pushed on through Taximaroa, San Andres, and other villages, with the easy gait and *insouciant* manner that distinguish the Mexican soldiers, — who make marches that would astonish any other troops, on the smallest amount of sustenance, — and slept that night at the *hacienda* of Querendaro.

The next morning our cavalry was engaged with that of the enemy; but the fight proved to be a mere affair of outposts; and for another day or two we continued our route unmolested, although hostile cavalry was seen hovering about our column. On the 25th of February, 1852, the army was marching over a difficult and dangerous road, and the head of the column had become engaged in a deep and narrow defile, when it was heavily attacked on both flanks. My two batteries were near the middle of the column: the infantry were thrown back upon us in confusion, and a panic began to spread among the whole command. Seeing how vain would be any effort to rally the disorganized infantry, and that the situation called for a diversion of another kind, I resolved that my artillerists should furnish it. At my command, they quickly dismounted and separated the pieces and carriages of two mountain-guns, having been previously well drilled in that manœuvre. They then took, one a wheel, another the trails and axles, a third another wheel, while four or five carried the pieces themselves between them with their lassoes: others followed with the implements and ammunition for the guns, and, struggling manfully up the almost perpendicular sides of the defile, remounted the guns, and opened a rapid fire upon the left flank of the enemy. This feat could not have been performed by any troops but Mexicans. In no other country is the lasso so skilfully used, and none but Mexican military saddles have heads to secure it; soldiers of other nations are not so good horsemen as Mexicans; and, finally, no other than agile, surefooted, unshod Mexican horses could have climbed that fearful ascent.

Like his rider, the horse of the country is trained to chase, and assist his master in overthrowing wild cattle of greatly superior strength; and the manner of breaking him to the saddle, of bitting him, of saddling and riding him, is diametrically opposite to all European methods, civil or military. As to Americans, except in the Far West, where the best riders adopt the Mexican fashions, equestrian exercises have fallen so completely into desuetude, that we have now only park-riding, which is but a poor imitation of the "Bois" and "Rotten Row."

This sudden artillery-attack shook the enemy, and gave time to our men to rally, who again pressed forward into the defile; while our cavalry, coming up in the rear, decided the event, and drove the rebels from the field.

Emerging from the defile, we saw the forces of the latter in line of battle in the plain, and formed to attack them; but, at the first shot from the much-dreaded artillery, they retreated, pursued by our cavalry, to Patzcuaro.

Under the walls of that town they made another stand: but the artillery again put them to flight; and we entered the city in triumph, where the president established his head-quarters, the rebels retreating to the mountains. Having dispersed the *facciosos* as they were called, and restored order in this beautiful State, until its next disturbance we could turn our attention to social enjoyment, in which we were aided and entertained by some of the very persons who had fought against us; and, the objects of the campaign having been attained, we returned leisurely to the capital.

There, having been badly wounded, I became the guest of a family from whom I received the kindest care.

While confined within-doors, my former friends often came in to while away the dull hours with agreeable conversation.

Among these was a young man who held a government office, and who had often questioned me about the different countries I had seen, and sought such other information as I was able to impart.

One day I asked him, in return, to relate to me his own experiences; and, complying at once, he told his little history, which, as it forms an admirable commentary upon the manners of the country, I may repeat in a free translation of his own language without being charged with digression.

"Commonplace and uneventful as my humble memoir may appear to you, colonel, who have had such large experience of all countries, it still has a moral, and perhaps implies a satire upon our Mexican society, of which I am an insignificant member. I am a native of Guadalajara. My parents died while I was yet young, after having given me as good an education as they could afford with their very limited means. They left me no money, but much taste for spending it

"I languished some time after their death, in a small provincial town, on a modest employment, which permitted me to ride a borrowed nag on the Paseo on Sundays and holidays, and to purchase my inexpensive toilet and *cigarritos*, until I arrived in this city. I had come to the conclusion in my humble retreat that Fortune at last must be weary of neglecting my claims to a more brilliant position.

"With a purse light indeed when compared to my hopes and expectations, I descended at the best hotel in Mexico, and ordered the best accommodations. I was conducted at once with welcoming salutations to an elegant though small apartment, furnished with taste and comfort; and at once understood that I had entered a fashionable, and, consequently, expensive house.

"'Ave Maria,' thought I: 'my destiny has changed at last, and I must conduct myself like a well born and nurtured youth; for, as everybody knows, such a one is a person for whom society does a great deal, while he does as little as possible for society, public consideration here below being in inverse ratio to one's usefulness.'

"Being left alone, I approached the window, and, looking into the street, perceived a young woman on the balcony of the next house, who smiled pleasantly at my appearance.

"Too well-bred not to understand such advances, I saluted the lady, who politely returned my courtesy. Emboldened by such condescension, I made a sign in our digital language, which meant that I thought her charming; and blew her a kiss.

"The young woman burst into a laugh, and retired, shutting the window. 'Good!' thought I: 'an adventure has already commenced. Really, the capital pleases me: I shall be enchanted to inhabit it.' As dinner at the *mesa redonda* was not to be served for an hour or so, I employed the intervening time in a street promenade; taking possession, as it were.

"The streets were filled with people intent on business or pleasure. The gay air of the latter, and the complacency of the *negociantes*, were pleasing to a stranger; while occasional glimpses of handsome ladies on their balconies, children returning from school, and other lively sights which diversify the streets of our city, gave me an agreeable impression. 'Ah!' thought I, 'here every one lives but for amusement: every thing seems *en fiesta.*'

"I have always thought that life is only understood in great cities. I regarded the passing crowds; and it seemed to me that already I knew these persons, who henceforth were to be my fellow-citizens. I murmured to myself the names on the signs of the shops; and even felt an impulse to salute the passers, and to inquire after their healths. Continuing my walk, I arrived at my hotel, and seated myself at the *mesa redonda,* near an old schoolmate whom I recognized. As was natural, we mutually informed each other of the motives which had ed us to the capital.

"'I have come here to occupy a government-office,' said I.

"'And I also,' said my friend Valdes, 'came with the same intention, but have already lost all hope.'

"'Why?' said I.

"'The place I was desirous of possessing,' answered Valdes, 'depends upon the minister of the interior.'

"'Mine also depends upon the same official,' I returned.

"'I have just seen him, and he announced to me that a rival possessing incontestable claims would be preferred to me.'

"'Know you who he is?'

"'I do not know his name; but he has written some articles upon the administration of his department for "The Siglo," and is a licentiate: he is also a relative of Gen. Bravo.'

"'Caracoles, hombre! it is I!' ejaculated your humble servant, with a sudden joy he could not conceal.

"Francisco Valdes made an exclamation of surprise.

"'Pardon me, my poor friend,' said I, concealing my joy under an affected air of modesty. 'I am in despair at having been the cause of thy disappointment; but that particular place has been promised me for a long time. I had, indeed, a claim upon it, as the honorable minister told thee.'

"'So you are the nephew of Gen. Bravo?' said Francisco.

"'I am, indeed, the nephew of my uncle,' said I gayly. 'But be not uneasy: I hope to acquire some influence with the minister; and thou shalt have the very first agreeable vacancy.'

"Dinner over, and feeling that sort of generosity that is natural to a victor, I would not abandon my friend Valdes to gloomy reflections on his defeat, but accompanied him to the Alameda. Although it was the fashionable hour, and all the *ton* of the city was airing itself in carriages, on horseback, or on foot, my friend seemed dejected and disgusted. He found the gardens badly laid out, the women homely, and the weather — here in Mexico! — unpleasant.

"The true sun of most men is not in heaven: it is in the heart; it is joy. Reaching a gentle eminence from which the eye could take in the city, the volcanoes, the lakes, with their floating *chinampas*, and the whole unrivalled panorama of our glorious valley, I could not help stopping, and uttering an exclamation of delight; but my companion only shrugged his shoulders with contempt.

"'I always did hate a great city,' said he. 'What is it but a comb void of honey; an ant-hill, whose population is forever laboring without reaching satisfactory results? Such is human life, — action, bustle, everywhere; but substantial results nowhere. Water runs; the wind passes by us; we grow old, and die; and all is ended. What law governs all this agitation? Why, chance. Some arrive at their destination without having taken their departure; while others are forever departing, but never arrive. The happy are those 'heavy fathers' and stage-uncles who stick to their parts. But look at those wretched *leperos*, so out of place in this gay crowd! They cower under the pelting of the storm while traversing the dreary path of life; and, when they arrive at the coach-office of destiny, there are no tickets left.'

"Somewhat annoyed by these allusions, I ventured to remark that the first condition of success in seeking place is the possession of talent; the poor in wit being like the poor in purse, — unable to furnish an equivalent for the enjoyment of a good position. But, seeing that my remarks piqued

Valdes, I added, 'Philosophy is out of place just after dinner: so let us digest now, and postpone business until to-morrow. Can we complain of life or of society while enjoying this perfumed breeze, or while listening to that murmuring brook? No one, Francisco, can claim to be exclusively happy or miserable. The rich have need of the admiration of the poor, the powerful of the approbation of the weak.

"'Look at these charming women as they pass. It is for us that they wish to appear beautiful; those sumptuous carriages are gilded but for our admiration; those lackeys are gorgeously liveried, not for their masters, but for us; and that old gentleman, who rides so badly, exposes himself to a broken neck only that we may be amused.'

"A cavalier of ripe age, dressed in a splendid Mexican riding-costume and mounted on a richly-caparisoned horse, appeared at this moment on the Alameda. It was easy to see that his steed was well trained in those acts of the *manége* taught by our *ginetes* to a *caballo galan;* and he threatened at times to bring his rider to grief. He caracoled gayly, frequently turning upon his tracks, snorting, and champing the bit, and often taking as many steps to the rear as to the front; which is the last degree of perfection in a horse of the *haute école.*

XXXI.

"THE old cavalier, ill at ease, tried to induce his fiery charger to rest a little from his gambadoes; but the horse snorted, threw up his head, and passed on. Valdes stopped to gaze at the retreating horseman. 'He looks like a pair of tailor's shears on horseback,' said he: 'he must be a very great man to possess the right to make himself so ridiculous.' I noticed that all the promenaders saluted the old gentleman with respect and deference; the ladies, especially, bestowing radiant glances upon him. 'Mean flatterers!' remarked Valdes. 'If he were a poor ranchero, they would point their fingers in scorn at him. See him, now, parading before that carriage! He strongly resembles a circus clown. I have a great mind to hiss him.'

"'Silence!' said I: 'he approaches. He is a person of importance: see his decoration!'

"'Ho, ho!' said Francisco. 'Let us view him nearer: we may extract some amusement from his capers. Such a caricature must not be permitted to pass with impunity.'

"'Take care what you do, Francisco!' cried I. And he, 'I am not a public functionary, but a free man, and may have an opinion of my own.'

"So saying, Valdes walked rapidly to a little green elevation bordering the path followed by the cavalier; but suddenly I saw him stop, step rapidly forward, and salute the old gentleman. At the same moment the horse made a volt, and the old man's hat flew off, and was carried some distance by the wind.

"Valdes ran in pursuit of the *sombrero;* missed it three times, and caught it at the fourth trial. He brushed it carefully with his sleeve; then ran to the ridiculous cavalier, to whom he presented it with a low bow.

"'What the devil can he be about?' thought I; and, curious to know the reason of this sudden change of demeanor in Valdes, I endeavored to gain admittance to the roadway through the crowd: but the old cavalier instantly quitted the Alameda, Valdes accompanying him, walking by the side of the *caballo galan.*

"I returned to the hotel, still mystified by what I had seen on the Alameda; and, meeting the landlord at the entrance, asked him the name of my fair neighbor, who occupied her balcony.

"'Ah, ha!' answered he, 'that little one?'

"'Yes, to be sure.'

"'She is *una señorita libre*' ('a free young lady'). 'She is called "Rita." Ah! indeed, with her coquettish airs, and her great languishing eyes flashing from under her *rebosito.*'

"Then, assuming a grave air, he continued: 'She has helped to spend more than one liberal inheritance among my quondam lodgers. I often have here unsophisticated young men travelling for information.'

"Hearing this account of my neighbor, I virtuously determined never to open my window, or to waft more kisses from it; and, night drawing on, ascended to my apartment, and began to work at some literary employment I had in hand. In about a couple of hours I rose, walked to the window, and cautiously looked towards the house of my *vis-à-vis*, having been attracted by the sound of voices.

"I saw a man, whom I recognized as the ridiculous cavalier of the Alameda, standing before the door of my fair neighbor, which was held ajar by an old woman, whom he was supplicating for admission.

"I could make out from their colloquy that the *vieja* (old woman) was obdurate; and she finally retired, repeating a Spanish proverb, signifying, that, when one has no teeth, one cannot expect to crack nuts.

"The visitor, however, still lingered under the window, apparently hoping for reconsideration of the refusal; when I heard a whispered conversation, interrupted by stifled laughter, in the chamber of the 'free young lady.' Suddenly the window opened, and Rita appeared, bearing a vase in which was a large bouquet.

"The gay old cavalier raised his head, and softly whispered her name; but a deluge of cold water and flowers prevented him from saying more. I could not refrain from bursting into a laugh at his discomfiture, which drew his observation toward me. 'Ah!' said he, 'it is, then, a preconcerted affair.'

"He then groped his way up the narrow street, keeping close to the houses, and, with a shame-faced air, disappeared in the obscurity.

"I did not avail myself of the opportunity to enter into conversation with Rita, who lingered invitingly on the balcony. My sense of dignity as an official of the government obliged me to adhere strictly to propriety; and, feeling sleepy, I re-entered my chamber, and shut the window. 'A courtesan!' said I contemptuously to myself while putting on my nightcap; 'to trade on one's beauty! I have ever detested the race; and, now that I know the truth, this one appears hideous. I must turn a deaf ear to her blandishments: it is quite easy to one of positive delicacy like myself.' So saying, I slept soundly. My dreams were pleasant: I imagined that I had been elected president, and, making a European tour after the expiration of my term of office, married a German princess with a nice *dot*, an army of three men, and the right to nominate half a deputy to the diet. Awaking the next morning, I found that both the sun and my pretty neighbor had already risen. She was seated near her window, engaged in embroidery, while she hummed a *jarabe*.

'Aforrado de mi vida! "yo te quisiera cantar,"
Por mis ojos son tiernas, y empezaran a llorar.'

De Guadalajara vengo, lideando con un soldado,
Solo por venir a ver a mi jarabe aforrado.'

"The last versicle was appropriate to her souvenir of myself, I thought; for she looked up, smiled, with a blush over her features, and, without acknowledging my rather distant salutation, lowered her head over her work with an air of sadness.

"I finished my toilet with care; for I had heard that the minister of the interior received at an early hour, in order to appear like a man of business-habits. I placed the letter of my uncle (the general) in my breast-pocket, and started for the house, which I entered, quite awe-struck with its magnificence.

"The high windows splendidly draped, the broad staircase, and roomy vestibule, announced wealth and power. I felt an innate respect for one so well lodged, my assurance diminishing in proportion to the size of the apartments I traversed; until my self-mistrust culminated on entering a vast saloon hung with silk, and superbly furnished.

"I delivered the general's letter to a servant, who prayed me to wait until his Excellency had finished his toilet. Left alone, I walked round the room, curiously at first, then with a furtive step. I was troubled, I knew not why. I consulted my watch, although I did not wish to know the hour; and at last seated myself mentally to rehearse the compliments I wished to pay to the great man, as I piqued myself on my knowledge of the world, and of the art of pleasing. 'All men,' said I to myself, 'are alike. Take plenty of vanity, ditto of egotism, a few grains of chance, double the same number of vices disguised as virtues, mix well together, and you have indifferently a king or a cobbler. The surest way to success is humility. One has but to listen when a patron speaks in order to be credited with wit and wisdom. Should his Excellency have his weak points, so much the better: they will be so many rounds of the ladder to aid me to mount.' As I ended my monologue, a door opened, and a gorgeous *robe de chambre* appeared. 'His Excellency!' said the servant.' We each made a step towards the other, and recoiled simultaneously. I beheld the same person who had been repulsed so scornfully by Rita the previous evening; while the minister clearly recognized me as the stranger who had made merry at his mishap! Both were embarrassed; but the minister first recovered his presence of mind, assumed a tone of dignified coolness, and remarked, 'You are the gentleman recommended by Gen. Bravo; are you not?' glancing at the letter which he held negligently.

"'I am,' said I trembling.

"'Ah! no doubt you have claims?'

"'His Excellency must have seen — in the letter — of the general,' I faltered.

"'Oh, yes! he spoke of some articles written for "The Siglo,"—true; but who is there that does not write for the newspapers now-a-days? A licentiate too: ah! that is not an uncommon distinction. Meanwhile, I will see. I wish to be useful to any one recommended by the general. Ah! come and see me, — some other time: just now I am busy.'

"Speaking thus, his Excellency waved me politely towards the door; upon nearing which, as I involuntarily obeyed his gestures, I suddenly comprehended that all would be lost in case I did not insist upon something at once."

XXXII.

"THE situation in which I was left in the preceding chapter was a critical one; and I nerved myself to meet it with the courage of despair. 'Pardon me, your Excellency,' said I; 'but the general gave me hopes that your protection would be accorded me.'

"The minister frowned. 'Have I promised any thing?' asked he coldly.

"'Nothing; but the general told me — he thought — by his advice I left the employment I had, hoping to establish myself at the capital.'

"'Do you know any one here?" asked the minister with an appearance of eagerness.

'No one,' I answered. 'I arrived only yesterday.'

"'Ah! really? I imagined I had met you somewhere.'

"By the bitter and angry manner and tone which emphasized this last remark, I understood that all hope had fled. I made a step backward, and joined my hands, articulating, 'Oh! why should I have seen what I did last night?'

"'It all seems like the translation of a verse of Ovid,' coldly remarked the minister.

"I twisted my hat in my hands nervously, and gazed around with a frightened air: a cold sweat bathed my forehead, and I essayed to make my exit, but, stopping an instant, ventured to say, —

"'May I ask his Excellency for whom my place is destined?'

The door opened, and the servant announced 'Don Francisco Valdes!' It was a ray of light to the minister. 'Behold my answer!' said he.

Francisco stopped at once with a stupefied air. 'I, Excellency?' said he.

"'I would not announce it to you yesterday, when I had the honor to meet you on the Alameda; I had not then fully decided: but, since that time, your respective rights to the place have been more fully ascertained.'

"'All right!' said I, thinking of the adventure of the vase. 'Oh meanness personified! and this is what is called society?'

"The door stood wide open, and I made but two steps down stairs and into the street. Reaching the open air, I collected my scattered thoughts, and relaxed my haste. There was, seemingly, a weight upon my chest. I felt at once furious and humiliated. It seemed to me that I must discharge upon somebody the grief that oppressed me.

"I imagined that all the incidents of my interview with the minister were written upon my forehead for every one to read.

"I hurriedly traversed the streets, the alleys, and the squares, casting furious glances on the houses, and on the people I met. Mexico, just then, appeared hateful. 'What a noise!' I murmured, 'what disorder! Why are those idlers abroad? no one works here!' And my thoughts reverting to my adventure, — 'Ah, ha! success in this place comes by picking up the hats of great men. City of injustice and debauchery, Mexican Sodom! thy prizes are only to be gained by parasites and sycophants. Cursed city! I shake thy dust from my shoes.' As I achieved this imprecation, I was rejoined by my successful rival.

"In his turn, Valdes had assumed the joyful air and deprecatory accent that I had put on the previous evening. 'Well,' said he, 'my poor friend, it seemed I deceived myself: my claims have at last been recognized.'

"'Hardly worth while to talk about claims,' said I: 'does not favor decide every thing here below?'

"'You thought otherwise yesterday,' he answered; 'and, by your own avowal, the unsuccessful are only the poor in wit.' He refrained from finishing his speech; but I bit my lips with spite at the justice of his remark.

"'For the future,' said Francisco with graceful dignity, 'count on me. The minister wishes me well; and, should any vacancy occur'— I could listen no longer; and, darting a disdainful glance at poor Francisco, I turned my back upon him, and hurried forward.

"Fatigued at last by desperate and aimless wanderings through the streets, I returned to the hotel, shut myself up in my chamber, and fell into philosophic reflection upon what had happened. 'After all,' I thought, 'why make myself miserable? My misfortunes only please the minister, who regards them as a kind of homage to his power. In afflicting myself, then, I am but the accomplice of his vengeance. My fortune has been compromised, it is true; I am without a place; my bill in this hotel is unpaid; and I have about cash enough left to buy a hook and a rope to hang myself withal: still it is more dignified to support my reverses manfully. His Excellency doubtless believes me now in bed, crushed by misfortune, and taking hartshorn to quiet my nerves. Well, I will disappoint him by passing a pleasant evening.' So saying, I rang the bell with all the confidence of a millionnaire.

"'Let me have an excellent supper!' I cried to the waiter; 'a roasted *chichalaka* (pheasant) and your best wine, — champagne and Burgundy. Above all, let the supper be well served. Go!'

"I drew my curtains, and lighted four new wax candles. A table was soon set with bright crystal on snowy damask, and I sat down to a supper that would have made a *gourmand* smile with pleasure. With the first course my spirits revived, and I convinced myself that the loss of such a place as that I aspired to was not irreparable, and that I could obtain another equally desirable and less onerous.

"At the second course I rejoiced that the minister had refused me a place, in which, had I accepted it, my high destinies would have been trammelled by the petty bonds of a subaltern employment.

"With the dessert I believed myself a prince living in an enchanted palace, while docile genii anticipated all my wants, and ministered to my desires.

"The generous wine quickened my pulses; my bosom's lord sat lightly on his throne; the pictures danced upon the walls; and the floor seemed to sway lightly under my feet with a dreamy movement, like the swinging of a grass-hammock.

"I jested with the waiter, who seemed charmed with my wit; and, finally, I tossed off my *chasse* and sallied into the street, occupying the whole broad staircase in my descent. The sky sparkled with the stars of our charming tropic night, and I thought that no city could be more beautiful. The very mansions around me seemed illuminated as if for a triumph: joy and benevolence were inhaled with the perfumed air. I politely saluted several passers, although they were utter strangers to me. I dropped a *duro* in the begging-box at the street-corner; laughed heartily at two *leperos* engaged in gambling for *clacos;* and entered a Punch show, crowded with *galopinas* (chambermaids), which I soon deserted for the open air. I walked rapidly for a space; then loitered, and began talking to myself:—

"'Wine is calumniated,' I said with enthusiasm. 'It is the best of God's gifts to man. It is not what some fanatics would have us believe, nor is its analysis what chemists assert. Wine is liquid sunbeams. It is the beautiful sky and invigorating climate of Southern Europe bottled, and brought to us here in the tropics. Ah, celestial fluid! it is thou that reanimates the sinking heart, and transforms vulgar brains into festive halls in which thousands of lovely visions glide through graceful dances.'

"Musing after this manner, I at length found myself in the

street of my hotel, entering it at the side opposite to that which I had generally used. Pausing at what I supposed to be the door of the hotel, I knocked for admittance. A window above opened; a head was thrust out, and immediately disappeared: the door was unfastened, and an old woman admitted me. I was still distraught, occupied indeed with thoughts suggested by my vinous dithyrambic, and mechanically ascended the stairway without giving it special notice. Before I realized my situation, I found myself in a chamber not my own, *vis-à-vis* with La Rita.

"To have excused myself, alleging that I had mistaken the house, would have been the part of a country booby: so I accosted my fair hostess as if I had come to make a call of ceremony. The old woman disappeared; and I found the young girl, on a near view, remarkably handsome. She received me graciously; and we were soon engaged in animated conversation.

"'Cielo!' thought I, 'this is a worthy crowning of my evening's pleasure,—*post Bacchum, Venus!*'

"Rita did not assume a character not her own, and, from the discussion of general subjects, soon glided into excuses for the life she was leading. I was not in a censorious humor: indeed, I re-enforced her arguments in her own defence, telling her, for example, that, in ancient Greece, women, her prototypes, like Aspasia and others, helped materially to form the manners of that cultivated nation.

"After an hour or more, I rose to depart. 'Do you remain long in this city?' asked Rita.

"'Alas!' said I, 'I thought so yesterday: but my hopes have been blasted; and thou, perhaps, art the cause.'

"'How so?'

"I related my story.

"'If that is all,' said she, 'I think I can arrange matters. I have hitherto, as you have seen, repelled the advances of his

Excellency; but, for thy sake, I will not only give him an interview, but will promise thee also that thy wishes shall be granted beforehand.'

"'Indeed!' returned I: 'then art thou my good angel!' And, bidding her good-night, I returned to my hotel with a profound contempt for honest women.

"The next morning I slept quite late; remaining in bed, indeed, until the servant brought me a note from the minister of the interior, couched in the politest terms, and asking me to 'do him the honor' to breakfast with him, so that he could explain himself upon the 'misunderstanding' of the day before. I understood at once from what quarter had come the change in his sentiments; and, while dressing, according to my habitual custom, addressed to myself this monologue:—

"'So,' said I, 'the place I wished for is to be granted, not to my talents, but to the solicitation of a lady of the *demimonde*. Well, what does it matter, since it has been conceded to the influence which my person and accomplishments have produced upon a woman? Women are our primal protectors. As infants, we are nourished from their bosoms; in middle age we are indebted to them for the delights of love; and, when we grow old, their care soothes our sufferings, and assists our infirmities. Is it not more honorable and agreeable to owe one's fortune to a young girl than to some old dowager who would marry you against your inclinations?'

"Having leisurely performed my toilet, I set out for the house of the minister; and, although I knew that I was much belated,—for I arrived long after the hour specified in his note,—I felt no uneasiness on that account. The day before I appealed to the justice and benevolence of his Excellency; now I came recommended to his vices: so I was not the least troubled.

"The minister excused himself for having asked me to breakfast at so early an hour; saying, that, upon a reperusal of the general's letter, he saw more in it than had met his eye on its first reading, and even recognized a mistake of persons on his part. He added some complimentary remarks on my literary works, and announced that a commission for the place would be issued to me the same morning. On my part, I gave proof of an excellent appetite; flattered my host like a man of wit and tact; approved of every thing about him without exaggeration; and, at the close of the meal, left the minister enchanted with my parts.

"As to Valdes, he could never again get the *entrée* at the minister's; and, after several ineffectual attempts, he resigned himself to his fate, and returned to his village.

"When my uncle, the general, knew of the appointment of his nephew, he merely remarked, 'I was sure of it: the minister of the interior can refuse me nothing.' He wrote, nevertheless, to thank his friend, and accompanied the letter with a handsome present.

"I continue to keep on excellent terms with both my patron and La Rita, who also maintains her place in his regard. His Excellency and myself are frequently seen on horseback together: and, thanks to his lessons, I have already become a tolerable cavalier; although I thought I had won a right to that distinction long before I came to the capital, having had the usual experience of all my countrymen in that exercise.

"Perhaps, my colonel, at the conclusion of my little memoir, you would like to know my opinion as to the best mode of succeeding in life in our country, to which my experience has been confined. I will tell you in the words of my invariable answer to all young men who question me on that subject: 'Merit is one's best Mæcenas and patron.' I have always said it, and have proved it by my own example. I sometimes add, that it is only in high principles that one should seek for success and happiness."

XXXIII.

THE spring of the year 1852 was now at hand, and the time propitious for a change to a more northern climate, which, for various reasons, I was desirous of making. About this time, also, happened the contingency for which I had provided when I accepted service in the Mexican army. This was the retirement of my excellent patron and friend, Don Mariano Arista, from the presidency.

Accordingly, I resigned my commission, receiving on the occasion numerous testimonials both public and private, and prepared to leave the republic, in which I had led a somewhat eventful life, and had always been treated with uniform kindness and hospitality. Besides the sunny skies, the unrivalled climate, and the magnificent scenery, of this portion of our globe, so favored by bountiful Nature, and eulogized by Humboldt as unique among the countries he had visited, I left behind me many kind and steadfast friends, and a few families to whom I felt truly attached, and whom I hoped again to meet.

There is a nameless and indescribable charm in Mexico which holds every one who has lived for a term of years within its boundaries, and which begets a longing to revisit it which never fades. The Spaniards who returned to their own country after the revolution which separated the colonies from Spain were especially affected with this nostalgia, we are told; and there is a proverb which corroborates the statement:

"Si en Indias fueres, sea en donde los volcanes vieres" ("If you ever go to the Indies, let it be where the volcanoes are").

Having completed the preparations for my departure, I left the city in company with a young Californian returning from the placer with a notable sum in dust, — his two-years' harvest, — whose acquaintance I had made in the capital. Besides ourselves, there were nine other passengers by the diligence, all natives of the country, mostly commercial gentlemen bound to Vera Cruz. Not one of them was armed; for the sons of the country have an idea, that to resist robbers only provokes them to greater atrocities.

All went well with us until we arrived at the stopping-place at Perote, where the passengers slept, on the last stage to Vera Cruz. Next morning, the coach started; and the nine insides, including myself, were resuming our interrupted dozings, when two shots were heard in quick succession. The coach stopped: there was some hard swearing; and all got out into the road.

There was nothing strange to be seen, however, except two dead bodies riddled with buck-shot, which lay, one on each side of the highway, where they had been tumbled by the right and left barrels of my fowling-piece, in the hands of my companion Twichell, who was seated beside the driver.

The driver said there was a third person, and recognized one of the *rateros*, (foot-pads), who he said, the evening before, had questioned him at Perote about the passengers and their nationality.

These two had seized the heads of the leaders of our team, while the third man tried to cut the traces; and only the prompt action of Twichell had saved the passengers. Yet they were all highly indignant at my comrade, and myself who sustained him, dreading, as they said, the revenge of the robbers. They had come prepared for robbers, with pinchbeck watches, and but little money in their pockets. But we only laughed at them; and soon the coach began its descent through the defile of Cerro Gordo, near which place of glorious memory for Americans the attempt had been made.

Arriving in due time at New Orleans, I was soon on my way up the Mississippi, and entered the "belle rivière."

Among my fellow-passengers on the steamer was Lieut. Thomas J. Jackson of the United-States army, who seemed, at first, a remarkably quiet, reserved, although very intelligent officer, and with whom I soon became acquainted; for there is everywhere a sort of *cameraderie* among officers of the two services which attracts them to each other in a crowd of strangers. For several days the inland voyage continued; and our nights were partly spent upon the hurricane-deck of the steamer, engaged in conversation.

One of these conversations was so peculiar, that it fixed itself in my memory; and subsequent events proved it worthy of record; although, I confess, I hesitate to put in writing any thing which seems to border so nearly on the marvellous.

One clear starlight night, as we glided along the calm river, our conversation turned upon the firmament and its countless orbs that looked down upon us. Jackson asked me if I had ever been induced to take a flight from the study of nautical astronomy, practised by all naval officers, into the realms of astrology. I replied that I had always been interested, more or less, in those mathematical studies required in nautical calculations; and that, from the exact rules demanded for working the various problems of the ephemeris, I had sometimes, to amuse the idle hours of a sea-life, worked out the nativities of my shipmates. I had even taken Zadkiel's Almanac, and used his rules, but without believing in the science of judicial astrology. Jackson, however, was not so incredulous; although it was evident that he had not then decided fully within himself as to the truth or falsehood of this exploded science.

"Why," said he, "should we be ridiculed for believing in

this, as in other occult sciences, in this nineteenth century? Magnetism! magnetic somnambulism!—who shall say that the science of aerostation will not be made practically useful to mankind? Why should not the buoyant and elastic element surrounding our earth be made the vehicle of transportation from clime to clime for man and his increasing necessities? I will go farther, and ask, Who can doubt but that it will eventually be so used, like its twin-element upon which we are now afloat? The means of directing those forces which we know exist have not yet been discovered; but that does not prove that the air will not some day find its Fulton or its Watt. The imperfect vision of things often appears to the intelligence before the things themselves. The learned are free to confess their ignorance; but they should not elevate it into a principle. They may understand and explain an immense number of phenomena; but the causes of these often entirely escape them, or they are compelled to take them upon trust as insoluble mysteries. Ask these savants the why and the wherefore of the natural actions they investigate, and they assume a solemn air, and refer you to the fabulous ages of science. It is much easier to deny any relation of spirits to matter than to demonstrate it.

"If the illuminati of the middle ages have not made sciences, at least we cannot deny they have made poetry. Sentiment led them into the sphere of illusion, it is true; but illusion is often the shadow of truth. Let it be remembered that Kepler was an astrologer. The mathematician Cardan relates that the events of his life were announced to him through dreams, presentiments, and apparitions, by his familiar genius, and by the movements of the stars. And these were strong-minded men. Even Napoleon believed in his destiny, and is said to have carried his belief in the supernatural farther than his historians will admit. Those bright orbs above us are living creatures. Each one of them is animated by a certain intelligence gifted with forces, and they act directly upon our planet. Each ray of light falling to earth finds its destination in the animate world. Not a living being, not even a flower, but has its patron and guide on high in one of those orbs suspended in ether. Why should not this wonderful influence transmitted through space, this communion of souls as it may be called, this correspondence of the spheres, forming a universal bond of union, determine also the destinies of the beings they are known to influence? Whenever one of those worlds approaches another, does not each endeavor to draw the other within the sphere of its attraction? And who, in this day, will deny the Newtonian theory?

"To foretell events, to pierce the heavy mist that conceals from us the secrets of fate, is a universal longing of the human heart. This longing is felt in the hut of the savage as well as in the palaces of the great. So fierce and universal a desire must be one of Nature's mysteries. She has already opened our eyes to so many, it cannot be that she means to deceive us in this one.

"If we do not read in the great book eternally open before us in the skies, as we have already done in that book the leaves of which are in the strata of the earth, it is because we have only learned to spell, as yet, in the alphabet of mystery."

Before we parted at Pittsburg, a day or two after this conversation, I had given Jackson the necessary data for calculating a horoscope; and, in the course of a few months, I received from him a letter, which I preserved, enclosing a scheme of my nativity. As any one who may have calculated these schemes by the rules must know, a horoscope may be interpreted in various, even contradictory terms, by different persons; and this was no exception to the rule. The only reason I had for remembering it at all was, that our destinies seemed to run in parallel lines; and, so far, it was remarkable. It was this peculiarity that caused Jackson to communicate with me, and the reason why I laid it carefully aside for a re-examination.

The several planets were placed in their respective houses above and below the horizon; and Saturn being near the meridian, and approaching a square with the moon, great danger was to be apprehended by the native at the period when the aspect became complete. Mars also bore a threatening aspect; while Jupiter was below the horizon, and semi-sextile, which was not altogether unfavorable. There was no trine, and the sextile was weak. Altogether, from the evil aspect of the square of Saturn, which threatened an opposition, — that most dreaded of all the evil aspects of the heavens, — the scheme was quite dangerous and malign.

The precise time and nature of the threatened danger, requiring a second calculation, accompanied the scheme, prognosticating the culmination of the malign aspect within some ten years, or during the first days of May, 1863; at which time the native ran great risk of life and fortunes: but, in case he survived that peril, the ominous period would never again recur.

In his letter Jackson says, "I have gone over these calculations several times, as their result is almost an exact reproduction of my own. . . . It is clear to me that we shall both be exposed to a common danger at the time indicated."

Having but little faith in the almost-forgotten and altogether-repudiated science of astrology, I took little heed of either his scheme of nativity or his letter, regarding the former as ingenious, but as merely a proof of an ardent and somewhat enthusiastic temperament; while I little imagined, at that time, that the rather unpolished and rugged exterior of Lieut. Jackson concealed a character destined to become famous among his countrymen.

XXXIV.

SOON after the events of the Italian campaign of 1858, ending with the battle of Solferino, I found myself at Strasburg in company with several officers returning to Paris, who had served either in the French army, or in that of its allies the Piedmontese. These gentlemen were of various nationalities and ages, and met every evening at the Café du Lion, where the campaign, and other subjects congenial to military men, were discussed, according to the custom in Continental Europe.

My particular comrade and friend was a Russian colonel, who had served in the artillery of King Victor Emanuel, partly for exercise in a professional way, and partly, I think, to ease his mind by an occasional shot at the Austrians, to whom, like many of his countrymen, he certainly bore no good will. One evening, the tables being all filled, as we were about to leave the café to take one on the sidewalk, we were politely invited by an elderly officer with the epaulets of a *chef de bataillon*, and wearing several orders, among which we remarked that of the iron crown, — now seldom seen, — to take seats at his table. Accepting the hospitable invitation, we were soon at ease; and the conversation became quite animated.

Military discipline happened to be the theme; and the Russian at once vaunted that of his master the czar, depicting the stolid devotion of the Russian private soldier, his perfect submission, and total indifference to death, although the army is entirely recruited from the class of serfs.

I ventured to remark that all this might be true, but that the French soldier also possessed a deep sense of moral obligation towards the necessities of discipline; and, in addition to those passive qualities, had, usually, skill and knowledge sufficient to enable him to act when deprived of his officers, which, possibly, the other could not do. I also said that I had never heard of any considerable mutiny in the French army like that of the British navy at the Nore, for example; or of such disorganization as that of the British army at Badajos.

The old *chef de bataillon* then said it was true that examples of the kind were very rare in the French army, but that he had known of one such in his experience; and that, if we had the patience to listen, he would give us the details.

"It happened in this very city," added the old officer; "but all accounts of it were suppressed by the government of the time, and, as far as I am aware, have not as yet passed into the domain of history."

As I have never met with any account of this transaction, I will venture to transcribe it here, as given by its narrator: —

"In the memorable year 1815 I belonged to the Army of the Rhine, which, having valiantly fought during the summer of that year, fell back upon Strasburg, numbering fifteen thousand men, under the command of Gen. Count Rapp.

"The place was invested by the Austrians; but, in consequence of the political aspect just then, there was a truce between us. The Bourbons had returned under the allied auspices, and had made many concessions, which were unfavorably regarded by the army, among which was the surrender of some strong places and a quantity of war material. Our general also received an order to disband and disarm the Army of the Rhine; which it was difficult for him to execute, there being heavy arrears due the troops. After much negotiation with the royal ministers,

Rapp sent his chief of staff in person to Paris; but a deaf ear was turned to his remonstrances and warnings, and he was compelled to return with but four hundred thousand francs, — a sum totally insufficient to discharge the arrears. His arrival at Strasburg at once destroyed all hopes of a peaceful accommodation with the troops; and, although he succeeded in obtaining an additional amount of a hundred and sixty thousand francs from the municipal authorities, the mutiny at once burst forth.

"At eight, A. M., of the 2d of September, about sixty non-commissioned officers of the different regiments of the garrison assembled in one of the bastions of the place, and drew up a paper, stating that the Army of the Rhine would consent to obey the order for its disbandment, only upon the following conditions: viz., first, that the officers, sub-officers, and privates should receive *all* the pay due them; second, that all should depart on the same day, taking with them their arms, baggage, and forty rounds of ball-cartridge for each soldier.

"This programme having been approved by the meeting of delegates, five of their number were appointed to call upon the commanding general in order to communicate this unanimous decision of the troops.

"The five delegates repaired to the palace; and, after some hesitation, were admitted to the presence of Rapp, who received them in his bath, and listened to their respectful announcement until the term 'conditions' was mentioned. This word made him furious; and, springing up, he exclaimed, 'Conditions! You wish to impose conditions on *me?*' The anger of the general awed the delegates, who had not as yet lost all respect for authority; and they took their leave.

"The delegation then made their report to the rest of the non-commissioned officers, about five hundred in number, who immediately proceeded to adopt further measures, well knowing that a man like Rapp could never be intimidated. They had already committed themselves by their action, and felt that they must carry the affair to a termination of some kind, if they wished it to be successful.

"Accordingly they informed the soldiers of their respective corps of their repulse, and received from them further instructions. The meeting, held upon the Place d'Armes, unanimously resolved to depose their officers temporarily; and, having elected other officers in their places from the sub-officers, chose as chief, for the time being, the sergeant-major of the Seventh Light Infantry. This man was named Dalhousie, of remote Scotch, but immediate French ancestry, and was well known in the army as a person of capacity, courage, and a certain soldierly loquacity peculiar to himself. Having been informed of his election, he addressed his comrades in the following pithy speech: —

"'Comrades! you wish to be paid your arrears in full? Am I right in saying that is your object in assembling here?'

"'Yes, yes!' shouted all present.

"'Well, then,' said Dalhousie, 'if you promise to obey me implicitly, to abstain from license or disorder, to respect property, and to protect everybody, I swear by my head that you shall be paid to the uttermost farthing within twenty-four hours!'

"This short allocution was received with applause; and the new general-in-chief proceeded to officer the troops afresh, choosing the drum-major of the Fifty-eighth of the line as his chief of staff.

"The troops then returned to their barracks.

"The *générale* was then beaten; and the whole army, excepting the grand guards, pickets, and smaller guards, — cavalry, artillery, and infantry, — appeared upon the Place d'Armes in imposing array under their new officers. Meanwhile, Gen. Rapp, informed of the revolt, sallied forth from his headquarters, accompanied by his staff, and proceeded to the same place to stop the seditious movement. The operations of the troops, however, had been conducted with such celerity, that he arrived just as the columns, followed by the populace, were debouching upon the square by all the streets leading to it. They were immediately formed in line of battle by battalions in mass, and commanded to fix bayonets. The cavalry drew sabres, and two full batteries were loaded with grape, before the very eyes of the general.

"Whenever Gen. Rapp attempted to address the troops, his voice was drowned by loud vociferations; and the guns were kept trained upon him and his staff as they shifted their ground. One artillerist, especially, adjusted his piece so carefully and persistently, following every movement of the general, that the latter advanced, and addressed him thus: 'Well, miserable, do you wish to kill me? Fire, if you dare! Here I am, at the muzzle of your gun!' — 'Ah! *mon général*,' cried the soldier, 'I was with you at Dantzic. I would freely give you my life; but my comrades want their pay, and I am compelled to act with them.' And he ominously blew his port fire.

"It was here in this very square, gentlemen," said the old officer, warming up with his story, "that Count Rapp, deafened by the clamor of the troops, who seemed to be intent only upon preventing him from being heard, and followed by a tumultuous throng, finally decided to return to the palace.

"The troops kept close behind him; and, as soon as he entered the gates, all the different entrances were occupied, interior and exterior guards were detailed and posted, and sentinels doubled at every post, including the staircase leading to the general's private apartments. At the same time the telegraph and the military chest were taken possession of, and another guard sent to the Maison Rouge, the lodging of the Austrian general Volkman, the commissioner, for his protection. The drawbridges were raised; and all communication with the country outside the place was cut off, or permitted only by passes signed by the new commandant. The new chief of staff, with a trumpet, repaired to the headquarters of the allied troops, and signified to their general, that, while he continued to observe the truce, the garrison would use no hostile act towards his troops; but that, if they attempted to profit by the misunderstanding between the French general and his soldiers, the latter would resist with their whole force. Dalhousie established his headquarters upon the Place d'Armes, and created two commissions, — one upon subsistence, composed of commissary-sergeants; and the other upon finances, of sergeant-majors. They were declared permanent, and deliberated upon the most suitable modes of maintaining public tranquillity, and assuring the city against the possibility of surprise either from without or within.

"The guards of the citadel and of all interior posts were doubled, and the cantonments outside the place re-enforced. The troops bivouacked on the public squares, and no military precautions which the most zealous prudence could suggest were forgotten. It was forbidden for a soldier to enter any place in which spirituous liquors or beer were sold, under pain of death; and the same penalty was denounced against any one guilty of pillage, disorder, or insubordination. In order to further assure the public tranquillity, a bulletin was ordered to be issued every six hours, containing full information of the situation of affairs. The military chests were examined, and estimates of the necessary sums required to liquidate the arrears of pay made out in full. Dalhousie convened the municipal council, to which he made full representations of the reasons which led the army to revolt against its superior officers, and besought its members to take counsel together upon the subject of raising the funds necessary to discharge the arrears.

"Meanwhile the troops maintained an ominous silence, holding no conversation with their former officers or with the citizens; which conduct, so rare among French troops, occasioned great uneasiness, and plunged the city into deep despondency.

"Dalhousie at last received a message from the council, informing him that they consented to supply the necessary funds; thus yielding to their fears what they had refused to prayers.

"The division and brigade generals and other officers who had been deprived of their 'commands,' having made trouble by their efforts to bring the troops back to obedience, were shut up in their quarters, and guarded. The citizens were at last re-assured by the continued good order which prevailed among the troops; and the following 'order of the day' was issued: 'All goes well: the citizens have provided funds, and the payments have commenced. (Signed) GARNISON.'

"The *sobriquet* of Gen. Garnison was given to Dalhousie. The secret instigators of the insurrection now saw that the expected riot and bloodshed would not be inaugurated unless they succeeded in exciting an *émeute* among the troops: so they sent a chasseur to the Place d'Armes to proclaim that Gen. Rapp had attempted to smuggle money out of the place; and that, in consequence, he must be put to death as a traitor. This effort was defeated. The troops imprisoned their chief in order to carry out their plans; but they harbored no animosity against him. His reputation as a man of honor remained intact, and his integrity was no more doubted than his courage. Such open provocation to murder excited distrust, and the troops only became more circumspect. Similar efforts to excite mobs among them failed of their desired effect, including a direct attempt to assassinate the general.

"An event that occurred about the same time did much to quiet the turbulently-disposed among the troops, and to dispose them to return to order. The enemy's line received strong re-enforcements, and sallied from its cantonments before the place, approaching the division in observation without the walls. This apparent concert between the movements of the Austrians and events within the city, which it would appear improbable they could have been cognizant of, caused much speculation among the garrison. Re-enforcements from the place were sent to the outside division, and demonstrations made, which had the effect of checking the hostile movements of the enemy. It may be that the Austrians did not care to meet so redoubtable an enemy as the Army of the Rhine; or perhaps they preferred to await the measures adopted by their partisans within the walls. At any rate, the enemy returned to his original position; while the garrison continued, calmly and persistently, to pursue its proposed end, — the payment of its arrears. Strasburg presented a spectacle of perfect order in the midst of disorder, and of severe discipline maintained in an army in revolt. Dalhousie sent to Rapp a deputation, composed of the sergeant-governor of the place and six general sergeants, which was received by the general with some asperity. He pronounced them the dupes of designing men, and unworthy to wear the French uniform. Their spokesman told Count Rapp that it was true they were in revolt; but that the rest of the armies had been paid off, and they only asked for their just dues, — the poor pittance for all their sacrifices of blood and risk of life, and which was necessary to pay the expenses to their homes. Rapp answered that he had represented their case to the ministry, but that he was unable to procure more than the four hundred thousand francs, which they were welcome to divide among the different regiments. This they positively declined, saying that the whole arrears must be liquidated. The interview was ended by Gen. Rapp's ordering the deputation from his presence, telling them he blushed at the idea of holding further discussion with mutineers.

"It is my belief that Rapp was annoyed by the news that

his compatriots, the Strasburgers, had yielded to fear what he could not obtain from them by entreaty.

"At last the loan was effected, the paymasters received the money, and the agitation subsided. Payments were made to the troops in the usual form, which having been completed during the night, the *générale* was again heard in the morning; and all the posts and guards were withdrawn from the palace, while the whole garrison assembled on the square as before. Gen. Garnison then read a proclamation addressed to the soldiers of the Army of the Rhine, in which he complimented them on their boldness in asserting their rights. This boldness had compromised them with the civil and military authorities; but he said that no danger menaced any one in consequence, save the sub-officers, who had controlled the revolt in order that equal justice might be done to all. He then appealed to them to preserve good order and discipline, in order that the sub-officers might have immunity from punishment. It was then announced, that having served with honor, having received their pay in full, and being Frenchmen, they must deliver up their horses, arms, and government-stores, and submit themselves to the orders of the king.

"The sergeant-general, Dalhousie, then ordered the two divisions of infantry, the cavalry, and artillery, to defile before him; and conducted the whole force to the prefecture, where white standards were distributed to the regiments. The troops then returned to their barracks and to the authority of their officers, who immediately repaired to the palace to tender their congratulations to their general, Count Rapp.

"Dalhousie was there present; and the general generously gave him a pardon in consideration of the order and discipline he had preserved while the army was in revolt. I am entirely ignorant of his after-life. Thus ended a mutiny without precedent in our military annals. I have never thought it was instigated by the Austrians; for they had no motive for so doing. The Bourbons were in Paris, the emperor a fugitive, and foreign diplomats were at the moment making out the new map of humiliated France. A plot against the life of Rapp seems yet more improbable. Austria, it is true, might have desired to occupy Strasburg temporarily; but the advantage would hardly have compensated for the sanguinary combat sure to have been provoked by an attempt in that direction. No: it appears to me more simple and natural to look upon the whole affair as an explosion, a revindication, perfectly legal in principle, made by men who could not be supposed to possess great regard for the unknown power which had changed their colors, and which, to fill up the measure of its impolicy, wished to disarm without paying them. This would have been too great an humiliation for men who had performed their duties so well, and who kept aloof from the politics of the day.

"In my opinion, the revolt was inevitable, under all the circumstances of the case; but we must admire the discipline which triumphed over all its imminent peril, and secured to its leaders an almost glorious impunity. All this illustrated the excellent spirit which distinguishes our sub-officers and soldiers, and which permits them to respect a substitution of power impossible in aristocratic armies."

In thanking the *chef de bataillon* for his narration, we both agreed that the mutiny of Strasburg could never have taken place in any other army than the French without degenerating into a scene of fearful license and demoralization; and we separated for the night, with an offer from the old officer to introduce us on the next morning to another institution of the French army.

This was the *doyenne* of those very useful ladies, the *cantinières*, then at the dépôt of the fourth of the line, — Madame Thérèse Jourdan, *veuve* Patru, at that time ninety-five years old, who, notwithstanding her great age, suffered no particular infirmity, enjoying all her mental and physical faculties. She had entered that regiment as *cantinière* when fourteen, and had never since quitted it. Her husband, Capt. Patru, was killed at Lutzen; and after his death she had resumed the *bidon*, which she had retained until about three years before we saw her, her great age no longer permitting her to serve *la goutte* to the soldiers. She enjoyed a small pension, contributed by the officers of the fourth, in gratitude for her services to the regiment. These services had been meritorious and extensive indeed; for she had been an eye-witness of all the great scenes recorded in the history of the armies of the republic and of the first empire.

XXXV.

RETURNING home in 1860, one of the last of those o whom I took leave in Paris was Major Philip Kearny. "You return," said he, "to take part in a long and sanguinary civil war. The men of the South will consent to no other solution of the questions at issue. For years they have accustomed themselves to the idea of an inevitable collision in defence of what they regard as their constitutional rights, as set forth in the pestilential doctrines and impracticable theories of Calhoun. Abstractions they certainly are; but the South will expend all their strength and wealth in their support. The politicians, both North and South, have so complicated the affairs of the nation for their own personal ends, that they cannot be adjusted by peaceful measures. The Gordian knot must be cut by the sword. Ignorant of the art of war in all its varied aspects as are the Northern people; despising every trained soldier as a charlatan; easily imposed upon by the most ignorant pretender to skill and experience in our profession, as they must necessarily be, owing to their lack of military education and exercises, — I have still a presentiment that they will emerge victoriously from the contest. I know the Southern people well. I acknowledge, that, man for man, of the two peoples — for we are now two distinct peoples — they are the best soldiers: still, I know, that, in the administration of public affairs, there is nothing practical about them. In the end, their warlike energies will be wasted in the field from sheer ignorance of business-matters, such as the commissariat and its innumerable details; and hence they will gain nothing by the superior martial qualities of their soldiers, which are undeniable. Go! You will be on the winning side; and I shall soon be with you on the other side of the Atlantic. Somehow we will be triumphant; and, should we live to the end of a three or four years' war, we shall see the country settled on a new basis, stronger and more united than ever."

I quote these words of Kearny to show the prevailing sentiment among the old officers of the army and navy as to the result of the political *imbroglio*, and the probable duration of the war. The people of the North could not or would not then believe that any danger was threatened to themselves by the state of public affairs, and to the last hour went on with their business and social enjoyments in perfect confidence that they would be left undisturbed to pursue the even tenor of their way. They were confirmed in this security by the politicians intrusted with the government, who assured their constituents that there would be no war, or a very little one; and, thus re-assured, they kept on in their usual avocations with all the absorbing devotion to affairs that distinguishes our countrymen. The conspiracy grew and strengthened in the Southern States; while the imbecility of the administration encouraged the secessionists to perfect all their plans for a vast insurrection, until the attack on Fort Sumter aroused the sleeping North to a sense of the real condition of national affairs.

All this has become a part of our annals; and I shall confine myself to what I saw and experienced in the momentous events that succeeded the direct attack by the Southern conspirators upon the nation's life, and the consequent uprising of the Northern people. Stimulated by the attitude of the North, the administration resorted to feeble and uncertain measures for defence, while continuing to assure the world, through the medium of the State department, that the war would be but a trivial affair of sixty or ninety days at farthest. How weak and contemptible these measures were was illustrated in the hastily-equipped and undisciplined military mob which met its final discomfiture at Bull Run. This disgraceful affair, however, made it plain to the North that the men of the South were in terrible earnest; that soldiers enlisted for three months' service were incompetent to check the insurrection; and that the much-vaunted militia-system could not be relied upon to furnish either officers or soldiers for regular warfare. This latter national institution broke down at once, for the sufficient reason that it was impossible to mobilize it for service, although the people had been told by militia generals and Fourth-of-July orators, from the time of the Revolution, that it was perfect as a system of military defence. This was believed, because it is pleasant to imagine that we are all citizen-soldiers, subject to no such requisitions upon our time and personal service as are made in other countries, intended to familiarize the population with the rudiments of the military art, notwithstanding the same expedient had been tested and failed in 1812 and 1846.

True, the same system prevailed at the South; but it must be remembered, that, in that section, there flourished a higher martial spirit; for in the war with Mexico, fourteen years before, the Southern States furnished more than forty thousand men to the general service, while only about half that number was contributed by the more populous North.

The danger was imminent, and must be met; and, instead of a useless domestic military organization, a system still more objectionable was adopted, — that of volunteer regiments in sufficient number to fill the quotas of the several States, officered by persons selected, not for their professional skill or experience, but according to the pecuniary aid they could render in raising and equipping recruits, or their political influence. Men, material of war, and money, were lavishly offered: for the people had said to themselves, "This sort of thing must stop;" and they far outran the government in war-spirit and determination.

Like others of my countrymen, I had already offered my services to the General Government; but was assured they would not be required, as no increase of the navy was contemplated. Having passed the age at which my enlistment as a private soldier could be legally permitted, and feeling bound to aid my country to the extent of my ability in the trials she was about to enter upon, after having been educated to the profession of arms in her service, I tendered my service to the governor of the State of my residence, and was appointed colonel of the Seventh New-Jersey Volunteer Infantry.

I joined my regiment at Trenton, and was mustered into the army "for three years or the war" on the 31st August, 1861; entering upon my duties immediately at the camp near that place. Recruits came rapidly in, all men of the best class, — young, patriotic, and athletic, principally from the agricultural districts, — and all eager to begin their new career, and to acquire a knowledge of the duties of a soldier. They were far superior to those who enlisted at a subsequent date, when the highest bounties could attract to the service only inferior material. These men seemed to be conscious that they must take the affairs of the country into their own hands in order to retain their liberties, as well as to repel the charge of neglect of their honor which had been made against them.

My ranks were soon filled up to the maximum strength; and in less than a month we arrived in Washington, and encamped on Meridian Hill. Instruction now began in earnest; and in a few weeks I had the satisfaction of seeing my raw recruits transformed into tolerably proficient soldiers. I applied at once the principles of discipline I had learned in a hard school — the United-States navy — firmly and uncompromisingly; as I knew, that, once taught, they would never be forgotten. No fault was condoned or pardoned; but certain punishment, swiftly and surely applied, followed every infraction of the rules established for the government of the army. In a very short time the men understood this: and the result was eminently satisfactory; for punishment ceased almost entirely. It was very hard for these young men to stand sentinel for eight hours together with loaded knapsacks, to be made "living statuary" on a pork-barrel for a pedestal, and to endure other penalties known to military discipline; but the lessons of such experience were lasting, and the recruit who had once gone through the course enjoyed immunity ever afterwards. The general condition of the army at this time was deplorable; and the large force collected, although of excellent raw material, but little better than a mere mob. Desertion was a common occurrence among officers as well as soldiers; and the streets of Washington were filled with persons in uniform, who, by their reckless behavior, evinced not only total disregard of military discipline, but also of the claims of respectability, and even decency.

Of the regular officers of the army, few had ever seen a whole regiment together in the field; while their knowledge of garrison-duty was acquired in some frontier post in the Far West, or a fort occupied by two or three companies. Gen. McClellan was charged with reducing this mass of heterogeneous elements to order; and he accomplished his task in about three months, converting the mob into an efficient and disciplined army. When he assumed command in the summer of 1861, the troops in and around Washington consisted of about fifty thousand infantry, seven hundred cavalry, and six hundred artillerymen, with thirty guns; while their only organization was the same defective one of "provisional brigades" as at Bull Run. There was literally no nucleus of regulars to form upon; for the army had been utterly disorganized by secession. It was necessary, therefore, to begin *ab initio*, to form an army on a scale which the nation had never dreamed of. To say that McClellan acquitted himself creditably in this colossal work is to accord him scant justice: for the fact is, that his achievement was one which entitles him to a place in the first rank of soldiers; and its excellent results were apparent in the army up to its final dissolution.

He at once established a stringent police-system, applying it to all ranks; sent inefficient and objectionable officers before boards of examination; instituted a course of instruction; and kept the troops in their respective camps and posts. Grand guards and picket-duty was regularly performed; and, in course of time, the troops offered a creditable spectacle to the military critic. Without dwelling on this subject, let it suffice to say, that, at the end of three months, McClellan found himself at the head of an efficient army of a hundred thousand infantry, ten thousand cavalry, and twelve thousand artillerymen, with five hundred guns. There was, besides, an engineer-corps with pontoon and wagon trains, conducted by competent officers of the quartermaster and commissary departments; and the ordnance was abundantly supplied with reserve ammunition and supply-trains. This bare statement of the enormous amount of labor achieved in an incredibly short space of time hardly conveys an adequate idea of its proportions, except to practical military men; and, for this reason, McClellan's reputation is higher abroad than at home. What I have summed up here by no means comprises all this intelligent officer's labors in the period named; for a system of defences was planned and executed under his direction, by which Washington was completely covered from attack, the works forming a line of circumvallation over thirty-three miles in extent. These earthworks — consisting of detached and engaged fortifications connected with curtains, provided with bastions, redoubts, and wide ditches — were armed with heavy cannon, and were estimated for a garrison of seventy thousand men. Later they saved the capital from capture by the confederates, and permitted Grant to keep a tight grasp upon the throat of the waning insurrection before Petersburg, without weakening his army by detaching troops for the defence of Washington.

In point of discipline and organization, the Army of the Potomac made no improvement under the successors of McClellan, although it achieved more decisive results in the field: and we have the emphatic declaration of the most illustrious of them, — Meade, — that, "had there been no McClellan, there could have been no Grant; for the former fashioned the weapons with which the work was performed."

At this point I have thought it best to close the record of my military service. The career of the Army of the Potomac is matter of history; and I could add little to the numerous and detailed accounts of its sufferings and its triumphs. But there is another and more potent reason which bids me pause here. I could not tell the story of my connection with that army with the judicial impartiality which should characterize the historian and the narrator of grave events. I could not withhold denunciation of incompetency and perfidy. I could not write of the first two years of the war without giving utterance to righteous indignation, aroused by the wickedness of men in high places, which hampered the army, and protracted the civil strife far beyond its necessary limits.

I served in the army until after the battle of Chancellorsville, participating in all its important engagements, and, the greater part of the time, commanding a brigade. At the battle above named, I was an involuntary witness of an event which had an important bearing on the issue of the war, and which has been the subject of prolonged controversy. I refer to the death of Stonewall Jackson. The circumstances under which I acquired the right to give testimony in the matter were somewhat remarkable; and I here give a full statement of them.

The left of my brigade-line lay near the plank-road at Chancellorsville; and, after night had fallen, I rode forward, according to my invariable habit, to inspect my picket-line. The moon had risen, and partially illuminated the woods. I began my inspection on the right of the picket-line, progressing gradually to the left, where I stopped to rectify the post of a sentinel not far from the plank-road. While thus engaged, I heard the sound of hoofs from the direction of the enemy's line, and paused to listen. Soon a cavalcade appeared approaching us. The foremost horseman detached himself from the main body, which halted not far from us, and, riding cautiously nearer, seemed to try to pierce the gloom. He was so close to us, that the soldier nearest me levelled his rifle for a shot at him; but I forbade him, as I did not wish to have our position revealed; and it would have been useless to kill the man, whom I judged to be a staff-officer making a reconnoissance.

Having completed his observations, this person rejoined the group in his rear, and all returned at a gallop. The clatter of hoofs soon ceased to be audible; and the silence of the night was unbroken, save by the melancholy cries of the whippoorwill, which were heard in one continued wail, like spirit-voices; when the horizon was lighted up by a sudden flash in the direction of the enemy, succeeded by the well-known rattle of a volley of musketry from at least a battalion. A second volley quickly followed the first; and I heard cries in the same direction.

Fearing that some of our troops might be in that locality, and that there was danger of our firing upon friends, I left my orderly, and rode towards the confederate lines.

A riderless horse dashed past me towards our lines; and I reined up in presence of a group of several persons gathered around a man lying on the ground, apparently badly wounded. I saw at once that these were confederate officers, and visions of the Libby began to flit through my mind; but reflecting that I was well armed and mounted, and that I had on the great-coat of a private soldier such as was worn by both parties, I sat still, regarding the group in silence, but prepared to use either my spurs or my sabre, as occasion might demand.

The silence was broken by one of the confederates, who appeared to regard me with astonishment: then, speaking in a tone of authority, he ordered me to "ride up there and see what troops those were," indicating the rebel position. I instantly made a gesture of assent, and rode slowly in the direction indicated, until out of sight of the group; then made a circuit round it, and returned within my own lines. Just as I had answered the challenge of our picket, the section of our artillery posted on the plank-road began firing; and I could plainly hear the grape crashing through the trees near the spot occupied by the group of confederate officers.

About a fortnight afterwards, I saw a Richmond newspaper at the camp at Falmouth, in which were detailed the circumstances of the death of Stonewall Jackson. These left no doubt in my own mind that the person I had seen lying on the ground was that officer, and that his singular prediction — mentioned previously in these pages — had been verified.

The following is an extract from the newspaper account: —

"Gen. Jackson, having gone some distance in front of his line on Saturday evening, was returning about eight o'clock, attended by his staff. The cavalcade was, in the darkness, mistaken for a body of the enemy's cavalry, and fired on by a regiment of his own corps."

Then, after detailing what took place after the general fell from his horse, the account proceeds: —

"The turnpike was utterly deserted, with the exception of Capts. Wilbourn and Wynn; but, in the skirting of thicket on the left, some person was observed by the side of the wood, sitting his horse motionless and silent. The unknown individual was clad in a dark dress, which strongly resembled the federal uniform; but it seemed impossible that he could have penetrated to that spot without being discovered, and what followed seemed to prove that he belonged to the confederates. Capt. Wilbourn directed him to ride up there and see what troops those were,— the men who fired on Jackson; and the stranger rode slowly in the direction pointed out, but never returned with any answer. Who this silent personage was is left to posterity," &c. — *Richmond Enquirer, May* 12, 1863.

Jackson's death happened in strange coincidence with his horoscopic prediction made years before: but the coincidence was, I believe, merely fortuitous; and I mention it here only to show what mysterious " givings-out " we sometimes experience in life.

PUFFS FROM PICKET-PIPES.

PUFFS FROM PICKET-PIPES.

AFTER the disastrous repulse of Burnside before the confederate works at Fredericksburg, the Army of the Potomac returned to its cantonments in Stafford County, Va.; and the work of its re-organization began under Hooker, who had succeeded to the command only to repeat the blunders of his predecessor at Chancellorsville.

The place chosen for the winter encampment of the army was a *cul de sac* between the *embouchures* of the Potomac and the Rappahannock; which rivers formed the two sides of a triangle, of which it was necessary to guard the base only to be perfectly safe from an attack. The disadvantage of the position was, that the army could not leave it without crossing the wide and deep Rappahannock, the fords of which were all carefully guarded by the vigilant enemy.

The country north and east of Fredericksburg was guarded by a strong picket-force of our troops, extending from the Rappahannock to the Potomac; while our cavalry patrolled its front for twenty miles along the left bank of the former river.

Picket-duty was performed in turn by detachments from all the corps of the army, comprising a brigade of infantry; and a general commanded the whole grand guard, whose temporary headquarters were at a farm-house a few hundred yards to the rear of the line.

Fires, and smoking even, being forbidden while on picket-duty at the advanced posts, a pipe was invented by some ingenious soldier, the muzzle of which was turned down. instead of upward, as in ordinary pipes; and, this being covered, no fire was visible to any person in the vicinity of the smoker. These were called picket-pipes; and were skilfully carved by the men from laurel-roots, and from a soft white stone common in that region.

The farmhouse mentioned was resorted to by the loungers on picket-duty; and beneath its roof many a thrilling tale of adventure on the debatable ground in our front, travelled in every direction by our scouts and outpost patrols, and those of the enemy, was told to eager hearers.

Story-telling is a favorite amusement both of soldiers and sailors in their idle moments; and a skilful narrator is sure of attentive and interested listeners in such an audience, especially if he relates his own personal experiences, as not uncommonly happens.

I have often regretted that I did not take notes of many "yarns" I have thus heard from the lips of some who possessed the talent of story-telling not inferior to that of the Eastern professional *raconteurs* I have often seen in the coffee-houses of the Levant, whose language I could not understand, but whose graceful and vivid pantomime could hardly be misinterpreted.

One fine moonlight night at my headquarters, during my turn of duty on picket, a group of officers were enjoying their pipes, when it was proposed to vary the evening's amusements by story-telling, — it being stipulated that each one should draw upon his own experience for his material; and, the party being tired of euchre and other games, the proposition was received with universal favor.

As in military councils and court-martials, the youngest was deputed to speak first; and a young lieutenant of infantry accordingly began, with the usual apologies of youth and inexperience, as follows: —

THE LIEUTENANT'S STORY.

LIKE most of my comrades in the volunteer army, I was not brought up to the military profession, but adopted it under pressure of the times which have found us all so unprepared. Indeed, I may say that I never have thought seriously of adopting any career involving great trials, hazards, and privations; least of all, the army.

After finishing my education, I passed the time as agreeably as I could at home and abroad, without a thought that my idling was ever to end, or our country to be disturbed in its seeming ease and quietude.

Only the year before the breaking-out of this war, being in Paris, I lodged at the Hôtel de Bade on the Italian Boulevard, where I met persons of an entirely different class from those who frequent those *caravanseras* in which Americans delight to spend their time and their apparently inexhaustible supplies of ready money, without, I fear, receiving in return a *quid pro quo*, in most cases.

Strange to say, I had never, as yet, witnessed a scene said to be the gayest in the world, and which every one who visits the rollicking French capital is familiar with from the start, stranger or Frenchman, although I had been for several years an *habitué* of Paris.

The truth is, I had most agreeable society at my command, and cared not to resort to public amusements to pass away time, then of some value to me, employed as I was in acquiring educational and social information, varied by amusements peculiar to the French people, but hardly appreciated by foreigners. Shall I say that the latter are hardly sufficiently advanced in civilization to profit by the advantages alluded to? the majority, at least, of those who visit France in the capacity of ordinary tourists.

I had heard among my acquaintances that intrigue of the old sort — that of which we read in works of fiction and the like — was dead at present in Paris, and that new fashions had taken place of the old *modes*, not only in dress, but in manners.

It was, then, simple curiosity, or that indefinable feeling which moves us toward any thing unknown or mysterious, that impelled my steps to the Rue Lepelletier, to witness, for the first time, the great *bal d'opéra*. I entered the *salle* soon after its opening at midnight. I was in plain evening-dress, and, of course, unmasked; and strolled about for some hours, amused and diverted by the motley scenes around me, the grotesqueness of the maskers, and the vigorous and exaggerated style of the dancers, — whole quadrilles seeming to have lost their senses.

Soon wearying of these gymnastics, imported from the Latin quarter, and that of Breda, I strolled out into the lobby.

At the door I was detained by a crowd of revellers; and on the domino of one of them — a female masker — my button became so entangled, that it was necessary to tear it (the fabric) in order to extricate ourselves. The fair mask herself gave me the needed assistance, and endured the tearing of the rich texture without a protest, as if it were indifferent to her. I had already seen enough of the ball. The mien of the masker interested me. We exchanged a few words, which convinced me of her intelligence; and, willing to be amused, I finished by offering my arm, which was accepted with *nonchalance*, rather unpropitious, I thought, for the perfection of a better acquaintance.

We finally took seats in a cabinet occupied by a few couples, who seemed entirely too much interested in their own affairs to desire to interfere with our privacy. For my part, I imagined that my fair partner was of that large and influential class in Paris whose proverbial extravagance and "speed" have won for them a name of which I could never see the aptness, — the "half-world."

I could now examine at leisure the appearance of my companion, so far as it was not concealed by her mask and the folds of her domino. I could see that she was tall and slender, and that her movements were undulating and full of grace. Her toilet was admirable, although severely simple. Her domino was of black satin, the *camail* trimmed with exquisite lace, — the fairy net which had caught me at first, — and her mask of the same, with a thick *barbe*, through which I could see neither her hair, nor even the tint of her complexion.

She was irreproachably *gantée*, and her small feet delicately shod with slippers that might have been worn by Cinderella. Her air was that of a woman, not of the half, but of the whole world, who was accustomed to good society, and unfamiliar with these assemblies. We began to converse; and, to my astonishment, I found that my name and country were not unknown to her. However, I would deny neither: indeed, I saw it would have been useless.

The lady knew me, as the saying is, "like a book," and sketched my character and some of the incidents of my life; urged me to correct certain faults she pointed out to me, and of whose existence I was fully conscious; and, in short, gave me most excellent advice, without inflicting a single wound on my *amour propre*.

Every trace of hesitation and apathy soon disappeared; and she showed such sagacity, such refinement, such delicacy of expression and of feeling, that I was stupefied.

Gliding from topic to topic, she passed in review society, literature, the opera, and the publicists of the day, relating many anecdotes *à propos* of each, and uttering the most sparkling witticisms with a grace of attitude and manner quite irresistible.

Dazzled by such brilliancy, I kept silence, and merely listened in delighted wonder.

"Is it possible that I do not know you,— you who know me so well?" I said at length, impatient of my enforced passiveness in our *tête-à-tête*.

"You do not know me, I assure you," returned the mask. "If I should show you my face, you would see it for the first time."

"Where, then, have you learned what you have revealed to me? Are you a sorceress?"

"Perhaps; or I may have divined what I have said to you by my knowledge of human nature. Do you fancy yourself the only object of my study?"

I did not dare to discuss the question; and the demand gave me no time to reply in fitting terms.

She changed the subject, opened a new chapter, and exhibited herself under a new face. Never did chameleon change more quickly, or with better effect. Engrossed by the conversation, I heeded not the jests of the passers, nor replied to several direct attacks by the merry maskers; and, when the last harlequin and pierrot retired arm in arm, was startled to hear an intimation that the ball had closed, and that it was necessary for us to withdraw.

"Already!" exclaimed my new acquaintance.

We had been talking for five hours.

"Permit me to see you home?" I said.

"Impossible!"

"Shall I never see you again?"

"I will think of it."

"You will not tell me who you are?"

She made a gesture of negation.

"Ah, cruel one! you take possession of me, turn my head, and then abandon me as a child throws away a toy of which he is weary. Well, I shall not submit. I will follow you, learn who you are, and force you to avow yourself, to receive me, to love me. After such a delightful evening as we have passed together, I cannot look forward to indifference and oblivion between us. Decide, then, and accept my escort, or I will force it upon you! Come, decide!"

"You would not do that, I am sure; but, if you did, I should succeed in evading you. On the contrary, you must leave me here free, and give your word of honor not to seek to know me, or who I am: in that case, I will make you two concessions greater than you could have hoped for; although, indeed, I had long since resolved to grant them when you had earned them."

"What are they?"

"I will return here next Saturday; and I will give you my portrait until then. You can look at it when I am no longer near you. Do you consent?"

I made her repeat thrice the promise to return. I received from her hand a card photograph in a sealed and perfumed envelope; and, such was my eagerness to behold the lineaments hidden by the mask, that I rushed towards a gas-burner, and tore open the envelope. The original took advantage of my movement, and disappeared in the dense crowd hastening towards the entrance of the opera. After a hasty glance at the portrait, I returned to the spot where I had left my companion; but she was already gone, and a search for her would have been hopeless.

I went to the Café Cardinal on the Boulevard, and drew forth my picture again. I was stupefied by my good fortune. The portrait represented a most lovely and bewitching face and form, — a poet's dream. "Thanks to Minerva and to Venus!" I said under my breath. Such a divine face, and such an intellect! I could hardly believe it possible; yet here was the ocular proof. Like a miser, I bore my treasure home, and tried to sleep. I could not. I gazed again and again at the beautiful face, recalled the five hours that had sped so quickly, and decided that I could not wait a week to see my inamorata. I must discover her immediately, or lose my senses.

You may laugh, gentlemen, but most of you know not the fierce ebullitions of the *sang Gaulois* in the veins of a youth of nineteen. Now, indeed, I should patiently wait for the rendezvous a week, perhaps a fortnight.

Next morning, taking with me the precious photograph, I visited three somnambulists and two clairvoyants. Each told me a different story, and sent me in different directions to search for my mysterious beauty. I must try again. The card I received did not bear the name of the photographer; but it must have been made at some one of the several fashionable establishments of Paris. I visited them all. First, Nadar. I had no eyes for the curiosities and marvels assembled in his *atelier*, which is one of the sights of Paris; no admiration for any other beauties than those of my mistress. I drew out my *carte de visite;* asked the master whether it was his work, and whether he could name the original of the picture, or give me any other information concerning it.

"Monsieur," said the artist, "if I made this portrait, and did not sign it, as is my usual custom, I must have done so for especial reasons: if I did not make it, I have no right to claim the merit of its production. You understand? I regret to say that I cannot reply to your question. As to naming the person you desire to know, that would be still more out of the question. We are a sort of father-confessors, we photographers, and never reveal the secrets confided to us. I am indeed *dé-*

solé that I cannot oblige you; but a little reflection will convince you that I am quite in the line of duty."

From Disderi, from Ken, from Dagron, I received the same answer in substance; and my visits to other establishments had no more encouraging results. I went home in despair.

Where or to whom should I address myself for a solution of the mystery? After some hours of perplexity, I applied to an intimate friend, who finally introduced me to a gentleman distinguished for his perspicacity and intelligence, and who knew his Paris *à fond*. My friend informed me that this person's sagacity amounted almost to the Scottish gift of second-sight, while his amiability was proverbial.

My researches in different directions had occupied all the intervening days; so that it was on the last day before the *bal d'opéra* that I met this gentleman, by appointment, at the Café Foy.

He heard my story to the end without saying a word, only looking meditatively at the famous swallow, painted by Horace Vernet on the ceiling of that celebrated restaurant, for some time; and then the oracle spoke: —

"Go to the rendezvous to-morrow; and, as soon as you see your domino, say to her, 'It pleases me: I am enchanted with it. Present me.'"

Here was another enigma for my already puzzled imagination; but in vain I entreated my Mentor for an explanation.

"I will be at the ball," said he. "I will wait in box number twenty at precisely three hours after midnight. Come then, and tell me the effect you have produced, and you shall know all."

I was forced to be content with this direction and assurance, and retired from the interview with grave doubts as to the faith of my friend.

Saturday, midnight, the hour for the opening of the masked ball at the opera, came at last, finding me punctually at my post, eagerly looking for the black domino. I must have had a very *distrait* air; for I was honored by many comments by the crowd, which I thought very ill timed. It seemed as if a tawdry sultana, who seemed to have marked me for her particular prey, would never cease persecuting me.

At last I caught sight of the sheen of satin, and of a tall, graceful figure, which could belong to no other than my *domino noir*. Parting brusquely from my Oriental houri, I advanced towards her, grasped her hand, and led her aside with a palpitating heart.

I quite forgot the enigmatical phrase I had been instructed to utter; and it only occurred to me when she announced to me her intention of retiring early from the ball.

Hoping to retain her by these words, which I imagined to be a sort of "Open sesame," I repeated them to her. The lady was evidently surprised, complete woman of the world though she was. She made a movement as if embarrassed, but remained silent for a few moments.

"I do not comprehend you," said she in a troubled voice.

"You seem, on the contrary, to comprehend me admirably;" much better, I thought mentally, than I comprehend myself. "What is your reply?"

The answer was confused and hesitating: it rendered matters more obscure between us than ever: and soon after, in a place where the dense crowd hardly permitted individuals to be distinguished, the lady wound suddenly, like a hare, through the groups, and disappeared.

I was eager to have all this explained, as you may suppose; and hastened to box number twenty, where I found my friend and guide in the ever-changing and mysterious kaleidoscope called Paris.

I believed that I had lost my inamorata forever, and was somewhat inclined to reproach him as the cause, even while imploring him to conceal nothing from me if he did not wish me to become an inmate of Charenton. His coolness provoked me.

"My dear young friend," said he, "I was not mistaken, as you have seen; and you shall be enlightened on the situation without further suspense.

"The woman who captivated you was neither more nor less than a marriage-broker. She has a commission (among others) to unite a poor young girl to a rich young man. She has intellect: the girl has beauty. She begins the spell of fascination in person, wearing a mask; for, notwithstanding her elegant figure, I will lay a heavy wager she is old and wrinkled: the face will finish the work. By the aid of love for beauty in the abstract, you could have been so blinded to the deception, that the affair would have gone on until it was too late to withdraw. That is the whole mystery. I suspected it at once from your story. No girl of sixteen, such as that portrait represents, could have the skill and knowledge of the world of your siren. I advised you to apply the test; and it has succeeded. You may now imagine what these women of the world, disappointed as to matrimony, are capable of.

"I once knew a certain countess who possessed two or three *chef d'œuvres* of art. She lay in wait for amateurs, intimating her possession of these treasures, and her desire to sell them. When they came to view them at her apartments, she received them charmingly, and showed the pictures skilfully disposed in a dim light. Then, accidentally as it were, she introduced them to a magnificent creature, who looked her part as well as the countess played hers. She often failed, of course, and results were not always what she hoped for; but, if the plan succeeded once or twice, her profit was considerable.

"Your domino belongs to this school. Thank Heaven! your eyes have been opened before it is too late. Believe me, I am sufficiently rewarded if I have succeeded in unmasking this daring imposture; and you will, I know, do me the favor to warn other possible victims of this one of the many snares that beset their paths.

"It would be very disagreeable to a worthy man to find that he was married to a pretty fool, when he thought he had secured both beauty and intellect in the same person."

The Mentor then took his leave, and I suddenly came upon the intimate friend I have already mentioned. I was now completely cured of my illusion, and warmly thanked him for an introduction to so clear-headed and sagacious a man as he who had just left us. "Ah!" said my friend, "he is indeed surprising in his wits, and has the most superb *sang-froid* I ever saw in mortal man. Last summer, at Baden, I had played heavily, and lost so much that serious consequences threatened, which rendered me more desperate. Your friendly adviser was in the *cursal*, looking on with his usual imperturbability. At last I was reduced to a single louis, and turned to him madly, demanding his advice where to bet my last coin. "My friend," answered he gravely, "as you ask me as your friend, I can only answer the appeal by advising you to — put it in your pocket."

At the close of the lieutenant's story, few comments were made. The *dénoûment* was rather unexpected to his auditors, most of whom were scarcely well enough informed to appreciate so peculiar a phase of life in the most refined capital of the world.

The puffing of the pipes alone indicated that many of the company were not napping; although the story had produced a soporific effect in a few cases.

An artillery-officer of the regular army was the next volunteer *raconteur* in our nocturnal confabulations. A section of his battery lay not far in our rear; and he had strolled to our biovouac that night in quest of amusement, and to escape from the monotony of his camp.

We will entitle his narrative

THE ARTILLERY-OFFICER'S STORY.

I AM a graduate of the United-States Military Academy at West Point, and a Virginian by birth. It is likely that most of the people of my native State would deem me recreant to the land of my fathers, and an invader of the "sacred soil." But I think that true patriotism consists in something broader than one's obligation to any single State of our glorious Union, and can very well support the odium, if any justly falls upon me. I have never believed the mad doctrines of Calhoun and his followers, who have succeeded in shifting the theatre of war from their own States to poor old Virginia, who now endures its terrors and devastations. Neither do I approve of the conduct of many of my former brother-officers in raising sacrilegious hands to destroy the fairest fabric of human government ever devised by man, and thus violating their military oaths.

But I will not detain you, gentlemen, by entering into a discussion upon the merits or demerits of the two great parties now contending for the mastery in this our fair and great country, but will enter at once upon my story.

Fifteen years ago I was at the Military Academy, in the lowest class; of which Leonard Mason was also a member. Our parents resided in Williamsburg; and it so happened that we entered the institution at the same time.

The life of most men, let us hope, is brighter at its close than at its beginning, emerging from the grossness and cruelty of the schoolboy and the passions of youth into the light of reason and knowledge; but he of whom I speak was not so fortunate.

The height he reached was amidst thunder-clouds; and the road before him was no lighter, though his ascent was only misty, and his starting-point lay open to the sun.

He was, indeed, a glorious boy, with spirits inexhaustible as long as his pocket-money lasted; and both spirits and money were ever at the service of his friends. He was "too clever by half" for the majority of his companions, and was snubbed and bullied in consequence, but had a little knot of ardent admirers all his own. Such is the lot of most wits at school, where practical jokes and drinking-songs are chiefly acceptable, and higher kinds of humor are stigmatized by the all-degrading term "facetiousness."

"What may your name be?" drawled a cadet corporal to Leonard Mason shortly after his installation at the "Point" as a raw "plebe;" the question being an official one.

"It may be Sancho Panza; but it isn't," replied the youth; and he was punished immediately after for the repartee.

He soon became popular among the cadets, however, by reason of his many good qualities, — his generosity, activity, and beauty, — a gift which prepossesses boys in favor of its possessor, as it does the lowest classes and savages, in an eminent degree.

I seem to see him now at "Bennie's," where every enemy of the digestive organs had abode, "standing treat" to all comers with a smile of welcome, or bounding over the plateau, with his golden hair streaming in the wind, and his eyes lit up with the light that glows from a happy heart.

Almost all Virginians are especially good at every thing in the sporting way; and their devotion to cards almost reaches the dignity of a *culte*. Leonard Mason was emphatically a son of the Old Dominion in this respect, and was also passionately fond of every game of chance. He would have raffled off his teeth if he could have got anybody to put in for them; and was constantly devising ways and means of evading the army-regulations against gambling. He cut slips of paper, inscribing them with the names of running horses, on the eve of every great race, for "sweep" purposes; and, despite the strict discipline to which we were subject, contrived to use them secretly. If a pack of cards was discovered and confiscated, Leonard was sure to have introduced them. He cut dice out of India-rubber (to secure silence in playing), and invented a hundred games with slate and pencil, for school-times. Having secretly manufactured a cribbage-board, he was one night engaged in that enticing game with a friend, after taps, by the light of a tallow dip carefully veiled; and so absorbed were the two in their amusement, that they did not perceive the approach of the "rounds." Suddenly they heard a terrible voice above them, — "Two for his heels!" for Leonard's adversary had omitted to mark the knave; and the "rounds" had become so interested a spectator, that he couldn't help rectifying the error. They were very much alarmed at the time; but Leonard Mason never took the incident, as did the other, for a warning.

But "we all have our weak points," we all said; and his is the pleasure he takes in losing his own money, or in winning other people's to spend it for their entertainment: and for my part, when I look back, there were none whose companionship I enjoyed more than that of Leonard Mason.

When we had climbed to the senior class, Mason had grown graceful and handsome, and his many accomplishments were fully recognized. It would have been impossible to select a more deservedly popular man than he. He excelled in his studies; he was an excellent soldier, a fluent speaker, a tolerable musician, a passable poet, a good cavalier, an excellent pool-player; and, in short, promised to become one of those "admirable Crichtons" who from time to time dart meteor-like athwart the academic course, and then disappear, utterly lost in the darkness of the outer world.

In all our exercises and manly games, Leonard Mason was pre-eminent among his fellows; and often, as I saw him at the finish, breathless, and with heightened color, his broad chest rising and falling like a wave, I thought I had never seen a more splendid specimen of young manhood. His sparkling eyes, and honest, hearty laugh, inspired the belief that he was one who would not slip or fall from honor even on the "turf" itself. In our stolen pleasure-trips to Bennie's, or across the river, he was always the leading spirit; and at the former place, where shakes the well-worn bagatelle-board on its uncertain legs in the sanded parlor, his egg-flip and apple-toddy were allowed to be the best. And where the lawn slopes down to the river's edge, there he sang the songs we loved to hear, such as suited careless youth. He was the soul of all our jovial company. As we stole home to the cadet-barracks after one of these nights out, and effected our entrance, I said, —

"You make the hours fly fast, Leonard: that's one o'clock."

"The quarter to only, I'll bet a dollar," said he.

After our graduation, I gave a supper-party in honor of the great event, at Delmonico's, in New York. Leonard Mason did not arrive at the time appointed, and we sat down without him; for nobody waits on such occasions.

We began to talk of the absent, as the mode is; and I, thinking there could be no harm in a playful kick at such a favorite, offered to lay a wager that Mason was detained by cards.

"I wouldn't like to be his adversary," said one.

"Nor I his partner," said another, "lest Old Nick should fly away with us with pardonable freedom; for he has the Devil's own luck."

"Yes; and the Devil's own play too," said a third sulkily.

"It doesn't keep him from the duns, at all events," added the man next to me. "I dare say some pertinacious tailor is waiting for him now on the staircase; and that's what makes him late, after all."

Much distressed by this news and the tone of these remarks, I requested further information. I learned that Mason was not so popular as he used to be; and since he left West Point, some months before, had joined a fast set, to whom it was supposed he had lost considerable sums; was certainly in pecuniary difficulties, and very much changed in manners and appearance. Further information was cut short by the entrance of Mason himself.

If I had not been expecting him, and no other, I doubt if I should have known him, so altered was his person in a few short months. His face was very pale and haggard; his eyes — brighter than ever — were set in deep, black circles; and his clothes hung loosely on his limbs. He welcomed me however, with all his old cordiality, and threw about the arrows of his wit as usual: they were more barbed than of old; the sheet-lightning had become forked.

The conversation turned upon a graduate of the Military Academy who had taken holy orders. The same fellow who had complained of "the Devil's own play" announced his intention of following the example.

"Strange," said Mason, "that such 'fast' men should take holy orders! and, still more singular, how rapid is the metamorphosis! The French prints, the gold-mounted whips, the colored clothes, are sold at a frightful sacrifice; and a brand-new divine launched the next morning. What a pity to throw away that exquisite taste of yours" — addressing the man who had announced his intentions — "on the merest black and white!"

The latter had on a gay red necktie.

He said many things of this sort in a semi-savage manner

for a moment; but one of them moved his chair to give us room.

"Eleven; now then for a ten!" roared the dealer. "Fifteen — curse my luck! — and nine; overdrawn, by Jove!" A peal of joy arose from the others.

"You only pay me a V, though," said one mournfully.

"An X for me," said another; and "You pay me sixty dollars, — thirty on each card," added a third.

They were playing, then, a good deal too high for me; and, as I should have thought, for Mason also. I declined, therefore, to join the party; but stood with my back to the fire, and watched the game.

Vingt-et-un, like other matters which depend mostly upon luck, is a serious trial of the temper; and the present company seemed not to have much patience to spare: they were more or less in wine too, and exhibited a great contrast in their manner to the quiet and friendly fashion in which cards are, and should be, usually played among gentlemen. The chief cause of this was, that they were playing for higher stakes than they could well afford; that is to say, gambling.

The eternal "Make your game," and "I double you," were the only words spoken by Mason, as dealer; but he spoke them like a curse. Despite the heat of the room, and his intense excitement, his face shone beneath the bright light of two or three gas-burners as white as alabaster, and his thin hand shook over the pack like a lily on a dancing rivulet. He kept the deal a short time, losing heavily; and, when he was player, he clutched at the cards before they reached him like a drowning man catching at straws.

I shaded my face with my hand, for I was deeply pained, and watched him intently. He had usually "stood" upon his first two cards without drawing another; but he seemed suddenly to change his plan, and "drew" again and again.

"Nine — sixteen: surely you must be over," said the dealer.

"No, said Mason, "thank you! I stand."

Now, on that occasion I happened to see that Mason *was* over, — being twenty-two, — and that he received the stakes instead of paying them. My blood rushed to my head, and I thought that I heard my heart beat for a moment at the sight; but I dismissed the thought that his act was intentional, and watched in hope that it would not be repeated.

No, thank Heaven! he is "over" this time, and throws up his cards with a sigh; and now he wins; and now, as I live, he is "content" at twenty-five, and again receives instead of pays. Not twice nor thrice this happens, but twenty times. He is cheating whenever there is an occasion to cheat.

The night — or rather the day — wears on, and still the players sit unwearied: their lips are parched, their eyes are heated, and they scarcely can take up their cards. But not till dawn breaks in through the thick curtains and athwart the flaring gas-lights does any one leave his seat: then two hurriedly depart; and the rest drop off their perches presently, like moulting birds; and I am left alone with him who was my friend and playmate, and who cheats his guests and companions.

"Devilish dissipated, ain't it?" said Mason, yawning.

"Devilish!" I echoed.

"And what cursed luck I've had! A hundred dollars ready money and two hundred and fifty of autographs gone besides. But, Lord love you! I've had worse luck than that, and shall have again; and, if I don't mind it, why should you, old chap? Don't look so confoundedly virtuous," he added angrily; for I was looking all I felt: "you've done the same before now."

"Never the same, Mr. Mason," I replied.

"What do you mean?" said he hastily, but without remark

ing on the way I had addressed him. "You've never gambled: do you mean to say that? I like your impudence."

"Gambled, perhaps," I answered, "but never cheated, sir."

At that word his wan cheeks burnt like two living coals, and he dropped into an arm-chair beside me without a word; while a sort of convulsion seemed to pass over his whole face, and his breath came and went with difficulty.

"Mason," I said with pity and some emotion, "be a man! You were drunk, and knew not what you did. You lost command of yourself, or you could never have done such a foul deed, I know."

I saw with joy the tears gathering in his eyes, and, with my face averted from him, appealed to his old nature as forcibly as I could.

I told him what a hold he once had on all the hearts of his old associates, and how men's backs were turning on him now. I bade him judge how his whole self was changed by his own altered features and the strange companions he had chosen.

He only answered by a silent passion of tears. I was obliged to put to him some bitter questions for the sake of that I had in view.

"Does any one know of this beside yourself, Leonard?"

He shook his head.

"Is this the first time in all your life that you ever did this thing?"

"The first, the first!" he moaned.

I thought, and still think, that this was true; that he cheated in a sort of despair, and in a frenzy, rather than according to a preconceived and customary plan.

"Have you a Bible in the room, Leonard? Good! I have it here. Now swear to me that you will not touch dice or card again for two years; swear, I say," for I saw he was about to refuse; "or for your own sake, as well as that of others, I will proclaim what I have seen to-night, not only to your friends, but also to our military superiors."

Leonard Mason took the oath, and kept it; for he left New York that very day for Washington, and, having graduated in the cavalry previously, applied to be sent to his regiment, then on the western frontier of Texas. I was in the artillery: and so, for some years, we were widely apart; and it was only across the memory of my brightest academy-days, and especially over their scenes of pleasure and excitement, that his shadow fell dark and cold.

Only two years since, I visited my home at Williamsburg on a short leave of absence; and, being well acquainted with all the old Virginia families of the neighborhood, was invited to the house of an ancient acquaintance of my own.

Cleves Court was the seat of Col. Landon Carter, a Virginian of the old style; and there he dispensed the proverbial hospitality of the Old Dominion in a right royal fashion. The colonel had "one fair daughter, and no more;" and I had known Clara Carter from childhood, our families having been quite intimate for several generations.

Clara was not quite pretty, but had vivacity, and a thousand charming graces of manner many times more attractive than mere beauty of person. She was tolerably accomplished, and was reputed to have a handsome sum in her own right over and above what expectations she might have from her father. More than once I had thought of an alliance with this desirable young person myself: but she had once caught me practising an address to a young lady aloud, arrayed in cadet uniform, before a mirror in a drawing-room at Cleves Court, thinking I was *solus;* and she never forgot it. Whenever afterwards I strove to be tender, she would give her imitations of my looks and gestures on that occasion; and I, knowing how little laughter is akin to love, soon stifled my flame in my military studies, and began to take a life interest in the army. Still, however, I felt very anxious for her happiness; and it was with some terror, and much astonishment, that I discovered, on my arrival at Cleves Court, that she was engaged, and that the fortunate suitor was Capt. Leonard Mason.

Col. Carter, it seems, was not altogether satisfied with her suitor or his prospects; but Clara had set her heart upon him, and it was at her own disposal. To my half-joking questions about her lover, she gave me such replies as convinced me, that, in manners and attractions at least, he was the same who had charmed us all in youth; "but he looks so pale and thin at times," she said, "that I can scarcely bear to look at him."

An early day was appointed for us to meet at Cleves Court, the colonel thinking it would be agreeable to both parties on the score of our comradeship at West Point; and I was impatient for the time to arrive. "If he blushes or looks confused at seeing me," thought I, "it will be a good sign: that sad business at college will still haunt his memory, and prove him to be not inured to shame. It was his first and last and worst error, perhaps; and who am I that I should bring the sin of his youth against another man? How many of us in early life have committed faults, and even crimes, and yet have reached harbor and smooth water! and what right have we to send another, who is about to join us, back again upon the stormy deep?" Full of these magnanimous reflections, I arrived at Col. Carter's, finding within-doors that gentleman himself only, who bade me seek the young couple in the garden. They were walking together under a trellis of roses at the farther end, and never heeded my footsteps as I came along the gravelled walk toward them.

He had his arm around her waist, and was combating, it seemed, some opinion or scruple of hers; for his musical tones, although I could not hear their sense, caught up and overpowered hers.

On a sudden Clara gave a little scream, and pointed to me; and then I knew that it was I who had been the subject of their debate. As they came forward, she endeavored to disentangle herself from him; but he held her firmly as before.

Mason had changed much, and showed the marks of time and service: his complexion was bronzed, and he was heavily bearded.

"What a time it is since we met!" said he. "Why, when was it that I saw you last?"

"In New York," I replied. "You must remember that, Mason;" for I was not pleased with his coolness and effrontery.

"Yes," he said, "to be sure it was in New York; and we had some ridiculous quarrel about *vingt-et-un*."

"Well, don't do it again: for that is just my age; and I don't want to be quarrelled about," said Clara. And the dinner-bell — tocsin of peace — began to sound.

At the table we heard as much of the captain's history as he chose to tell. He spoke of his Indian fights, of Camanches and Lipans, and the excitement and adventure of frontier-life. He poured out quite a river of anecdote, all of which he finished off by some prudent or moral reflection; lamented this man's passion for play, another's thirst for drink, and the absurd extravagance of a third: in fact, acted the part of a model son-in-law to be to perfection.

But in the evening, as we smoked our cigars, after the old colonel had retired to rest, and Clara had followed his example, he was, to me, more natural in his communications.

He then spoke of the intrigues and marriages made "on spec" in society; of his colonel's fondness for "brag" and "poker;" of the ease with which money was to be made at the Metairie races by the crafty; of the "smashes" that had occurred in his regiment: and, in fact, laid open the whole *repertoire* of a fast military man.

His old humor was quite gone; but a bitter wit overflowed his talk, and an utter disbelief in goodness and good men pervaded all his language. This he addressed to me, "as one man of the world talking to another:" so and so and such were the real truths, — the sort of horrible, hopeless gospel always heralded by that particular expression. And yet when he drew himself up to his full height, and wished me good-night with his old bewitching smile, I pressed warmly his outstretched hand; and, long after the echoes of his footsteps had died away on the oaken stairs, I sat over the fading embers with my mind fuller of sorrow than anger because of him.

I had the darkest foreboding about this marriage. I had little doubt but that Mason was a fallen star, who would fall lower yet, and drag down with him another, pure and bright, and dear to me. Yet I liked him still: what wonder, then, at her affection, who knew his strength, and not his weakness? "How often do we see men like these," I thought, — "men without a prayer, who have twenty pious lips to pray for them; without love, — to call such, — and yet so wildly adored; without one great or wise or beautiful thought, and yet diffusing almost a glory by their presence! With one look of love they wipe away a hundred wrongs; and, when they die, their image is enshrined in many hearts, and not less tenderly because these may have been broken." I had no right, without more evidence, to compare Leonard Mason with such men as these; and yet I did so. It is not hard to find out in the army what an officer's life has been: but I did not consider myself justified in prying into the captain's past career in the South-west; for I knew that I had been a rival, and feared lest jealousy might prompt me in the matter quite as much as a regard for Clara's happiness.

Their marriage took place a short time after my visit to Cleves Court; and they went North for a wedding-tour.

I received a most eligible appointment as instructor of

artillery at Fortress Monroe; and frequently paid visits to Col. Carter, who urged me to come whenever I could. The childless old man, who had given up the light of his home, told me it was pleasant for him to be with one who had known and loved his daughter,—for he knew of my old affection for her better than she did, and would gladly have encouraged it,—and we talked of the absent one continually.

Month after month passed by without any sign of their return; and Clara's letters grew more vague, and Leonard's were quite silent as to their movements. He wrote that he found living at the North more expensive than he thought, and generally requested to have more money. Once, even, he wrote me a private epistle, "as one man of the world writing to another," about the possibility of getting at the property of his wife, which, according to my advice, had been put quite safely out of the gallant captain's reach. Then the letters of both ceased altogether. Post after post had Col. Carter begged of them to write; and I myself had not been backward in appealing to Mrs. Mason's filial feelings, or in pointing out to her husband the hazard of offending his father-in-law. But six months elapsed without letters from them. I then became convinced that he was preventing her by force; cutting off, for some purpose of his own, her intercourse with her parent: and here all my considerateness for Mason vanished, and I made every inquiry about him I could think of. Knowing that his leave of absence had expired, I found out at the war department that Capt. Leonard Mason, —th Cavalry, had resigned his commission; that his resignation had been compulsory, to avoid trial by court-martial on account of some gambling transactions which had come to light since he left his regiment in Texas: "And indeed," said my informant, the secretary of war, "they were some of the worst cases that ever came under our notice."

My suspicions being thus verified, I volunteered to the

almost frantic father to go in search of the lost sheep, or rather, of the wolf and lamb so unfortunately paired. I would not take him with me, because he was the last man in the world fitted to cope with Mason; but he gave me the fullest powers to act for him, and, if it could possibly be done, to bring about a separation.

I went on my sad errand, among the throng of pleasure-seekers (for it was now the summer), up the noble river which Leonard and I had often ascended together in our cadet-days. The grand scenery of the Highlands looked as imposing as of yore: all things around were beautiful; and every heart save mine seemed to be full of joy. The noisy glee of a knot of young cadets — which vividly brought to mind my former experience — contrasted most painfully with my sad forebodings. One of them forcibly reminded me of what Leonard Mason once had been when we had climbed together to the "Cro' Nest," and, while we rested, he sang to us "Excelsior." Then I doubted not that the words of Longfellow were appropriate to the singer as to the place; and, as I thought of him and the vanity of the prophecy, my heart grew heavy with fear.

I naturally intended to seek the Masons at Saratoga, as this was the last place from which tidings of them had been received; and it was, moreover, the resort of the gay set among whom I expected to find them. The first afternoon of my arrival was spent in fruitless inquiries; but the next day I fell in with a person who had seen them both at this celebrated watering-place, and who knew Capt. Mason. He assisted me in seeking them; but we found that they had left a day or two before, and had gone to New York. To the great city, then, I proceeded on the evening train; and, as soon as I arrived, lost no time in renewing my search, but without success.

The next day, by the merest accident, I encountered a person who knew everybody, and had seen Mason without knowing his name.

"Why, they are here, sir! I saw them last night: I am sure of it. They were both playing together in a private room at M——'s," — naming a noted hell, in which ladies were sometimes admitted by special favor of the proprietor, since an M. C.; "the gentleman very pale, and with black beard and hair, and sunken eyes; the lady not handsome, but lady-like, and with a musical voice."

"Good heavens!" said I. "And did you ask their name?"

"Oh, yes! M—— told me, — Stuart; Captain and Mrs. Stuart."

"Thank God!" I said. And yet the next moment I doubted whether it would not be better that they should be there than not to find them at all, or to find them doing worse.

Accompanied by my acquaintance, who had the *entrée*, I went to the private room of the "hell" that evening. I sat down at the gambling-table among others, holding my head low, as if intent upon the game, and watched the company as they entered. Presently the man I was in search of came in, with a lady, thickly veiled, upon his arm; and the two took seats opposite me. Yes, it was she, but deadly pale and quiet, looking more like a wax automaton than the light-hearted and self-willed Clara I had known. She had been fond of jewelry, and used to wear it in profusion; but there was not an ornament about her now, except her marriage-ring, which I saw as she stretched out her hand to receive her winnings or pay the banker. She seemed utterly careless about the matter herself; but, when more fortunate than usual, she looked up from the cloth into her husband's face, as if to glean from it a beam of joy. They evidently played in accordance with some systematic plan; but they did not prosper. I saw Leonard Mason's face darkening, and his teeth setting tighter, with every failure to win his stakes. At last, with a terrible but suppressed oath, he rose, and walked rapidly from the room, motioning to his wife to follow him.

Conversation is not usual in these places; but, when he had gone, one of the initiated present made the remark, —

"The captain's scheme doesn't answer. He said he should break the bank as surely as P—— did last summer."

"Ah!" said the dealer imperturbably, "P—— did not go away with the money, though; and as for the captain's new system, it's as old as the hills."

It was strange to hear the banker thus proclaiming his own invincibility; but he knew well how fast the devotees of the table were bound to him; and, indeed, he was answered by a general laugh. I had already risen, and was following the couple out of the room. They walked into Broadway, and entered Union Square. The moon shone brightly; and her rays were reflected in the basin of the great fountain, which was rippled by a light breeze. The scene was peaceful and lovely. The square was vacant at that late hour; and, as I advanced towards the Masons, I was reminded of the time I first met them together in the garden at Cleves Court. The way in which he laid his hand upon her arm at my approach recalled the manner in which he refused to be shaken off on that occasion. I saw in that grip that he was recalling to her mind certain previous directions, and that he had calculated upon a meeting of this sort.

"Captain Mason, or Stuart," I accosted him, "I have matters of a very serious nature to speak to you upon." At that intimation his pale cheek grew whiter; and I felt sure, at once, that he had done something to be afraid of, besides the things I knew of.

"Mrs. Mason," I continued, "to you also I have some weighty messages from a father you may possibly never see again."

"Address yourself to *me*, sir, if you please!" burst forth her husband violently; but she broke in with, —

"Tell me, for God's sake! is he ill, is he here, sir? O Leonard, Leonard, let me see our father!"

"He is not ill, madam," said I; "though he is broken-hearted. But, if I return to him without you, I do not doubt that he will die; and at your door, Capt. Mason, who have not suffered his daughter to write to him, his death will lie. Shall I go back and say that his son-in-law dare not pass under his own name, and that his daughter is compelled to become a professional gambler in the public hells of New York and Saratoga?"

"You will return to him," replied Mason savagely, "with a bullet through your heart, if" — But here Clara, in an agony of tears, and half swooning, entreated to be led home; and we bore her between us (for she could not support herself) to their apartments on the third floor of a neighboring street. They were almost without furniture, and not altogether clean, but with a glass of flowers here and there, and a few other traces of the "grace past neatness" which rarely forsakes a woman. Papers and cards covered with figures showing the average numbers of times certain cards had turned up at faro proclaimed the systematic gambler, not the mathematician; but they were all delusive calculations for discovering the philosopher's stone, — the way to win. Mason carried his wife, still sobbing piteously, into an inner room, and, returning instantly, motioned me to a chair, and demanded my business.

"May I ask, sir, on the part of Col. Carter, why you have not corresponded with him these six months, — not even to inform him of your having left the army?"

"You know as well as and better than I, sir (for I believe you put your meddling hand to it)," he replied, "that he refused me a pecuniary request, made on the part of his own daughter; and I did not choose that she should have any thing more to do with such a hard-hearted old miser."

"Now, supposing," said I, "*as one man of the world talking to another*, it was rather in the hope of bringing the old miser to your terms? and supposing that your plan has taken effect, and that I am instructed to pay you half your demand — that is to say, twenty thousand dollars — upon condition that Mrs. Mason returns to her friends?"

I had expected an outburst of rage at this proposal; but he only turned himself to the cabalistic documents upon the table, and, after a little consideration, answered calmly, —

"No: I must have thirty thousand!"

Col. Carter would have given double that sum; but I was so enraged by this coolness, and want of feeling, that I expressed myself with an eloquence that would have carried every thing before it in a criminal court.

"Swindler, cheat, felon!" I cried, — and at the word "felon" I saw him shake "like a guilty thing," and pursued my advantage, — "yes, felon, whom to-morrow I could consign to a life-long imprisonment, how dare you make conditions with me?"

But he recovered himself almost immediately, and bade me leave the room.

"To-morrow, sir, will see me far from this city with her whom your unselfishness is so anxious to divorce from her husband.

"Do you think," he added with all his ancient bitterness as I crossed the threshold, "that I have not heard of the friend of the family, the confidential adviser, the Platonic lover, the rejected suitor, before now?"

My indiscretion had thus broken off a treaty which promised to be more favorable than I had dared to hope. If Clara could have been induced to leave him, the business might have been by this time equitably, or at least legally, settled; but what was to be done now?

I went again to my acquaintance of the night before; for it might be that Leonard Mason had compromised himself so deeply, that the fear of the law would bring him to reason. His all-absorbing passion for play might have led him within its liabilities. I stated my case to this person, and asked if he could assist me.

"Certainly," said he, a bright thought seeming to strike him. "Come with me."

After a short consultation, we went to the headquarters of the police, where I procured the help of an officer; and we returned to the lodging of the Masons. Leaving the officer outside, I entered, and found the captain alone, as before, but with several trunks and boxes about him, evidently prepared for immediate departure.

"Well, Capt. Mason," said I, "I am come once more to repeat my offer of last night."

He laughed quite scornfully, and replied, —

"Since you are so hot about it, sir, you must now give forty thousand for the lady. I will take no less; and in two hours it will be too late. Go to your hotel in the mean time, and debate the question of 'love or money.'"

"You do not move from this place unless I wish," I answered. At a sign from me, the officer entered; and I continued: —

"You are now arrested for living under an assumed name, and for confining your wife under duress; and you will be detained in prison until other and *far graver* charges which may be brought against you shall have been substantiated."

The last sentence had a great success, as I could see by his changing color; and he replied, with an appearance of his old frankness, —

"You have out-manœuvred me, I confess: withdraw your forces, pay me the sum you proposed at first, and I will perform my part of the business."

The officer retired at my request, and he addressed himself to me: —

"Shall I take an oath before you? or will my word suffice?"

"Sir," I replied, "the results of the last oath you took in

my presence have not been such as to induce me to ask you for another."

He said nothing; but a flush came to his face which reminded me of that which had reddened it in his rooms years before. I drew up a document for him to sign, which was a literal copy of one I had received from a lawyer, and which had been already prepared in anticipation. It bound him by the strongest tie — his own interest — never to claim Clara as his wife again. He signed it; while I, on my part, gave him a check for the money. At that moment, in came his poor wife in her bonnet and travelling-dress.

"You may take those things off again," said her husband calmly: "we are not going away."

She looked from him to me with a sort of hope just awakening in her tear-worn face.

"You are going home to your father, Clara," he added.

"Thank God, thank God!" she said; "and thank you, Leonard! How happy you have made me! We will go together to him and the dear old place, and never leave him: we will forgive and forget; won't we, dear husband, won't we?"

"Mrs. Mason," said I, "your husband cannot accompany you. It would not be possible for your father to see him, even if he chose to go; which he does not."

The truth is, I was at that time very inexperienced in the female character, and was secretly vexed that she should cling to this rotten tree; nor did I then comprehend that woman's love cleaves to its chosen object through disgrace, neglect, and crime.

"I leave not my husband, sir," she said quietly, "until death doth us part."

She stood erect, and laid her hand upon his shoulder, but with a mournful look: it was the dignity of love, but also of despair. He quietly and coldly put her arm away.

"It is better for us both, Clara," he said. "I wish it to be so. I would rather," he added with some effort, "that you never saw my face again."

She gave a short, sharp cry, and fell heavily upon the floor.

For many days she lay fever-stricken and delirious; and I was unable to remove her.

Fortunately I knew a most amiable and accomplished lady in the city, who volunteered her assistance to me; for I was left her only protector, Capt. Mason having departed, no one knew whither. My sympathizing friend secured the attendance of one of that sisterhood which devotes itself to the alleviation of human suffering in whatever form it is found; and Clara was nursed by a Sister of Charity, who scarcely ever left her bedside.

When, at last, she returned to consciousness, the face hanging over her was that of her own father: it was his tremulous voice that answered when she called, "Leonard, Leonard!"

Nevertheless, when the mist over her mind cleared away, she did not refuse to be comforted, even at first. Whatever others might have said against her husband, whatever proofs of his unworthiness might have been shown to her, she would have rejected; but his own renunciation of her cut, like a sharp sword, her heart-strings from him.

She never asked to go to him again. He became to her an ideal being. The portrait she possessed of him, the lock of golden hair, the love-letters he had once written to her, were memorials of a far other than he who had said, —

"I would rather that you never saw my face again."

She was taken back to the old house, and grew resigned, and, in time, almost cheerful. She must have suffered many and terrible things; and her nature recovered itself slowly at the touch of kindness, as the drooping flower opens gradually to the sun.

The old man became almost young again, and scarcely ever left her. He was fuller of kindliness towards me than ever;

but not so his daughter: and I was not wanted at Cleves Court, I saw; and so discontinued my visits.

I had a difficult mission to perform when I left Cleves Court for Saratoga; but I did my best, and with no motive but her good to inspire me.

Just before this war broke out, I was travelling on duty in the West, and embarked at Baton Rouge for Natchez. It was late in the evening when I went on board; and, without noticing a party around the card-table in the "social hall" of the steamboat, I went to my stateroom, and to bed. I was fatigued, and slept sound until morning; when I was aroused by a hubbub on the gang-plank, the steamer having stopped at a wooding-station. I looked forth from my little window, and saw a man hustled violently ashore by the indignant passengers amid many an oath and execration. Reaching the levee, he turned his pale face, and shook his fist menacingly at the crowd on the deck. That was the last time I saw Leonard Mason. I went into the saloon, and found the passengers and clerk of the boat engaged in examining the contents of a valise they said was his, — "the cheat."

An "advantage-box," loaded dice, marked cards, were successively drawn forth and detected by these experts, who had lost heavily the night before, and had watched the professional gambler, and exposed him. I thought of the days, not far distant, that we had passed at the Military Academy, and how terribly altered was that skeleton form I had just seen ignominiously expelled from the society of his fellows from the strong and sprightly nervous frame of the young cadet; and the soul too — but that was past human ken or judgment.

What has become of the lost one since I know not; but have heard, that, like most Southerners of military education, he is now in the confederate army.

THE MAJOR'S STORY.

FROM my childhood, my friends, I have been a soldier, and my earliest recollections are of the barrack and the camp; while my youth was accustomed to the field and the bivouac. In fact, I have been that much-maligned personage, a soldier of fortune; which means, in most cases, a soldier of *no* fortune at all.

Once in my life I resolved to relinquish the profession of arms, and to adopt some peaceful calling; but inexorable fate drove me back to the career which I began, as I have said, almost in childhood.

After having given my sword to several European powers, and also lent it to the Turk, without finding myself any better off than when I began, I determined to visit the land of promise to all adventurers like myself, and came to this country to seek a home and a family. I had always been a dreamer, and to acquire these blessings was the dearest wish of my heart; while the hope of its realization had been my only solace in many a dreary bivouac, as I lay on the ground covered with my cloak, gazing upward at the stars, with oftentimes many a poor fellow stark and stiff in his gore around me.

The expenses of the voyage had absorbed all the little ready money I possessed; and I landed in New York penniless, having nothing but a stout heart and strong limbs, that had so often stood me in good stead.

It was the autumnal season; and I strolled all day through

the busy streets of the great metropolis of the Western World, studying the new scenes that met my eye; and, as the shades of evening fell, I stretched myself on a bench in Washington Square to rest.

I did not fear observation; for I was utterly unknown. I was pale and careworn after my voyage: and my clothes were by no means new,—"my beaver gone to seed;" my shoes, like those of Julian St. Pierre, "minus half their soles." I saw the yellow leaves of the maples drop from their boughs as the breeze swept through them; and a shudder ran through my heart at the sight. They were hurled round and round by the tiny currents of air; and at last borne away, Heaven only knew whither. "Such," thought I, "are my hopes;" and I compared myself to the tree from which they had been torn. In the green springtime of life my heart had put forth its blossoms and its branches, and many a bird of love trilled its sweet song amid its fresh foliage; but all had gone. The young plant had withered; and the winds beat upon it, lone and melancholy. Brooding over such thoughts as these, I clasped my hands over my eyes to shut out the gleams of the pale stars, and wept silently.

I thought of my youth and its golden visions, and how, like the diamond frost-work that is melted by the sun, they, too, had "vanished into thin air." I thought of the struggles I had endured, the perils I had passed; of how I had labored and fought, not for myself, but for others; and, worse than all, how my proud heart had been obliged to bow to the

> "Spurns
> That patient merit from the unworthy takes."

It was a bitter thought; but I pressed my hand upon my breast, and said to myself, "It is well."

I then imagined myself married and the father of a family, although still in the humblest pecuniary circumstances. I imagined, that, my speculations having failed, I was a beggar. In fancy, I reached my humble abode after a long and weary walk. My wife came out to meet me; and my children clasped my knees, and flung their little thin, white arms around my neck. I thought of the morrow, — of their wants, and my destitution; and, though my heart dropped tears of blood, my lips wore a smile, and I cheered them with words of hope and love. I bade them good-night with many kisses; and we slept, and dreamed those cold, gray dreams that hover over the beds of poverty.

The next morning, after eating a scanty breakfast, I went forth to earn the pittance of a laborer. My heart hung in my bosom like a lump of lead, and I bit my lips to hide my agony. My rent was due, and I had not a farthing to pay it. I thought of my pale wife and little children; and imagined them shivering in the cold air, houseless and friendless.

Wrapped in these painful fancies, and walking with my face bent towards the ground, I suddenly spied a little piece of paper, looking like a bank-note, lying on the pavement.

I grasped it eagerly; but, alas! it was only a ticket in the Havana lottery! I kept it, nevertheless, and that day asked a barkeeper what No. 33,661 had drawn.

"Have you that number?" asked the barkeeper with an air of surprise.

"Yes: here it is," I answered.

"That ticket, sir, has drawn eight thousand dollars; and you have only to go to the firm of P—— to get your money."

Who could describe the thoughts that rushed like meteors through my bosom? I was as rich as I wished to be, and could now hurl back with scorn the taunts of those who had oppressed me. I hastened to my home, while the ground seemed to fly beneath my feet. My wife's face was livid when I approached; but, when I told her of my fortune, she burst into tears.

She could not speak for joy; but, falling on her knees, she clasped her thin, white hands, and thanked God for his blessings. She spoke not a word; but the mute heart's prayer rose upwards, sweet and fragrant as the incense from the holy censer. I could not even smile; but my eye was again lighted with the gleams of hope and joy.

I thought, that, in a day or two, we were all on our way to find a home in the West. As we sped up the lordly Hudson on the magnificent steamer, my arm clasped the waist of my wife as we sat on the hurricane-deck: and as we watched the buildings of the great city, and the spires of her churches, and the tall masts of the shipping, as they faded into the clouds, I thought of those whom I had befriended, and who had requited my kindness with contumely; and, ah! how merrily rang the supper-bell on board the boat! and how savory was the smell of the food upon the ample table! My wife's cheeks were pale no longer; the children prattled gayly; and we all sat down together and enjoyed the repast. Thus sped day after day till seven had passed, when we reached our destination.

I soon found a settler itching to escape from even advancing civilization, and of him bought, with the proceeds of the lottery-ticket, nearly five hundred acres of rich land, good farm-buildings, and all his stock and agricultural appurtenances.

We were soon installed in our new residence, and were happy, — perfectly happy. The first night of our occupancy I sat on the balcony of my little house, smoking my pipe, and gazing on the beautiful scene spread before me. The tall trees around the house seemed to bow and do homage to me as to their master. I could hear the lowing of the kine in the cattle-yard, and see the broad fields teeming with abundant crops. They were all mine now. I saw the brook that ran silvery in the pale moonlight as softly as a dream. I thought how, on the morrow, I would take my gun, and wage a crusade against the game that chirped on the prairie in shot of my very door. After these pleasant musings and anticipations, I went to bed with a heart light as a feather, and dreamed sweet dreams.

The next morning, just as the sun was tinging the summits of the hills, and the birds were singing their early songs to the light of day, I awoke, started, and found myself still in Washington Square.

I had been sleeping all the while, and the lottery-ticket was but a figment of my dream. My hat had fallen from my head, and was nearly filled with dead leaves. Among them was a piece of paper. It was a fragment of a boy's kite that had been caught in the trees and blown to pieces. On it was written, in a schoolboy's round hand, *"Patience and perseverance will accomplish every"* — and here the sentence broke off. It was evidently a leaf torn from a boy's copy-book: but I gave it a long, wistful look; and, while my visions faded away forever, I resolved to profit by the aphorism.

The sun had just withdrawn his face from the bloody plain of Shiloh. The conflict, which had raged for two days with unceasing fury between the armies of Grant and Buell and those of Johnston and Beauregard, had terminated in the defeat of the latter, which, under cover of the approaching night, was fleeing before its victorious foe.

Yet our victory was not a great one, as by it we simply regained the camps from which we had been driven; though, in point of fighting, the case was doubtless in our favor. The confederates chose their own time and place of attack, pounced upon an inferior force, and performed a feat that military writers declare is impossible against a well-disciplined army, — effected a complete surprise. A stronger combination of adverse circumstances could hardly be imagined than that which operated against the Union army; yet we finally repulsed them.

I rode forward with the pursuing cavalry. Vain had been the courage of the rebel troops; fruitless the exertions of Johnston, who met his death on the field: his army was now in hurried retreat. The shouts of the victors, the shrieks of the wounded, and the feeble moans of the dying, the wild ravings of thirst, cries for succor, and even prayers for death, were all unheeded by the eager hosts intent on pursuit and escape. Since the evening I had spent in Washington Square, matters had prospered with me: my dream had been realized. I had settled in a growing Western State, married, and had a small family. But this great struggle in which we are now engaged came on. My military knowledge and experience were called for, if not appreciated; and I was forced by circumstances to take part in the conflict. Although my property lay in the South-west, I never hesitated an instant which side to take. I enlisted in a regiment of cavalry recruited in my State, and was appointed adjutant by our colonel, who, innocent of all knowledge of the art of war himself, was not blind to the advantage of having an old soldier at his right hand.

The enemy's retreat was conducted in good order, and his rear-guard covered the army with undaunted coolness. Our cavalry cut down or dispersed many stragglers; but their farther advance was checked by a steady line just visible in the approaching dusk, and a volley which emptied many saddles. Suddenly I felt my horse reel and tumble under me, and my own strength fail; and instantly both horse and man measured their length upon the sod. How long I lay bereft of all my faculties I know not; but, returning to consciousness, I found myself near a heap of mutilated corpses.

The first object which caught my eye was a canteen suspended to the side of a dead rebel officer, and glittering feebly in the pale moonlight. Inspired by hope, I crawled to the body of the confederate as quickly as I could, and seized the envied treasure. I was not disappointed; for the canteen held some excellent whiskey, a small quantity of which greatly revived me.

Sitting down near the place where I had lain by the side of my poor horse, which had been slain, I began seriously to reflect on the predicament to which the fortune of war had reduced me. I first examined my body and limbs in search of the wound which had so inopportunely placed me *hors du combat;* but, finding no visible hurt, I concluded (what was really the case) that the soreness in my head, and my late swoon, were due to a contusion I had received from the fall of my horse. I recalled perfectly the circumstances of my fall; and, as these were sufficient to account for all the bruises I had sustained, further conjectures were useless. My position was not an agreeable one. I knew the bitterness with which the war was waged by the confederates, and the risk I ran of being either massacred upon the field, or starved to death in one of their vile prisons; and these considerations made me pluck up my spirit, with the determination to use my best efforts to save (what I had the utmost respect for) my neck, but to bear my fate, whatever it might be, with manly fortitude. I soon decided upon the plan of action to be pursued in case I was taken prisoner.

In the course of my military career, I had seen too often the immense value of a knowledge of medicine and surgery to the professional soldier, and had pursued my studies in that direction during the intervals of garrison-life and other leisure times. I had a general smattering of the principles of the healing art; had frequently assisted at important surgical operations; knew the best styptics in use; and had acquired a practical knowledge of phlebotomy. In my present dilemma, these accomplishments might prove very useful.

Accordingly, I resolved to dub myself a surgeon *pro tem-*

pore, and to pass as such with the enemy; trusting that my quality of non-combatant would rescue me from the fate which would inevitably follow the avowal of my real rank. Escape was impossible if the patrols of the enemy returned, even if my limbs had been supple enough to bear me on a retreat. We had been led far in the advance, and I was entirely ignorant of the position of either army. My best policy, then, was to remain where I was; and I adopted it, hoping that the federal army would first come to the field to collect their wounded. In the mean time my reveries were unbroken, save by the occasional cries of the mutilated wretches who surrounded me, several of whom were menaced by the turkey-buzzards, which already thronged the field in quest of their loathsome prey.

A cry of agony suddenly struck my ear; and, looking in the direction whence it proceeded, I saw a young man on his back, striving fruitlessly with his feet to drive away some of those carnivorous birds of which I have spoken. My first impulse, as I dragged myself towards him, was humane; nor did the sight of his gray uniform check its operation. I soon scattered the carrion birds; and, having administered a drop of my precious cordial to the parched lips of the sufferer, began the duties of my assumed profession by an examination of his wounds. Both arms were severely injured by a musket-ball. I soon bound them up, — a shirt from a neighboring corpse supplying me with the requisite bandages, — the confederate officer (for such he was) regarding me meanwhile with looks of mingled surprise and admiration.

At last an exclamation burst from his lips, and he almost overwhelmed me with a torrent of thanks. Modestly waiving the subject of my own deserts, I inquired if he had any hope of soon being removed.

"Ay, indeed!" cried he. "John Middleton would have been here long before this, but for some insuperable obstacle." And, glancing at my uniform, he added, "Do you keep up your spirits; for, although my arm is unable to defend you, the word of Tom Yancey has weight with my comrades, and you shall see that a rebel may possess a grateful heart. But what do I see? Surely my eyes deceive me, or I recognize the canteen of Bill Davis, of my regiment!"

I explained how it came into my possession.

"Ah! then he has fallen at last! — Poor Davis! the merriest fellow in the regiment, and a true lover of old Bourbon."

His enumeration of his comrade's virtues was interrupted by a shout from a distant part of the field; and the dawn, just then breaking, showed us four or five confederate soldiers cautiously seeking among the wounded. Yancey at once declared that his friend John Middleton was approaching, and requested me to answer the call; which I did. In a few moments the party came up. I must confess that I felt rather uneasy as the crisis of my fate approached, notwithstanding the assurances of my new friend.

The rebels, however, took not the slightest notice of me, their whole attention being engrossed by the wounded lieutenant; but when they had heard a relation of his sufferings, and learnt the kindness he had received from a federal officer, not even the Union uniform I wore could save me from the thanks and sympathy of his grateful friends.

A litter was prepared for Lieut. Yancey, while two stout confederates supported me in their arms: the glass of friendship circulated for the last time, and we prepared to leave the gory field. At this moment a rebel officer rode up, and, catching a glimpse of my hated garb, appeared much astonished at this unwonted display of confraternity. He was soon acquainted with the circumstances of the case, and, turning to me, highly complimented my humanity and skill.

"This is indeed an auspicious meeting, sir," said he. "If you are indeed a surgeon, your services are this instant required by one who will justly appreciate them."

Not anticipating that my skill would be so immediately put to the test, I felt extremely awkward. I might be called upon to perform an operation in which my ignorance would be manifest. I had, however, "staked my life upon the cast, and must abide the hazard of the die." Bowing to the officer, therefore, I expressed my readiness to make myself useful in any capacity.

A stray horse was soon caught. I was helped to mount him; and bidding adieu to Middleton and Yancey, who were profuse in their acknowledgments and kind wishes, I accompanied the officer, who was attended by two orderlies. We struck into a narrow and devious path leading through the woods. After riding about four miles, we arrived at a log farmhouse, in a clearing, around which several horses were picketed; while the number of officers and orderlies constantly passing to and fro showed it to be the temporary headquarters of an officer of high rank. This discovery did not lessen my apprehensions. We alighted; and the officer who accompanied me, and who had remained silent during our ride, threw his gray cloak over my shoulders, doubtless with a view of screening me from the observation of the rebels; whispered me to be of good heart, and to wait his return; and left me in the rude veranda of the log-cabin. Nodding assent, I seated myself on a rough wooden bench, and looked around. Several officers lounged about, smoking, and conversing on the events of the battle. A middle-aged confederate near me was talking with a young man; and some of their words reached my ears, although they spoke in a low key.

"A confounded hard day's work we have had of it," said the eldest. "The Yanks fought like lions. The fortune of the battle fluctuated more than once before we lost it."

"Ay," replied the youngest: "we had it all our own way on Sunday; but the re-enforcements coming up under Buell gave them the victory at last."

"That blasted gunboat greatly annoyed us," said the elder,

"by her broadsides. Our division was almost decimated by her shells. But for her, I think we should have broken the enemy's line."

"Their batteries were splendidly served," returned the junior officer: "we took six of them six times, which were retaken as often, at enormous cost to us and to them."

"The federals were badly demoralized on Sunday evening," said the first. "Their soldiers were huddled together under the high bank of the river, and could not be persuaded to face us by their officers. There was inextricable confusion among them; and the gunboats not only saved them, but, setting the woods on fire, caused the death of many of our wounded."

"The re-enforcements of Price and Van Dorn," said the younger, "were neutralized by the arrival of their Tennessee army, and all our expectations destroyed. The slaughter yesterday was terrible!"

"It was Greek meeting Greek. My men saw, and even hailed, their own neighbors in the deadly struggle. Poor Johnston! A braver or an abler soldier never drew a sword. He was left on the field, and B——"

"Hush!" interrupted the younger man. "The general now lies in this house, wounded in the hand: our stupid surgeons have been these two hours trying in vain to stanch the blood which flows from it; but the hemorrhage defies their efforts. Unless it is speedily stopped, he is in danger of following his colleague."

The colloquy was broken off by the entrance of the officer who had brought me to the cabin, and who made me a sign to follow him. I had heard enough, however, to satisfy me that the person to whom I was about to be introduced was no other than Gen. B——, now, since the death of Albert Sidney Johnston, commander-in-chief of the rebel army.

The certainty was by no means calculated to augment my self-confidence. But I had no time for reflection. My conductor led me into a narrow entry, at the end of which was a low door: this was opened to us by an old woman; and we entered a small room, one side of which was occupied by a rude bed, where lay a man of middle age and stature, with a stern but not ferocious countenance, in which was something which checked familiarity, and inspired the beholder with a feeling of respect bordering upon awe.

On the back of a chair was thrown his uniform of confederate gray, the collar simply adorned with the insignia of his rank, and his sword. Two officers, seemingly of rank, were seated at a little distance, anxiously regarding a third person, who was kneeling, and applying to the wounded limb cloths which were absolutely saturated with blood. The old woman resumed her station at the fire. The general slowly raised his eyes at our entrance, and fixed them steadily upon my face for a moment; when, as if satisfied with the scrutiny, his features relaxed from the expression of *hauteur* which they had worn, and he addressed me in a weak though clear voice: —

"I am told, young man, that your humanity has been already exercised in behalf of a fallen enemy. I also require the aid of your healing art. Pray, may I ask where you received your medical education."

"The little knowledge I possess, general," I replied, "has been acquired in Belgium."

"You are, then, a native of that country, I presume," said the general, "and not an American."

"Pardon me, general," I returned: "I am by birth an Englishman."

"'Tis well, sir. I resign myself to your treatment; that is, if you will condescend to give the benefit of your surgical skill to a rebel."

"'Tis my duty as well as my pleasure, general, to relieve suffering, whether I find it in a friend or an enemy."

"Mr. —— " (I did not catch the name), said the general

to the kneeling man, "you will prepare yourself to follow implicitly the directions of this gentleman; and," he pursued with a sneer, "you may chance to acquire a lesson in the practice of an art of which you now seem to know only the theory."

The abashed surgeon rose from his humble posture, and, as he relinquished his place, darted at me a look full of malignity, while I proceeded, not without some trepidation, to survey the wounded limb. My fears were somewhat alleviated on discovering that the hurt was not of a very serious nature. A musket-ball had traversed the fleshy part of the inside of the hand, and the wound owed much of its irritation to unnecessary probing; to allay which, and to stop the hemorrhage, seemed to be the first things to be done.

I called for some simple styptics, readily obtained; applied them to the wounded hand, and the bleeding stopped. I bandaged it securely, administered a composing draught from a portable camp medicine-chest at hand, and desired that the general should be left to repose. All instantly prepared to leave the room except the nurse and the crest-fallen doctor, whose name, I was told, was Mercier, a native of New Orleans. Col. Game, the officer who had been my conductor, and by whom the scowl of the indignant practitioner had not passed unheeded, fearing lest his envious feelings might induce him to counteract the good effects of my remedy, commanded him to retire; an order which he obeyed with visible dissatisfaction. I was then conducted into an adjoining room, in which we found refreshment awaiting us of a substantial kind, and a tolerable bed, which seemed to me the couch of a Sybarite after my recent fatigues. I did not awake until late in the day; when I again dressed the general's wound, and prepared him to enjoy the night's sleep. Early on the following morning I was aroused by Col. Game, who, having inquired in a friendly manner after my health, begged my acceptance of a plain gray frock-coat, "which," said he, "will not be conspicuous, and may spare you unpleasant remarks that some of our officers might feel authorized to make at sight of a Union uniform."

"It is not intended to place you under any particular restraint," he added. "You will give me your parole of honor to attempt no escape: indeed, the effort would be vain, and would only subject you to a penalty which even those disposed to serve you would be unable to avert. Take my advice, then, and be patient. The general's rest has been undisturbed during the night, the greater part of which I remained in his room: he feels much refreshed; and we shall all start this forenoon for Corinth, the general riding in a carriage. Upon arrival there, unless we are pursued by the federal army, he hopes that he will be well in a few days, with your aid; when it is probable that the first moment of his recovery will be the last of your captivity. We will now, if you please, visit the general, whose wound requires your attention to prepare him for the journey. Recollect that you have already gained two friends; and have a fair chance of securing a third, whose interest is of far greater value."

I readily gave my parole, thanking Col. Game for his good advice, and declaring that I should follow it implicitly; and together we entered the general's chamber.

I found the inflammation considerably abated, and the sufferer much better. Having renewed the dressing, I retired to the veranda and joined Col. Game, who introduced me to several officers of the general staff assembled for their frugal breakfast, and who received me with marked politeness. When the meal had been silently discussed, the much-worn carriage brought to the door and made ready for the occupation of the general, the company mounted; and, before noon, our cavalcade was slowly advancing toward Iuka and Corinth.

This last place is a strong strategic point. It lies in the

bosom of a semi-mountainous country, the surrounding hills forming an irregular circle from four to eight miles in diameter. The Mobile and Ohio Railway crosses the ridge formed by these hills, through a cut seventy-five feet in depth perpendicularly. Similar cuts of less depth penetrate the hills on the east, west, and south, where the different railways enter. Beyond these hills, in the direction of Pittsburg and Savannah, the ground becomes more level, and much of it is low and swampy. The country is diversified, the soil fertile; and there are extensive forests of oak, hickory, walnut, and pine. The principal military value of Corinth lies in the fact that it is a great railway centre for the different lines of the South-west.

As I rode near the carriage of the general with Col. Game, I had an opportunity of learning some of the reasons for the retrograde movement we were making, and was also instructed on many political points about which I had not hitherto been informed. We arrived late in the day at the town of Corinth; and orders were given, immediately upon our arrival, to strengthen the defences of the place, and to re-organize the troops, as their shattered regiments arrived, after their terrible losses at Pittsburg Landing. Col. Game and myself were quartered in a small two-roomed house near the headquarters of the general, into which we withdrew to partake of some refreshment.

Later, allured by the beauty of the evening, I was induced to cross the threshold, and almost unconsciously strolled to the farther extremity of the enclosure in which the house was situated. The little yard was surrounded by tall trees, through which an opening was scarcely perceptible, and was about an acre in extent. Finding a stump of a tree which had been lately felled, I sat down on it, and insensibly fell into my customary inveterate habit of revery. Time passed unheeded; and it is uncertain how long I might have remained in my brown study, had I not been suddenly aroused by a rustling sound. Springing to my feet, I gazed attentively around, but could perceive nothing to indicate whence the noise proceeded. I had begun to believe it was the work of imagination, when the same sound again arrested my attention. I started suddenly: and well was it for me that I did so; for the sharp crack of a revolver quickly followed the sound, and I was saved from its bullet only by my precipitate movement; for the leaden projectile grazed my head as it perforated my hat. I rushed in the direction of the report only to see indistinctly a dark form swiftly hurrying through the belt of trees encircling the yard. I halted, and was joined by Col. Game, who had heard the sound, and came to seek me; and who, on learning what had happened, warmly congratulated me on my escape. All search for the assassin at that hour being deemed useless, we returned together to the house. The suspicions of the colonel and myself pointed toward Mercier; but, having no confirmatory proof, we resolved to conceal our opinions for the present, and content ourselves with adopting precautionary measures against a similar attempt.

Lieut. Yancey soon called upon me, and insisted upon superintending the arrangement of my little comforts. He had nearly recovered from his wound in the right arm; and pointing to his left, which he wore in a sling, said, "You see, sir, I am still on the list of non-effectives: therefore you can avail yourself of my proffered services without the fear of encroaching upon my military duties."

I would not hurt his feelings by refusing his request; and soon his voice was heard in and about the premises, authoritatively demanding every thing requisite for my complete accommodation.

About a week elapsed, during which the general's wound had fully healed; and in the daily preparations he was making to receive our army, then advancing to besiege Corinth, he appeared to have utterly forgotten me, and the hopes of liberty which had been held out to me. Col. Game was absent at Iuka, and his return was uncertain: and, heartily tired of a life of unaccustomed inaction, I became uneasy and dejected; nor could the persevering solicitude of Yancey and his inexhaustible *gaieté de cœur* suffice at all times to relieve my depression.

In this frame of mind I would frequently wander into the suburbs of the little town to a grove of trees that had been spared from the fate of all the others in the vicinity by orders from headquarters, prompted by a recognition of the necessity that would soon exist for firewood and timber nearer the centre of the place than the surrounding forest when it should be beleagured by our advancing forces. A few log-cabins stood here and there around it. Here, screened from observation, as I imagined, by the friendly shelter of the huge tree-trunks, I indulged my dark fancies, and even suffered my ideas to roam beyond the bounds of this sublunary world; and, for a brief space, forgot the sad reality of my captive state. The grove, disturbed by no other sound than the sighing of the wind through its vaulted aisles, as it seemed to float in undulating sound, in its gloomy grandeur accorded with my soul's melancholy. Once, while in one of these reveries, I was suddenly aroused by the approach of footsteps. A figure muffled in a homespun cloak advanced, and, thrusting a slip of paper in my hand, hastily retreated, and was quickly lost in the gloom. Surprised at the incident, and anxious to ascertain the purport of the mysterious scroll, I bent my steps towards the outer skirting of the grove, and read as follows:—

"Do the chains of the rebels sit so easy on thy limbs that thou wishest to continue in bondage? If not, and if thou wilt break thy fetters, meet the writer of this at the rear of the cabin nearest the grove to-morrow at midnight. Burn this!"

There were certain mystic characters rudely traced on the paper, the meaning of which I did not understand; but I knew at once that the missive came from some one of those secret societies which had sprung up throughout the South, since the breaking-out of the great civil war, under various names. Some of these circles were formed to aid the Confederacy in the attempt to set up a government of their own within the limits of the United States; others had for their object the protection of the Union men of the South who adhered to the government of their fathers; while still others were instituted for the protection of deserters from the military conscription ordered by the Richmond government, which was and is exceedingly unpopular throughout Secessia, as you all probably know.

Having carefully perused the paper, I deposited it in my vest, and hastened to my quarters, where I learned with satisfaction that Col. Game had retired to rest. Seated in my apartment, I sought the missive, intending to burn it as requested; but it was not to be found.

I was greatly alarmed. I might have dropped it where it would have been picked up by some one belonging to the garrison: its import would evidently direct suspicion toward myself. My situation was a critical one; but I could do nothing: I could only await events.

Resolving, however, to try to recover the lost missive early the next morning, I threw myself on my couch; but sleep for many hours refused to visit my eyelids, and daylight found me wearied in body, and agitated in mind. I rose, however, with the dawn, and hurried to the grove, traversed its paths with rapid steps, and searched in every direction for the lost paper, but without success.

Bitterly execrating my carelessness, I returned home in a state of mind bordering on despair. Yancey was present at breakfast, which had been prepared under his auspices, but expressed no surprise at my early absence; although I remarked that he was more than usually attentive to my wants, — almost officiously so. As the thief sees an officer in every bush, so I trembled at every sound: the slightest noise, to my perturbed imagination, seemed the precursor of my arrest; and I hailed with pleasure the close of a day which seemed to me the longest I had ever known. The evening passed away less heavily. Yancey successfully exerted himself to dissipate my melancholy. About ten o'clock I escaped from the kind assiduities of my grateful friend by pleading an inclination for repose. When alone, I began seriously to consider my situation. The note of the stranger proffered me the means of enfranchisement: if these means proved such as I could in honor avail myself of, my duty to the cause I had embraced imperatively demanded my acceptance of them. I decided, therefore, to keep the appointment, and to let the result of my interview with the secret emissary govern my subsequent course. While I meditated on the uncertainties that lay before me, two hours almost imperceptibly slipped away: the hands of my watch, placed before me on the table, now indicated the last quarter.

I sprang up, wrapped my cloak around me, and, having extinguished the light, silently descended to the street. A few minutes' walk brought me to the designated spot; and the dark and indistinct outline of a human form beneath the overhanging gable told me that my mysterious correspondent was punctual. After a brief greeting, he told me in a low voice to follow him, as the place was ill adapted to the nature of our conference; and that he would conduct me to another, where we should be at least safe from casual interruption. I assented. My conductor led me by a circuitous route, studiously avoiding the principal streets, through several narrow and filthy outlets, to the western extremity of the town. Here we stopped amid the ruins of some cabins that had been once used for barracks, and afterwards deserted.

"We are now," said my guide, "near the spot I spoke of; but, as you are not one of the initiated, it is requisite that for a short time you should submit to have your eyes bandaged."

I did not offer any objection to this proposal. My pride would not allow me to recede, since I had gone so far in the adventure; and, having been blindfolded, my conductor caught me by the hand, and guided my steps. It was difficult to walk in this manner; and I found the path in which I was led both rugged and intricate. The distance, however, was short, apparently; and in about a quarter of an hour the stranger again halted, and struck three distinct blows upon a resonant surface with a stone, or perhaps the hilt of some weapon of offence. A hollow, almost sepulchral voice inquired, —

"Who comes there?"

My guide replied, —

"Uncle Sam!"

"Long live the Republic!" was the rejoinder.

We now descended half a dozen steps; when I discovered, by feeling with my hands, that we had entered a subterraneous passage, the sides of which were damp. It was not of great extent, as a few moments brought us into a freer air. Here I learned from my conductor that our journey had terminated.

He removed the bandage at the same time; and I saw that we were in a tolerably spacious vault, or cellar, partially illuminated by a lamp hung from the roof by an iron chain. Immediately under it was a rude table, round which, on coarse wooden benches, were seated six persons, enveloped in coarse, loose garments of dark homespun, which effectually concealed their figures; while all had their faces hidden by black masks, the *barbes* of which fell almost to their waists.

One, who seemed to act as secretary to this secret conclave, had several papers before him, and a pen in his hand, which I presumed was to be employed in taking notes of the examination to which I was evidently about to be subjected.

My guide pointed to a stool, intimating that I might be

seated; and, having whispered a few words to the chief person who appeared to preside, took his place, masked like the others, at the table. The chief then began his interrogatory by demanding of me my name, place of nativity, and my residence and rank. I instantly replied to the first and second question; and was about to answer the third, when my interlocutor said, —

"Spare yourself, sir, the pain of equivocating: we know that you are adjutant of the Sixth Illinois Cavalry, United-States Volunteers, and also the motives which induced you to assume the character of a surgeon: the stratagem was allowable, although its adoption unfortunately defeated a plan that would have essentially benefited the cause you have sworn to support. It is, however, in your power to retrieve the opportunity you were the innocent instrument of destroying."

"Put me to the test!" said I eagerly. "If the action be an honorable one, the dread of death shall not deter me from essaying it."

"Reserve this display of enthusiasm till the occasion comes to prove its reality," resumed the speaker of the conclave. "At present, you are enjoined to listen in silence to any communication we may think necessary to intrust you with; and, lest you should question our authority, learn that we derive it from the purest sources, — the voice of the persecuted Unionists of the State of Mississippi, which has nominated us to the legislative body secretly established in the mountains that surround us. An important blow at the Confederacy was meditated that would have paralyzed the secessionists, and redeemed the State from thraldom. Fortune seemed to favor its execution. The daring patriot to whom its execution was intrusted already saw within his grasp the glorious reward which his zeal would have merited from a grateful nation. At this moment you appeared, like a baleful planet, to wither his hopes, and blast his design. Mercier had" — at this name I started with agitation — " sworn to immolate our tyrant at the shrine of his country's freedom, and was about to redeem his oath, when you " —

"Great God, I thank thee," I fervently ejaculated, starting from my seat, glowing with indignation, "that thou hast made me the instrument of defeating the assassin's purpose!"

"Peace, fool, nor interrupt me with your cant!" vociferated the wily casuist, who evidently used his inflated language to conceal even to himself the vileness of his excuses for a cold-blooded murder. "Know that the end often sanctifies the means: that which you term assassination is but retributive justice. We have no time, however, to waste in words. Mercier, through your means, has become an object of suspicion: any further attempt on his part would be madness. You are bound to supply his place. Daily opportunities present themselves. Rank, riches, and freedom are the result of your compliance; death, inevitable death, the consequence of your refusal. Pause ere you decide!"

"My choice is already made," I calmly answered. "I would suffer a thousand deaths rather than owe my life to such conditions. I cannot see how you can offer such a base alternative to an honorable soldier. Do you pause, sir, and these gentlemen too, before you sully our glorious cause with such treachery!"

"Perish, then, in your obstinacy!" exclaimed a hitherto-silent member of the conclave, at the same time drawing a bowie-knife, and springing to the spot where I stood unarmed.

I felt that the crisis of my fate approached, and collected myself for a final effort. Practised in all athletic exercises, I quickly enveloped my left fore-arm in my cloak, and received the assassin's thrust unhurt; while a straightforward blow from the shoulder with my right arm dashed off the mask of my assailant, and levelled him to the earth. His features were those of the malignant and bloody-minded Mercier. To seize his knife, which he had dropped, and place myself in a posture of defence, was the work of an instant. Like a stag at bay, I resolved to sell my life dearly. I had, however, fearful odds to contend with; for six knives, formidable as my own, in the hands of as many infuriated demons, gleamed before my eyes.

The conspirators would not use fire-arms, because the reports would have betrayed them. At the instant before the threatened attack, a loud crash was heard; and the assassins stood transfixed with astonishment. A rush of footsteps followed; and, in another second, the vault was filled with confederate soldiers, at the head of whom I recognized Col. Game and Lieut. Yancey. The seven conspirators were removed to the city prison. We returned to the quarters; and I then learned from the confederate officers the following particulars:—

Yancey had noticed my depression of spirits, and, fearing it might lead me to the commission of some rash act, decided upon watching my movements. With this view he had followed me to the grove, in which, concealed behind a tree-trunk, he had witnessed the delivery of the secret note, which, being subsequently found, made him acquainted with the hour and place of interview. At this he likewise contrived to be present, and, having traced the stranger through all the labyrinths of his route, arrived shortly after him at the ruined barracks. The intricacies of the path, which impeded my progress and that of my guide, favored his concealment; and, screened from observation by the logs and rubbish that lay in the road, he managed to reach the entrance to the vault just in time to catch the signal and countersign. Possessed of these, and having noted the exact spot, he returned to the town to apprise the military authorities. On his way to the office of the commandant of the place he met Col. Game, who had just arrived, and to whom he made known his errand.

Not an instant was lost in mustering a special patrol from

the main guard, which, as has been seen, having forced an entrance, arrived just in time to save me from destruction.

The sequel is soon told. At an early hour the next morning a military commission assembled in Corinth by command of Gen. B——, before which the seven prisoners were arraigned. On the evidence of the papers seized in the vault they were found guilty of treason to the Confederate States, and of being spies within their lines, and unanimously sentenced to death.

I was also tried as a participant, but only for form's sake, and fully acquitted; the evidence showing that I had manifested the strongest abhorrence of the proposal made to me.

Corinth being then in a state of siege, the stern requirements of military law called for the instant execution of the sentence, which was carried into effect within two hours after its promulgation. I was released without exchange in consequence of the services I had performed, and received the thanks of the general. Col. Game and Lieut. Yancey went with me to the federal outposts; at which I was delivered up under a flag, and rejoined my regiment.

After the capitulation of Corinth to our army, and a consequent temporary lull in the military operations in that quarter, I obtained a short leave of absence, and visited my home in Missouri.

Here the worthy major hid his face in his hands, and seemed terribly affected by some inward emotion. After a little while passed in perfect silence by the whole circle of officers in respect to his evident grief, he resumed : —

I will refrain from distressing you, gentlemen, with the details of the irreparable and heart-rending misfortunes that had fallen upon me. Suffice it to say, that I found my home a desert, my house destroyed by fire, my flocks and herds dispersed no one knew whither, and my wife laid by stranger hands in a distant churchyard. Soon after, my children died one by one; and I am left alone again in the world. All this unutterable distress I owed to those incarnate fiends, the Jayhawkers.

The major rose from his seat, and strode out into the darkness. We soon lost sight of his tall form, but could trace his path by the clattering of his long sabre as he made his way towards a retired spot, doubtless to indulge his favorite habit of melancholy revery.

We all now stretched ourselves on our straw to enjoy a little sleep, without taking off our clothes, arms, or accoutrements; our horses, in charge of the orderlies, picketed near, ready saddled, as is the custom on picket-duty. But our slumbers were of short duration. I was first aroused by the dropping fire of the cavalry outposts and vedettes far away in the front of our infantry pickets: this was succeeded by the crack of the latter's pieces; and these again, after a brief interval, by the more regular and sustained fire of the reserves of the grand guard.

I then knew it was an attack in force, or at least a forcible reconnoissance; and sent information to the camps in our rear. The whole force of about two brigades was soon engaged with the enemy; and I again sent for re-enforcements, which soon arrived; and the enemy, having succeeded in ascertaining the position and force of our picket-guard, withdrew after a smart action of about two hours, in which our line suffered some losses.

I then rode to the front to re-establish the line, and to reconnoitre, in my turn, the battle-field; passing the many dead and wounded, who were already being removed to the hospital in the ambulances, or taken to the rear by their comrades for burial in a nameless grave.

The confederate dead lay thick in a ravine, the possession of which had been hotly contested. Emerging from this, myself and staff came upon a little elevated plateau that had been the scene of a charge of our cavalry upon the confederates.

As we reached a group of bodies, a young officer uttered an exclamation; and I saw stretched dead upon the ground the fine athletic figure of the major of the Sixth Illinois Cavalry. He had been pierced through the heart by a rifle-ball; and his features wore a placid expression that seemed to indicate satisfaction with the manner of his death. Near him, and just in his front, lay the corpse of a confederate officer, his head cloven by a sabre-stroke.

The artillery-officer was riding by my side, and dismounted to look at the features of the dead confederate. "Leonard Mason!" said he. "This is the end of my poor school-fellow!" And he could hardly conceal his emotion. Death atones for all errors; and let us hope, that, in this case, it was a relief to both the wrecked gamester and the unfortunate man who had evidently slain him by a strange fatality.

THE GENERAL'S STORY.

LORITO; OR, THE AVENGER.

ALMOST my first military adventure in the service which I had entered — the Mexican army — occurred at Queretaro, — a city since made famous by the execution of the unfortunate Maximilian, and his two unlucky generals, Miramon and Mejia.

Miguel — or, as he was then universally called, Miguelito — Miramon was, indeed, one of my pupils in the military school at Chapultepec, and noted, even at that early age, as a youth of uncommon spirit and genius.

A day after my arrival on a mission from my chief, the president of the republic, to whom I was then acting as aide-de-camp, I remarked to a friend that I had never heard the human voice so perfectly imitated as by a fine parrot who passed his time on a roost, or perch, outside a house opposite my lodgings, on the great square, or plaza.

My friend agreed with me in my opinion, and, informing me that there was a history connected with the bird, invited me to accompany him on a visit to his owner, who, although the possessor of a magnificent *huacamaya* and several other fine specimens of the family of the *psittacidæ*, seemed to value his little ordinary *lorito* more than all of them.

About four years since, said Don Manuel, — in answer to my request for his story, — my brother left us for the northern frontier to fight the savages; and the poor lad left to me Lorito as his last bequest. "Should I return," said he, "you will give him back to me: if not, keep him for a remembrancer; and, should he die, have him stuffed, and still preserve him in memory of me." I promised, and have kept my word. Lorito is still in my house; and, notwithstanding his age, which I do not know exactly, he appears to be likely to survive not only his first, but also his second master. I was at that time engaged in commerce; and, shortly after, receiving intelligence of the death of my poor brother, who was killed by the Indians, was compelled to depart for Havana on business of some importance. I resided then in this house, at that time the property of my aunt, who had living with her as companion a young girl, an orphan without kin, whom she had reared from a child, and to whose care I left Lorito, with many charges to take pains with his health and education.

I had not then ceased to look upon Engracia — which was the orphan's name — as other than a child, although perfectly aware of the sweetness of her disposition, and of the promise of great beauty she bore in form and feature. On my return, which was within a year, I was astonished by the loveliness of Engracia, which, as is common in our climate, had rapidly developed during my absence. I was also most agreeably surprised at hearing my parrot call my name, saying in a clear and audible voice, "Viva Manuel!" — a salutation taught him by the amiable orphan.

I was obliged to leave again very soon for Havana, and this time regretted more than before the necessity that compelled my departure; for, during my short sojourn, I fully appreciated all the good qualities of the beautiful girl. During the voyage from Vera Cruz, I found myself often asking whether Engracia was not the companion destined for me by Heaven, in case I was favored by fortune, and was able to return again to reside in my native city. I brooded long over the fact, that, when the time came for my adieus, my old aunt pressed me in a long embrace; while Engracia presented her cheek, which was rosy-red, then grew instantly pale; and that she supported herself by the wall, as if unable to stand,—a parting quite different to our first, at which she showed no emotion.

Of course I wrote regularly to my aunt, and never omitted to add some message for Engracia, who I knew read the letters to the old lady. At last, I wrote directly to my sweetheart, as I now considered her, begging her to keep my secret even from her benefactress, and telling her the day would soon come when we would mutually confide to the old lady our plans and hopes for the future. She loved me, for she gave her assent to my desire; and, if this was a fault, the poor child cruelly expiated it. After our correspondence had continued for some time, I thought it my duty to conceal the affection I felt for Engracia from my aunt no longer; and wrote to her that I cherished the design of making her my wife. This letter was unanswered. The poor old lady was already grievously ill when it arrived, and, indeed, died a few days after.

On her death-bed she embraced Engracia, and made known to her the contents of the letter. At any other time joy would have pervaded her heart; but now she bowed her head, and was silent. The dying woman then asked her if she knew of my love for her; and she acknowledged that she had known of it for some time. In answer to the questions of the old lady, she owned that she returned my love, and divulged the secret of our clandestine correspondence. My aunt listened benevolently, and charged the orphan to marry me, and to make me happy. Then, telling her that the thought of our union made her die content, she bade her adieu in the most affectionate manner, and asked for a notary to be sent to her bedside. Having dictated new testamentary dispositions as to her property, the notary gave place to the priest; and then began the death-agony. My aunt died that night. Her illness had been a short one.

Engracia wrote and despatched a letter, urging me to return immediately; but the ocean mails were tedious, and I did not receive it for a long time.

It was three months at least, after the decease of my aunt, that I learned the sad news from the orphan's letter; and even then my business was in such a condition, that it would have been ruinous to me to leave Havana without arranging it satisfactorily to myself and others.

Five months elapsed from the time of my aunt's death before I again set foot in Queretaro.

Meantime seals had been placed upon the movable property of the defunct, and her estate was unsettled; but I was named her universal legatee, except a small life-annuity to Engracia, which was her dower. The young orphan still resided in the house of my aunt, in which she passed her time while attending to her religious and charitable duties, as usual, and awaiting my return; her sole attendant being an aged female.

Let us not forget Lorito. Engracia still kept the poor bird, who maintained his position in the perch outside the window looking on the plaza, amusing the inmates of the house and the passers-by with his mockery of all the sounds he heard, and his persistent *bavardage*, rounding off his sentences usually with a loud "Viva Manuel!"

There is usually a large garrison kept in Queretaro, and the plaza is frequently used as a place of exercise. Lorito became acquainted with the braying of cornets, the rolling of the drums, and could distinctly repeat the commands given by the drill-officers to the recruits daily exercised on the square beneath him. His "Carry arms!" "Present arms!" &c., was the daily wonder of the loungers on the plaza. Notwithstanding that Engracia lived a solitary and unobtrusive life, only going out to church, or to visit the tomb of my aunt to pray, gloomy days were in store for her.

There was in the garrison a young officer, a notorious libertine, the son of a rich and influential family of Mexico, who had already distinguished himself by the profligate dissipation of a handsome patrimony. This officer, strolling one day near the cemetery, met the beautiful orphan, where she had gone to pray, and was struck with her elegant *tournure*, her graceful walk, and princess-like bearing. Although he could not distinguish her features, partly concealed as they were by a long and voluminous *reboso*, he followed her, and even accosted her in an almost deserted street.

Engracia deigned not either to turn her head or to hasten her steps, opposing to the bold advances of the lieutenant the most disdainful silence. She had not even the air of noticing his presence; while he continued to dog her steps, meanwhile pouring into her ear all sorts of commonplaces.

Engracia continued her walk homewards calmly, secure in the safety of the streets at noonday, and entered her house as if nothing had happened to annoy her: so that his barrack phrases of admiration fell upon deaf ears.

His trouble was not, however, entirely lost; for at least he had learned the residence of the beautiful *incognita*. In a place like Queretaro, it is not difficult to obtain all the other needful information about a lovely woman who has struck one's fancy; and the result of his researches in this direction was quite satisfactory to this vulgar Lovelace. He resolved, cost what it might, to bring to reason the haughty orphan, and to punish her disdain.

He made his plan at once, pushed a reconnoissance into the enemy's place itself, took account of the feeble resistance she could oppose to him, and resolved to risk the assault.

No one ever could explain the means he took to enter the house without observation; but he did so one evening, passed into the *patio*, — court-yard, — and, climbing a tree, got access to an empty apartment in the second story.

This room was separated from that of Engracia only by a

door in a partition. Old Antonia, who was deaf as a post, slept quietly on the ground-floor; and the invader knew she could scarcely hear thunder.

On this evening Engracia was not asleep: she was reading my letters, she says, for the hundredth time. Hearing a slight noise, she tremulously cried out, "Is it you, Antonia?" thinking it might be her nurse. No answer was returned.

Although gentle, timid even, Engracia did not lack courage. She took up her candle, saying to herself it was only her *dueña*, bravely opened the door separating the two rooms, and almost dropped the light on seeing the young officer.

"Who are you, sir?" she cried in as commanding a tone as she could assume; "and why are you here?"

The lieutenant took the candlestick out of her hand, and placed it on a table; then, smiling on the young girl, said, —

"You deigned not to listen to my protestations of love in the street; and I admit you had reason; for, undoubtedly, you wished me to understand that the place was very badly chosen. So I have found it necessary to come here without leave; for it would not have been granted, probably, had I asked it, ignorant as you must be of the ardent and sincere love I bear for you, and which I now avow, as well as that I have been forced to take this step."

"Sir, you most unworthily and cowardly abuse my condition, knowing that I am alone and unprotected; but I can yet make myself respected, even by you! As to what you call your love, know, sir, that I am the affianced of a man of honor, who, should he learn of your insult to me, would compel you to account to him for this odious proceeding!"

"Ha, ha!" laughed the officer. "And who is this happy mortal who pretends to dispute so adorable a beauty with me?"

"Viva Manuel!" cried the parrot, awakened by the sudden flash of light, dancing on his perch at sight of a stranger.

"Ah! he calls Manuel. Now, I will lay any odds that he has been taught that name by yourself," said the intruder.

"Go away, sir, or I will cry out!" returned the young girl with energy supplied by terror.

"Oh, no, indeed, my beauty! What! leave without having manifested all the passion I feel for you? You cannot mean it?"

"You wish, then, to bring scandal on my good name," said the girl in an appealing tone. "Sir, you will compromise me without accomplishing your unworthy intentions! Go, sir, I pray you, in the name of your mother, in the name of your sister, if you have one!"

The officer, still smiling, made an attempt to pass his arm around her waist, and to draw her to him. Engracia recoiled; but the officer advanced, and succeeded in seizing the affrighted and unnerved young girl. She cried aloud at this outrage, which was the signal for the parrot to make outcry loud enough to wake the dead; but old Antonia slept on.

Engracia redoubled her screams, and the parrot his unearthly clamor.

"Devilish bird!" muttered the lieutenaut angrily: "he will certainly cause the old woman to come up here!" And, cursing the poor bird, he dealt it a violent blow with his fist.

Engracia sought refuge in a corner, clasping her hands: her choking throat could no longer give voice to a call for help. The young man walked towards her, took her hands in his, and even dared to attempt to kiss her pale lips. Suddenly he imagined he heard a noise; and, before he could decide whether it was reality or an illusion, the parrot redoubled his cries vehemently. "To hell with thee, infernal bird!" said he, tearing him from his perch, and launching him forcibly from the window by which he had obtained entrance into the apartment.

The poor creature, hurled rudely by a vigorous hand, obeyed

the impulse like an inert object, and, without the power of opening his wings, fell into the garden near the wall of the house. Chance, or Providence, guided its fall close to the window near old Antonia's bed, who was, however, more awakened by the vibration of the room overhead than by either the cries of Engracia or those of the parrot, although the latter's were redoubled in a more piercing tone than before, being this time cries of pain. "What's the matter, señorita?" asked the old woman, opening her shutters. "Help, help!" cried Engracia as loud as her strength permitted.

The audacious libertine now understood that the game was up for him this time. "I leave you now, señorita," said he with suppressed rage: "but I will find you again; and, if you resist or complain, I swear I will kill you! It is for your interest to keep silence as to what has passed here, if for no other reason, to assure the safety of your handsome Manuel."

Saying these words he ran to the window, passed out, and, seizing the branch of the tree by which he had ascended, let himself to the ground. In another instant he had disappeared from the enclosure.

Antonia, having at last climbed to the room of her mistress by the stairs, found poor Engracia in a dead faint on the floor, having succumbed to the loss of strength and nervous prostration. The next day she had a burning fever, was delirious, and lay for some days in imminent danger. Old Antonia summoned the doctor, and cared for and nursed the poor girl as if she had been her own daughter. Meanwhile no one cared for poor Lorito, who had his wing broken by his sudden and violent expulsion from the apartment of his mistress. How was he cured? That is an ornithological secret: but cured he was; and, about a week after, Engracia faintly smiled at hearing the old cry, "Viva Manuel!"

I must now tell you why the lieutenant did not execute his

terrible menace. "I will find you again," said he, with flashing eyes, to Engracia; but he had never again sought her.

After leaving the house, he went to a supper at which he knew he should find his comrades. The guests were all sober enough when he arrived; but he, irritated by his failure, and mad with spite, began to drink inordinately. He was a little dashed at first; but, as the wine raised his spirits, he became communicative, then loquacious, and finished by recounting all the details of his rash attempt, concluding by reiterating in a drunken voice his threat to Engracia, — "I will find her again;" adding in a maudlin tone, "And, the next time, I will not fail."

"You will do no such thing, sir," said an officer calmly.

"You are jesting, I think," said the first.

"You shall not commit an infamous deed which will recoil on the whole of us. You shall not dishonor your uniform by ruining this poor child. Anyhow, it is a cowardly act; and I forbid it!" said the officer.

These noble words were warmly applauded by all present with voice and gesture.

But the lieutenant, stung to the quick, and more than half drunk, retorted, —

"Is it a captain, or a capucin, that presumes to address me in this manner? Are we listening to a sermon? or are we at a feast?"

The captain rose, and his friends followed his example. "Let him get over his potations," said he, unmoved. "He is now drunk. To-morrow he will be reasonable; and he will regret his words, and, yet more, his mad, silly threats."

"I shall do nothing of the sort!" roared the lieutenant, his eyes fairly bloodshot with rage. Moreover, I will soon show you whether I am drunk or not!"

So saying, he drew his sword, and rushed upon the captain. The latter easily parried the thrust with his arm, and, by a rapid turn of the wrist, seized the blade the miscreant would have buried in his body, and disarmed him. The others then threw themselves upon the lieutenant; and he was dragged away, hurling curses upon them all.

The affair became known, and the commanding-officer of the garrison placed the lieutenant before a court-martial. In some cases, doubtless, the offence might have been treated with some leniency; but this man had the most deplorable antecedents, which prevented the court from softening the rigor of their sentence.

Several times he had been punished for grave infractions of discipline, and had only succeeded in obtaining his epaulet by an act of distinguished bravery. Moreover, the authorities deemed it necessary to respect the opinion of the civilians, who regarded the sanctity of their dwellings as something not to be lightly violated by those who should have been foremost in protecting it. In this case the sentence of the court-martial was death; the prisoner's insubordination having been great, and his offence aggravated by repetition.

A relative high in office at the capital interceded for mercy, and brought powerful influence to bear in his behalf. The president refused, at first, either to pardon him or to commute the sentence; but finally decided to spare his life, but to bound his clemency. He ordered the colonel commanding the place of Queretaro to come to the city of Mexico, and communicated his will to him, directing him at the same time to preserve it a profound secret.

The condemned was to suffer military degradation, and also all the apprehension of execution: only, at the moment of giving the last command, the officer of the firing-party should not pronounce the word "Fire!"

The guilty person was then to be sent to the Castle of Perote to be immured in a cell, or to join a company of discipline composed of malefactors to labor on the public works, or be sent to fight the Indians in the North, as should be hereafter decided.

Meanwhile my poor Engracia convalesced slowly; but, as her health was re-established, consciousness of the past returned, and she was the victim of a deep melancholy. "He will find me," she said; "and, when he does, he will execute his terrible threat. But, even if he does not, how can I conceal from my affianced husband all the outrage and violence to which I have been subjected? It would be disloyal in me to do so; for I should have no secrets from him who has the right to all my love, as I wish, in turn, to feel myself entitled to all his esteem. And how can I meet without blushing and trembling the man who has dared to sully my lips with his kisses?

"Oh! should I find myself some time with him in a saloon, for instance! Horrible!"

Lorito, perched on his stick at the window, seemed to understand this monologue; for he uttered loudly his comment upon it, — "Viva Manuel!"

Meanwhile I was sailing over the waters of the Gulf, longing to reach my native land, and thinking the swift steamer that bore me onwards more slow than a clumsy Dutch galliot.

The day of the military execution, in conformity with the sentence of the court-martial and its supposed approval by the president, arrived at last; and the garrison assembled on the plaza of the city, upon which, as you may see, the front windows of our house look down. The hollow square was formed, and the condemned was escorted into its centre. First the sentence and its approval was read in a loud voice by the staff-adjutant; then came the military degradation, — a punishment yet more terrible to a soldier than the swift death which was to follow. At last, the priest, who had not left the side of the condemned, embraced and quitted him, and the firing-platoon took their station under a lieutenant.

The doomed man bore himself bravely, and with the courage of our race. He begged to be allowed to die with his eyes unbandaged, and earnestly desired to give the command to fire. The colonel commanding granted the first request, but refused the last for good reason.

The silence of the plaza was oppressive, broken at last by the harsh, quick command, "Ready!" "Aim!" "Fire!" followed in quick succession. The twelve muskets made but one report, and the unhappy culprit fell face forward on the stones of the plaza: several bullets had entered his heart, and death was instantaneous.

As the last command rang out, the colonel put spurs to his horse, uttering a sharp cry; and the gallant beast made but one leap towards the officer commanding the firing-party. The rider was pale as the corpse before him; and so was the officer, who stared into his colonel's face blankly, unmindful of the uplifted sabre he bore.

"Desgraciado!" ("Unfortunate man!") "why did you command 'Fire!' contrary to my express orders?"

"I, colonel? I did *not* command 'Fire!'" answered the officer, completely nonplussed.

The deathlike silence again prevailed, soon suddenly interrupted by a clear, trumpet-voice crying, "Recover arms!" "Present arms!"

It was Lorito, who commanded the military exercise, as was his wont, from his perch at the window.

He it was who had cried "Fire!" He had avenged Engracia.

In a few days I learned of this scene from the lips of my affianced in this house. Sighing, I pressed her to my heart, assuring her that to me she should always be the angel of purity I had so often dreamed of, and bidding her never again to blush before any one.

The poor wretch who would have dishonored us has expiated his crime. May God forgive him! Our marriage was celebrated soon after my arrival; and I have this boy, who was named for his father, "in order," says Engracia, "that, when Lorito salutes us with his favorite cry, I may not know which one he means."

Seated in the *xaduan* (hall) of my new acquaintance, I listened to this short and simple tale; at the conclusion of which the parrot took up the word, as the Spaniard says, and repeating a long rigmarole of military commands, drum-beats and rataplans, bugle-blasts, and a verse of a song, made an end with "Viva Manuel!"

MONTE; OR, THE ROBBERS.

SCENE. — The "Sociedad," — a private club-house on the Great Square of the city of Mexico.

Present. — Several loungers; myself, seated at a window looking on the square, sipping chocolate.

Enter Don Eusebio Lancry, a gay young Frenchman, — in American parlance, a "sport," — many years a resident of Mexico, whom I invite to seat himself at my table.

Don Eusebio. — AH, mi colonel! I know you are about to ask me where I have been for the last few weeks, and shall be most happy to relate to you my experiences for that time, or since I last saw you.

Myself. — It will give me much pleasure to listen, knowing you seldom say any thing not instructive or amusing: besides, I have heard that you had "fallen among thieves" lately.

Don Eusebio. — You have been rightly informed. I never again expected to enjoy this pleasure, I assure you. I will tell you all about it.

Well, some weeks since, I started for Vera Cruz, on business, and, returning, was captured by the *salteadores* of the *camino real*, and taken into the mountains near Plan del Rio. There I was stripped and searched: my repeater, a fine Breguet, was appropriated; and, finding only about ten ounces in money in my pockets, the rascals, enraged at my foresight, tied me to a tree, preparatory to putting me to death, because they could not find a more ample booty.

Myself. — And how did you escape from these gentlemen of the road?

Don Eusebio. — Just as I had given up all hope of ever revisiting my dear native land, or of seeing yourself and my other friends again in this world, and was endeavoring to recall some of the prayers of my childhood, the leader, or captain, of the band rode up; and I instantly put in a strong appeal to his sympathies, and, above all, to his desire for revenge, not that of blood, but of money. It was lucky, indeed, for me that the captain was the well-known Rafael Hernandez, an old acquaintance; and our recognition was mutual. We had last met at the great annual *fiesta* of San Agustin, which, as thou knowest, is the occasion for meeting every one of our acquaintances, and the true Olympian games of this silly Mexico.

It so happened that I had there encountered Don Rafael, and that our meeting resulted in a skirmish at monte, in which he lost a hundred golden ounces, which he paid on the spot like a true *caballero*.

He was quite another man, clad in the riding-dress of a ranchero, and surrounded by uncouth and rude brigands. Then he had been at San Agustin, where he was attired in the newest French mode, and accompanied by gay and beautiful ladies, to whom he handed out his gold to bet for him, on account of their better luck, with the most negligent and dashing air possible.

"Now, Don Rafael," said I, "can you not save me from the hands of these gentlemen, your subordinates, and, I doubt not, most honorable friends?"

"I have every disposition to do so, my dear Don Eusebio," returned this chivalrous rascal; "but"—

"Ah!" thought I, "there is a ' but.'"

"In our fraternity we have certain rules which even I dare not transgress, even to prove the sincere friendship I feel for you. One of these rules is, that nothing can be done by a member of our honorable society for the individual benefit of any single one of us, but that every step taken among us shall be for the good of the whole association. Unless, then, you can show me, that, by saving your life, I shall thereby confer an advantage on the whole *partida*, I must, disagreeable and wretched as it will make me, leave you in the hands of these gentlemen to do as seemeth best to them. True it is that this decision, to which I have consented only from a sense of its necessity, which has no law, irks me exceedingly in your case, inasmuch as I well remember, that, at our last interview, you promised me my revenge for the hundred bright ounces I lost to you at San Agustin. Those shiners I should like much to win back; but I see no way of doing so, as you have now no capital wherewith to commence a bank."

His last words restored my equanimity, and re-established my confidence in my own resources. I now saw my way clear out of my difficulties, resolving to at once practise upon the all-absorbing passion of the sons of the country for gaming. I immediately addressed Don Rafael thus: —

"My dear *compadre*, it is ill arguing with a man who has been tied to a tree, fasting for two mortal hours: induce these gentlemen, then, in whose faces I see already the evidences of a relenting spirit, to liberate me from my bonds on my parole not to attempt escape (this would have been impossible under the circumstances, but I made a great merit of offering it), and I will contrive a means of gratifying your very laudable desire, contribute to the amusement of your friends, and probably increase the funds in the military chest of your amiable troop. Without the least peradventure, I am confident of achieving the laudable object contemplated in the rule you mentioned, without causing its infraction by yourself."

The gang agreed to the proposition, and, I may say with

pardonable vanity, placed itself in my hands. Pen, ink, and paper were produced: and my first step was to draw upon the banking-house of Escandon & Co. for a thousand dollars, at thirty days' sight; which draft I made Hernandez indorse as security for my appearance in person, alive, before its arrival at maturity, half down, and the balance in three weeks, or sooner if required.

The note, with a letter, was despatched at once by a *mozo* well mounted, who returned on the following day with the money. We all then adjourned to a small and secluded *rancho* in the hills, and I opened my bank in due form. All entered zealously into my plan, which they said would enable them to amuse themselves finely while awaiting the opportunity for some new exploit in the way of their profession. Don Rafael was eager for his revenge; and the contest began.

I can truly assure thee it was the keenest encounter of wits I ever experienced in this country, in which my practice in this line has not been small. At the first *séance*, thirty-six hours were spent without sleep, and almost without tasting food. Drink was out of the question; and, luckily, there was none within reach of the rancho. At the expiration of that time, my nerves had become so tense, owing to the attention I was forced to give to the game, that I greatly feared a brain or nervous fever. With a little respite, however, I pulled through, and, much relieved, began again, single-handed, the fight against this band of devils, headed by the arch-fiend Hernandez. Finally, after a struggle perfectly unexampled in all my play at games of hazard, my Caucasian constitution and temperament triumphed over the mixed and mongrel organization of the modern Mexican; and, after four days and four nights of arduous exertion, I was declared the victor.

I won back not only the amount I had originally invested in the monte bank, my watch, and the small sum I had been robbed of by the villains, but also their own spare cash,— very little, to be sure,—half a dozen indifferent horses, and the deed of a house and garden in the city of Puebla (which I shrewdly suspect is mortgaged for its full value), a bag full of opened letters rifled from the diligences, a gold-headed cane, a case of surgical instruments, the wardrobe of a travelling actress, and a splendid lace cap and cloak that has served at the christening of some baby of wealthy and aristocratic parentage.

After the battle had been won, my mind was at ease; for I knew that these gentlemanlike scoundrels would religiously observe the sanctity of their gambling-debts; and I lay down on the hard hide bedstead of the poor rancho, leaving my stakes on the table we had used for play, without a doubt of their perfect security.

I was saved; and for full twenty-four hours I slept, uninterruptedly, the sleep of the just.

I awoke restored in mind and body; partook of chocolate prepared by a nice-looking *moza*, who acted as the Doña Leonarda of the brigands; and ordered up one of *my* horses. I then magnanimously divided among the robbers all the property I had won from them, generously adding a couple of hundred dollars of the five hundred received from the house of Escandon & Co.

At parting I received the congratulations of the band, with thanks for the amusement I had afforded them, and promised one and all that I would gladly give them their revenge in case of our meeting again. I then mounted and took the road hitherwards, piloted as far as the *camino real* by one of the bandits. I arrived only yesterday, and *me voila!*

I do not know why the rascals did not hold me to ransom, which they might have done, and reaped, perhaps, a large pecuniary benefit; but I suppose the high stakes for which I played — my life and liberty — added so much to the excitement of the game, that it possessed a corresponding attraction for them.

I most fervently hope, however, that I may never renew my acquaintance with Mexican brigands, or repeat my game of monte under the like circumstances; for all my strength was required to support the strain upon my mental faculties and nervous system, and never before did I so much feel the need of perfect repose as at this moment.

The sense of honor displayed by Hernandez and his band, any of them being ready to cut my throat in an instant without remorse at ordinary times, forcibly reminds me of the hero of one of your finest poets, — a man

> **"Of one virtue, and a thousand crimes."**

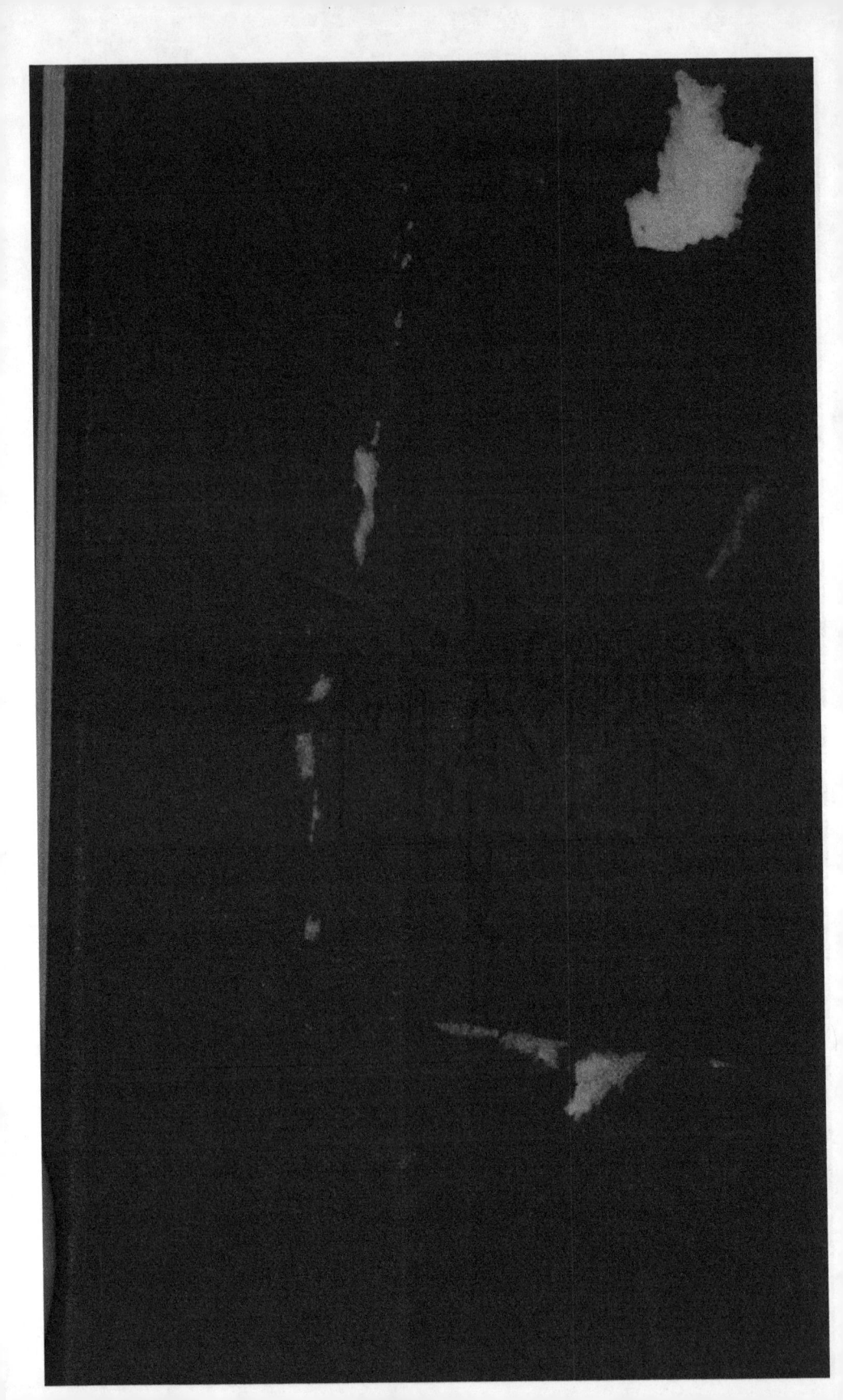

Check Out More Titles From HardPress Classics Series In this collection we are offering thousands of classic and hard to find books. This series spans a vast array of subjects – so you are bound to find something of interest to enjoy reading and learning about.

Subjects:
Architecture
Art
Biography & Autobiography
Body, Mind &Spirit
Children & Young Adult
Dramas
Education
Fiction
History
Language Arts & Disciplines
Law
Literary Collections
Music
Poetry
Psychology
Science
…and many more.

Visit us at www.hardpress.net

Im The Story
personalised classic books

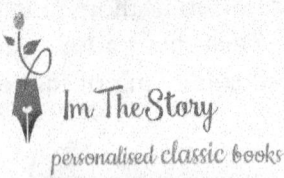

"Beautiful gift.. lovely finish.
My Niece loves it, so precious!"

Helen R Brumfieldon

★★★★★

UNIQUE GIFT

FOR KIDS, PARTNERS
AND FRIENDS

Timeless books such as:

Kids

Alice in Wonderland • The Jungle Book • The Wonderful Wizard of Oz
Peter and Wendy • Robin Hood • The Prince and The Pauper
The Railway Children • Treasure Island • A Christmas Carol

Adults

Romeo and Juliet • Dracula

- **Highly** Customizable
- **Change** Books Title
- **Replace** Characters Names with yours
- **Upload** Photo for inside page!
- **Add** Inscriptions

Visit
Im TheStory.com
and order yours today!